WALKING
ON
WATER

FOR

NANA

JOYCE

TID

WALKING ON WATER

A voyage round Britain and through life

GEOFF HOLT

SEAFARER BOOKS

SHERIDAN HOUSE

© Geoff Holt 2008

Published in the UK by Seafarer Books Ltd
102 Redwald Road · Rendlesham · Suffolk IP12 2TE

www.seafarerbooks.com

ISBN 978-1-906266-09-7 paperback

A catalogue record for this book is available from the British Library

Published in the USA by Sheridan House Inc
145 Palisade Street · Dobbs Ferry · NY 10522

www.sheridanhouse.com

ISBN 978-1-57409-276-9 paperback

A catalogue record for this book is available from the Library of Congress

Design, typesetting, maps, diagrams and incidental sketches:
Louis Mackay / www.louismackaydesign.co.uk

Editing: Hugh Brazier

Text set digitally in Proforma

Printed in Finland by WS Bookwell

As patron of RYA Sailability, I have worked with Geoff since he became its inaugural Chairman in 1995. A professional yachtsman before he was injured in a swimming accident as a teenager, Geoff not only has a passion for the sea, but he has selflessly devoted much of his life to promoting the charity so that others may share that same enjoyment

For many years, I have seen how the sport of sailing can enrich the lives of anyone and everyone, including those with disabilities. Sailing has the unique ability to offer freedom and independence to those who may otherwise face tough challenges in their own lives.

I have also seen how certain events have achieved wide public recognition, as happened when the UK's disabled sailing team won the gold medal at the Atlanta Games in 1996, and how that in turn increased awareness of RYA Sailability and inspired many others to take up the sport. Over 20,000 people with disabilities now sail at Sailability clubs throughout the country, and the number has been rising each year. Geoff Holt's successful voyage around Great Britain must now be added to the list of widely recognised and inspiring events.

To sail around Great Britain is a massive achievement for even the hardiest of sailors. To do so when paralysed from the chest down, sailing a 15-foot foot dinghy 1,500 miles during one of the worst summers on record, not only demonstrated his determination and sailing skill, but was a testament to his ability to conceive and execute a complex expedition. It was a tremendously courageous voyage – but typical of Geoff.

As with most great achievements, there is often a dedicated support team that contributes to that success, and Personal Everest is one such example. Geoff selected a highly motivated and professional team to support him with everything, from providing his personal care needs to driving the support vehicles and crewing his safety boat whilst at sea. They too are to be remembered and congratulated for the part they played.

Personal Everest touched the lives of many people, including those beyond our shores. It has not only inspired a new generation of disabled sailors in this country, it has demonstrated to everyone that disability need not be a barrier to achieving your dream.

Anne

HRH The Princess Royal
June 2008

Preface

Some time ago a good friend of mine, Trevor Jones, wrote a book and called it *Walking on Air*. Trevor was a helicopter pilot in the Royal Navy, and it was he who plucked Richard Branson out of the Irish Sea in 1987 when his balloon crash-landed after an attempt to fly across the Atlantic. A few weeks after the rescue, Trevor broke his neck in a skiing accident and became a quadriplegic like me. He's also a keen sailor. When his book was published in 1997, I remember thinking to myself, '*Walking on Air*, what a great title for a book, especially for a pilot. If I ever write a book, I'll call it *Walking on Water*.'

There have been many points in my life when people have said to me 'you should write a book', but I have resisted for a number of reasons. Finding the time was certainly one of them, but so too was the belief that I didn't have enough material. There are those who say that there is a book inside everyone, just waiting to be written. I'm sceptical – that's like saying there's an Olympic medal in each of us – and I certainly don't have the skill or patience required to win one of them! I also felt for a long time that I was too young to write an autobiography, conscious of all the great things that I still wanted to do that would be omitted if I wrote it too early.

When I completed Personal Everest, my sail around Great Britain, I felt the journey needed to be documented, not only as a means of thanking everyone who played a part in its success, but also to demonstrate what can be achieved, regardless of ability. But I also felt that the time had come to document my life story, although writing an autobiography aged forty-two still feels way too young. I console myself with the thought that I'll just have to write another when I have a new set of adventures and experiences that I want to share.

I have spent more than half my life as a disabled person. I am quadriplegic, and will have to use a wheelchair for the rest of my life. Like all disabled people, I have had to deal with many difficult physical and emotional challenges over the years. Some, such as getting out of bed or preparing food, are daily challenges presented by the disability itself, whilst others are barriers created by society – issues surrounding employment, personal care and housing, for example. But all are obstacles that need to be planned for and overcome, and I have explored many of them in the book.

Some years ago, the actor Christopher Reeve and I had a heated debate live on Channel 4 News. He had not long been paralysed following a horse-riding accident, and he spent much of his time and effort seeking a cure to paralysis and trying to walk again. I, on the other hand, although not desiring to live my life in a wheelchair, had become more accepting of the situation and was arguing that Reeve could better use his fame to raise awareness of issues such as access to employment, transport and everyday living for disabled people. Reeve stated, and I quote, that I was 'in denial with a capital D'. I realised then that disability meant different things to different people. For Reeve, it was the refusal to accept his condition and the hope of finding a cure. There's nothing wrong with that, but I choose to look at life from a different perspective.

The danger in refusing to accept your disability whilst searching for a cure is that it may somehow propagate a notion that walking is good, and being in a wheelchair is bad. Even the term 'cure' implies remedying a bad situation. Of course most disabled people would prefer not to be disabled at all – me too – but so long as we are afforded equal rights, we are not discriminated against, and we can work and live in an accessible environment, then who has the right to say we would be better off walking?

Given the choice between walking again but remaining

reliant on others to provide my personal care, and staying in a wheelchair but becoming independent, there would be no contest. Being independent and relieving my loved ones from providing that twenty-four-hour care would be my most sincere wish, even if it meant remaining in a wheelchair.

For more than two decades, I have existed only because I have the care and support I need as a person with a high-level spinal cord injury – and that care and support has been provided by my wife Elaine. There are not enough words in the English dictionary to express how lucky I feel to have that unconditional love and support.

I've been on many long journeys in my life, from physical ones like sailing the Atlantic as a teenager to emotional ones like coming to terms with a life-changing disability, but the trick I have discovered is to learn from each and every thing I do, and so long as I continue to test myself and embark on new challenges, then I will never stop learning. Writing this book has been a journey in its own right. Using only my right index finger, I have tapped almost a million keystrokes in writing, then editing, nearly 130,000 words. Apart from the physical difficulties of doing so over the past five months, it has forced me to open up some long-since closed boxes in my memory. It's been tough but cathartic too, and maybe, now that I have laid some of those ghosts to rest, it's time to be thinking about the next stage in my fortunate life.

Geoff Holt

I

I managed to gasp only a cupful of air as I was thrown out of my boat and into the sea. I lay there, face down, motionless. It was then a matter of waiting. Waiting for my lifejacket to inflate and turn me over, and waiting to be rescued.

My eyes were open wide and I could see shafts of daylight piercing the water around me, fading into the darkness below. The bitter cold of the water caused acute pain in my temples as the blood vessels to my head became constricted. I could feel the icy water creeping its way around the inside of my helmet and seeping around the neck of my drysuit. And still I waited. My lungs were bursting. Still my lifejacket did not inflate and still I remained face down, held up on the surface only by the inherent buoyancy in my clothes.

Everything had happened in slow motion as I fell out of the boat. First my head and shoulders were in the water, then my arms, my body and my legs followed. Once immersed, everything took on an eerie quiet – total and utter silence. I remained conscious and was acutely aware of my impending fate, but completely helpless to save myself.

Finding yourself thrown into a turbulent and cold sea against your will can be dangerous at the best of times. When you are quadriplegic, completely paralysed from the shoulders down, and plunged face-first into the water it very quickly becomes life-threatening. When the lifejacket you are wearing doesn't turn you over, and you have no alternative but to hold what little breath you have in your lungs whilst you stare in desperation and fear into the murky depths below, it becomes something straight out of your worst nightmare.

I had seen the rigid inflatable boat cut across in front of my bow, its yellow battle flag flying stiffly from its stern as it powered past, carrying a TV crew trying to find the best spot to film me from. Along with many other spectator boats that were out to wish me bon voyage that day, it was creating a terrific wash. My fragile fifteen-foot trimaran dinghy *Freethinker* was no match for the waves and confused seas which came at me from every direction and, together with a fresh May breeze, it was at the very limit of my ability.

That first pass by the TV crew's RIB had only added to the confused sea. I felt the back of *Freethinker* lift as the wash from the RIB began to pass under her stern. She then accelerated down the wave at terrific speed, sending salty spray everywhere, obscuring my view and completely soaking me as I sat perched in the tiny cockpit, only inches from the water. With weak arms, I fought to steer using the backs of my wrists on the tiller, but with little success – she was fast becoming uncontrollable. In an attempt to slow the boat down, I grasped the mainsheet in my teeth and frantically tried to free it, but the wind was so strong the rope was jammed tight in the cleat, and no matter how hard I pulled and jerked my head, I simply did not have the strength to release the sail. Having just about survived that wave, I looked over and could see the delight in the eyes of the TV crew: from their viewpoint, ahead of me, it must have looked most spectacular.

'Again, do it again,' I heard the cameraman shout to the RIB driver, clearly wanting to repeat the dramatic visual effect and capture it on film.

'No! Stop! Please stop!' I shouted as loudly as I was able, but they could not hear me. No one could hear my weak voice over the maelstrom of motors, wind and waves, nor could they see the fear in my face, hidden behind my helmet visor. I fumbled frantically with my clawed hands to press the tiny red *transmit* button on the VHF radio strapped to my chest. I could see what they were thinking and I knew the likely consequence. I needed to warn them to keep clear, but it was futile. With cold sea water spraying everywhere, using one wrist to try and steer, my teeth clenched on the mainsheet and the boat being thrown violently on the waves, even if I had managed to transmit my message, it was unlikely they would have heard me. It was too late anyway.

For the second time, the RIB cut across me, this time creating an even bigger wash behind it. With the wind blowing hard from astern, once again *Freethinker* surged at terrific speed down its wash. This time she accelerated even quicker, reaching the bottom of the wave and veering violently to starboard. In so doing, I overbalanced and was catapulted to my left. Unable to balance myself and with nothing to hold me, I found myself, not for the first time in my life, lying face down in the water, seconds from drowning.

Even though my head and face were under water, I remember a sensation of crying, because of the intense burning pain in my chest. I was aware that if I breathed in just one shallow gulp of water, with my already compromised lung capacity, I would probably die. I lay there, completely helpless, my paralysed body slumped on the surface of the water, just rising and falling with each wave that passed over me, waiting. I was seconds from drowning in the bitterly cold waters of the Solent. Less than fifteen minutes earlier, I had kissed my wife and son goodbye amidst wonderful celebrations as I set out from Hamble to become the first disabled person to sail single-handed around Great Britain. I had so much to live for – I did not want to die. And it is maybe for that reason that I cried too.

After what seemed an eternity, I decided that I would count to five – at which point I was going to breathe. I knew the consequence would be almost certain death, but I could fight it no longer. I mentally said my goodbyes to my family.

I got to four, and was drawing in what would have been my last breath, when I felt a strong pair of hands grab me from behind and turn me over. My lungs filled with air, not water: I was alive. Spike, one of my support crew, had thrown himself off *Everest One*, our team RIB, and swum to my rescue. Watching the footage on TV later that day, ironically filmed by the very crew that had caused the incident, my flirt with death had lasted no more than 35 seconds – but it felt like a lifetime.

Once safe in Spike's arms, and with the rescue boat alongside, my mind quickly turned to more immediate matters.

'Is she in neutral?' I bellowed at Andy, who was at the wheel of *Everest One*.

'Yes, why?' he said, clearly taken aback that I had emerged from a near-drowning incident only to start questioning his boat-handling skills.

'I just want to keep me legs,' I replied. Even though they do not work, the thought of having my legs chewed off by the boat's propeller, a very real likelihood had it been revolving at any speed, did not appeal. I needn't have worried. Andy had everything under control.

Despite being rescued from drowning, I recall no sense of relief, nor do I even remember thanking Spike for saving my life. I was immediately aware that being dragged from the water would not be the end of my problems. Indeed, it was only the beginning. Whilst I had been able to think only of survival as I lay face down in the water, once I began the slow trip back to the Royal Southern Yacht Club, where I had started my ill-fated journey just minutes earlier, my emotions were in turmoil. I felt sick, a deep nausea in the pit of my stomach, the same as you feel when bereaved, a helpless, empty, gut-wrenching feeling, yet numb, unable to cry out loud.

Even from some distance, I could sense the zoom-lenses of the photographers focused tightly on my face looking for my expression – any expression – and I was acutely aware of the many TV crews who would be broadcasting every agonising detail. I wasn't wrong on either count. When I later saw the television pictures, I felt that I had done a good job of putting on a brave face – my smile looked pretty convincing – but only I knew that behind that forced grin my world was imploding. Behind my eyes I was just ripping myself apart. I was aware that many people had followed the build-up and had seen the disaster that befell me that day, and that only compounded my feeling of shame.

'There's no going back now, you know.' The words of Her Royal Highness the Princess Royal were not only ringing in my ears, they were positively deafening. Some weeks earlier, on 21 March 2007, Princess Anne had launched my record attempt to become the first disabled sailor to sail single-handed around Great Britain. Herself a keen sailor and patron of RYA Sailability, the national disabled sailing charity that I was hoping to promote by accomplishing my sailing ambition, she had stood on a stage in London surrounded by my sponsors and publicly stated her support for my project. As her host that day, I saw the Princess to her car when she left. Just as she was about to drive away, she lifted her sunglasses, looked me dead in the eye and, in a voice that was not inviting further discussion, stated, 'There's no going back now, you know.' She didn't have to elaborate, I knew exactly what she meant. She had allowed me to put her name to my project and had thereby staked her own reputation on its success, and this was her way of telling me not to let her down. I have the utmost respect for the Princess, and I was determined to keep my side of the bargain.

Having royal endorsement was just one of many layers of responsibility resting on my shoulders that fateful day, and the Princess was just one of many people I felt I had let down. After the rescue, with me sitting perched on the inflatable hull of *Everest One*, held tightly around the chest by my project manager Ian Clover, we made our way slowly back up the River Hamble. It was no more than a mile but it seemed to take forever, and all I wanted to do was to get out of the glare of publicity and shut myself away. The incident had been witnessed by many people. Not least my sponsors and suppliers, who were using the opportunity to entertain clients and staff on a fleet of luxury motor cruisers. There was also a small flotilla of well-wishers out on the water and a large number of boats with members of the press on board, all of whom had come to witness my departure, not my fall from grace. Although it would hardly have cheered me at the time, I later learnt that immediately after my rescue, one of my suppliers, in an effort to lift the mood on a spectator boat, had been heard joking, 'If I'd known I was going to spend £3,000 on a funeral, I'd have ordered more champagne!'

I may have had some ups and downs in my life, but without doubt I shall remember Monday 14 May 2007 as the lowest. That may seem a strange thing to say, coming from someone who was paralysed as a teenager – but when I broke my neck it did not reflect on me personally, nor impact on my integrity. This latest episode was totally different. I had persuaded seven people to put their lives on hold to become my support crew, and they had left behind family, friends and even jobs to help me realise my ambition to sail around Great Britain, for no reward other than to be part of an historic expedition. I had persuaded a major law firm to give me money to fund my adventure and I had persuaded many other companies to provide me with specialist equipment and support. I had also told all my friends and family of my plans; they all believed in me and for months had been living every moment of the build-up with me. Most importantly, I had staked my reputation by persuading all these people – crew, family, friends, sponsors, the press and even Princess Anne – to put their faith in me. Everything hinged around me and what I had said I would do. My integrity, my credibility and the way I am perceived is of paramount importance to me. So it is difficult to find the words to explain the deep, deep feelings of shame, humiliation and embarrassment that I felt that day. I was completely and utterly distraught, yet numb and confused. Even though people were telling me it was not my fault, I felt my credibility as a yachtsman – and as a person – had been destroyed in an instant. I wanted to hide but there was nowhere to go.

Fifteen years working in PR and marketing had certainly provided me with the skills to 'talk the talk', and boy had I created a monster when I created the Personal Everest sailing project! At least the enormous press interest proved there was nothing wrong with my PR skills. But when you give your heart and soul to something, when you get people to support you and believe in you based solely on what you have told them, when you believe so strongly that your ambition is achievable, and then a freak accident nearly kills you a matter of minutes after setting off, your world feels like it has collapsed.

The media interest had grown significantly since I first announced my project in September 2006, and it had reached a crescendo on 14 May 2007. I was attracting national TV and radio coverage, not to mention pages in newspapers and the various sailing journals, all of whom had been generous in their coverage and their support of me. But with publicity come the inevitable critics. Naively I could see no negative aspects whatsoever in what I was trying to achieve, but that all changed the moment news of my near-drowning was broadcast. And because it was witnessed by so many members of the press, I attracted more than my fair share of critics.

Newspapers were soon receiving letters from readers keen to air their views, and comments were being left on various online message boards and websites. Of course many were messages of support but, at that time, I allowed myself only to read the negative ones. None more hurtful than those on the local *Southampton Daily Echo*'s website, which included such gems as

Why do the public warm to these nutters? Quite clearly the man needs help. Why should our brave rescue services have to risk their own lives to rescue these publicity obsessed imbeciles? *Anon*

or

How totally irresponsible, this man should be stopped, but no, it's PC gone mad. Bob should stay at home. *Anon*

I presume the moniker 'Bob' was a reference to my floating on the surface, which I must admit I find mildly amusing now, but not so at the time.

If I was hurt reading them, then I knew my wife Elaine would be too, so I consciously took a decision to keep them from her. I was also frankly embarrassed, and I didn't want to start circulating negative material at a time when I was trying to give the impression of strength and resolve. I took the comments very personally, especially when they came from people who knew nothing of me or my background. People told me to ignore the negatives and focus only on the positive comments, but it wasn't easy. I knew in my heart that the project was achievable, so it was surprising, upsetting and offensive that people were thinking these things. But my determination to continue was not about proving the critics wrong, it was about proving myself right.

Once back ashore, and with many of my well-wishers still present and enjoying the hospitality of the yacht club, I faced the inevitable postmortem press interviews.

'What happened?' – 'Why didn't your lifejacket inflate?' – 'What were you thinking lying face down?' – 'Are you going to continue?' – the questions were coming thick and fast. I don't recall my answers, but I do remember repeatedly saying that I was sorry. I just needed to get into dry, warm clothes and get out of there. Still wearing my false smile, I said my farewells and pulled the door closed on my motorhome.

By now it was late afternoon. The entire crew gathered together our belongings and we headed back on the twenty-minute journey to my house. I could only imagine what my team members and my sponsors might be thinking, and my mood sank still further. I was torturing myself with my shame, and I was aware that the people I had persuaded to support me would probably be questioning their own judgement at this point. And who could blame them?

We all sat and watched the local news on TV that evening. I was the lead story on both channels. I got to see the incident for the first time, which was extremely shocking, mainly because of the speed and apparent ease with which it had occurred, but the effect was greatest on Elaine. It's one thing getting back ashore and recounting the event, but when we saw those powerful images of me lying face down in the sea, looking like a corpse, Elaine burst into tears and left the room. I guess what made it worse was knowing that I was actually alive, holding my breath, desperately waiting to be rescued whilst fearing the worst.

I suggested to the crew that we all had an early night and reconvene the following morning to discuss what went wrong and what, if anything, would happen next. I didn't sleep well that night.

The following morning I needed to know the views of my sponsors and my crew. Was the attempt over before it had begun? My crew were first to gather. Early that Tuesday morning, Spike, Mike, Joel, Andy, Sarah, Ian and Elaine sat motionless in my living room, cradling cups of coffee while I waited quietly for their comments. It seemed strange even being back in our house. The previous day we had locked the front door with no intention of returning for at least two months, so sitting in the front room when we should have been well on our way seemed a little strange.

This disparate group, which had only come together in its entirety a matter of days earlier, had already developed a feeling of camaraderie and professionalism that you might find in a long-established sports team. If we had not fully connected earlier, the events of the day before had now bonded us totally. So when they unanimously agreed to support me and stated their wish to continue, it felt as though we had become one big family, a feeling which was to last throughout the project. My respect for each and every one of them never waned, and their decision to support me that morning signalled the start of my emotional healing.

I was further comforted by the unconditional support of my sponsors, the law firm Blake Lapthorn Tarlo Lyons. I spoke early that same morning to their senior partner. Characteristically, their first concern was for my health and wellbeing, which I found very touching. Once satisfied that I was unhurt, they gave their blessing for the project to continue, and from that moment they too became very much part of the family. I appreciate that it must have been a huge decision for them to make, especially considering any support for me would now face additional scrutiny by their staff and their clients. I had no prior experience of sponsors, but this was like no other law firm I had ever come across before – not for the first time in my life, I realised how lucky I was.

Despite being raised a Catholic and attending a Catholic school, I have long since lost any interest in religion. I've seen too much pain, witnessed too much suffering, endured too much injustice. I don't believe in fate either and therefore disagree with those who are adamant that 'things happen for a reason', but I do have the ability to see the positives in most situations, no matter how bad. OK, so it is difficult to find many positives when you break your neck at the age of eighteen and are faced with a lifetime in a wheelchair, but I managed to do so then. So it was never going to be as difficult to find a silver lining to this latest devastating episode in my life.

Having secured that reassurance from my crew and my sponsors, I was being given a second chance to prove that I could deliver exactly what I had said I would. I grabbed it with open arms, but this time I knew there would be no more chances. There was now an urgency to get the expedition back on track, and that gave us all a focus, but there were two pressing matters to be addressed.

Firstly, I had fallen out of the boat far too easily. Despite sailing this type of boat, a Challenger class trimaran, for nearly twenty years without any major incidents, I needed to know why it happened and how we could prevent the same thing happening again. There are about three hundred of these dinghies in the UK and around the world sailed by disabled sailors. Most are sailed on inland reservoirs and lakes, but I regularly sailed mine at sea, so I knew its capabilities.

Secondly, we needed to discover why my lifejacket did not turn me over. We did not have to wait long to find out. By 9.00 a.m. that Tuesday morning, a director from the manufacturer Crewsaver was on the phone. Less than an hour later, he and a colleague sat stony-faced in my front room. This was a very serious matter for everyone concerned, and we all knew it. The press had been full of stories that my jacket had somehow 'failed' and, to be honest, at the time I was livid that it had not automatically inflated. Lifejackets come in two main types; those that open automatically when you fall in the water and those you have to physically pull a toggle to inflate. Some twelve years earlier I had been given a top-of-the-range lifejacket by Crewsaver as a form of sponsorship when I had sailed single-handed around the Isle of Wight. These RIB jackets are the same as worn by the RNLI inshore lifeboat crews and are manually inflatable only. Unbeknown to the gentlemen in my sitting room, my jacket had been retro-fitted with an automatic inflating system because, as a quadriplegic, I did not have the physical strength or dexterity to pull a toggle. So when Crewsaver kindly agreed to provide all of our lifejackets for our latest trip, they replaced my old RIB jacket with a new one. I had presumed it was an automatic jacket just like my old one, while they presumed I had only ever had a manual jacket. Critically, neither party had checked, and the result was clear for all to see. We all agreed that it was better for the facts to emerge now than in a coroner's court.

With the problem identified and everyone involved desperate to find a suitable solution, Guy Page from Crewsaver kindly spent a day with us pool-testing a variety of different lifejackets with a variety of clothing combinations until we found one that did work. It was a huge relief and meant that we could cross that job off the list.

The next urgent task was to address my stability in my boat. It is extremely dangerous to tie or fasten anyone to a boat, for should the boat capsize their chances of escape are seriously compromised, especially someone unable to physically help themselves like me. Spike and Ian spent many a long hour sketching a variety of designs before finally agreeing on a collapsible framework that would be assembled around me. Once I was comfortably seated in my tiny cockpit, a pair of aluminium bars would be fastened to form support under my arms and thereby greatly increase my stability, but it would still allow me to float free if the boat became inverted. Within a day, the design had been manufactured and fitted to the boat. We were ready to go.

Unfortunately the weather had worsened since our false start on Monday. At first this was not a problem: it gave us time to address the matters of my lifejacket and the roll bars. However, by the end of the week, when all the jobs were done, we started to wait for the right weather conditions. When we had completed our original risk assessments, we decided that the maximum wind strength for me to sail safely would be about 15 knots. It was not quite that simple, because we also needed to take into account tides and sea state, all of which affected the performance of my boat and could impede any help that I might need from *Everest One*. It was blowing above 20 knots for most of Friday and early Saturday morning. Unknown to us, this delay waiting for the weather was only a taste of what was to come but, now that we had everything ready to go, it was frustrating indeed. The press coverage, certainly at a local level, was intense. Every day the regional newspapers had been telephoning me and running stories. Was I going to continue? Was it true that I was calling the whole thing off? When were we restarting? And the most amazing headline of all: 'I nearly died because I was wearing the wrong trousers.' We needed to go, and soon.

On Saturday 19 May, it looked as though the low pressure

system was moving away quicker than expected and would be followed by more gentle winds. Hourly assessments of the Met Office website and analysis of their synoptic charts gave us an inkling of hope that we could once again set off. On the Saturday night, only five days after the false start, we called a crew briefing and then notified our sponsors, immediate close friends and family that we would be leaving. This time there would be no press pack calling for 'one last photo', and no radio presenter pushing a microphone under my nose. As much as I had courted the press – and, in general, they were incredibly supportive of me – we had to do this departure in our own time. Five days earlier the situation felt out of control, and we were determined that would never happen again.

At midday on Sunday 20 May, at the public slipway at Lower Swanwick on the banks of the River Hamble, I was very quietly lifted into my boat. It was a bright, warm spring day with only a few locals launching their dinghies from the water's edge. We carried out all of my pre-sailing checks and then, followed by my 22-foot support boat, for the second time in a week I sailed off down the River Hamble, followed by a light breeze from the north. And so began the biggest adventure of my life.

2

I was born on 24 February 1966 in Farlington, Portsmouth, and christened Geoffrey Trevor Marden Hoad at St Colman's Church, Cosham, in August the same year. At the time of my birth, my mother, Patricia Hoad, was barely twenty-one years old. An attractive and ambitious young fashion model, she was married to Robin Hoad, a haulage contractor. Somewhat inauspiciously, I was named after Robin's brother, my uncle Geoffrey, who had been killed a few years earlier in a motorcycling accident at the age of eighteen. I had one older brother, Richard, born in 1963. Richard and I had anything but a stable upbringing, but our relationship as brothers was perfectly normal – that is, fighting and arguing continuously throughout our childhood. However, maybe as a result of some unstable times as children, we now have a respect for each other and a closeness that strengthens with the passing of time.

My earliest memory – I was about four years old – is being struck by a hit-and-run driver and left for dead in the middle of Waterworks Road in Farlington. Richard and I had just bought our ice lollies – I had chosen my favourite, a FAB – from an ice-cream van across the street. Even as a child I never did understand why he always parked on the opposite side of the road where there were no houses. Having paid for our ice lollies, and holding mine firmly in my small hand, trying not to let it drip, I recall seeing the ice-cream man look in his mirror and say it was 'OK' to cross the road. Richard ran first and I followed. He made it across safely but I was struck by a Land Rover which did not stop and I was left, unconscious, in the middle of the road. The next thing I remember was waking up on my Nana's sofa just as the ambulance arrived. My right leg had been very badly broken, and I had some head injuries. I remember feeling scared, I was in great pain and I was calling for my mummy.

By this time in my life, my mother Patricia, or Patti as she preferred to be known, had long since left Richard and me to be raised by her foster mother, Harriet Carter, our beloved Nana. Already in her sixties by the time I was born, Nana single-handedly looked after Richard and me for the first eight years of my life. My mother had left us with Nana to pursue her own life which, at that particular time, did not include her two young sons.

My leg was so seriously broken there was even talk of amputation, but it was saved by a previously untested operation which rebuilt my right tibia and fibula with several metal plates and pins, with pretty good success. Unfortunately the surgery made the broken leg grow much faster, eventually resulting in a right leg half an inch longer than the left, but at least I kept the leg, even though it was to cause pain and discomfort throughout my later childhood. Having been notified of my accident, my mother – whom I had not seen for several months – burst into the ward at St Mary's Hospital, Portsmouth, laden with presents for me, crying hysterically and openly blaming my Nana for allowing the accident to happen. I wasn't particularly interested in the presents, nor did I understand why my Nana was in trouble, I was just so pleased to see my mummy. But, as happened so often in the early years of my life, she left as quickly as she arrived. I guess she was there less than an hour, but I recall feeling much better for her visit. After a week or so in hospital I returned to Nana's house with my leg in plaster. To this day I find it hard to accept that no one seemed interested in finding the driver of the vehicle. It was a clear case of hit and run, and could easily have resulted in a tragic death.

Richard and I shared the back bedroom of No. 32 Waterworks Road, a semidetached council house that Nana had called St David's, in a fairly quiet part of north Portsmouth where suburbia meets industrial estate. Apart from Nana, the only other occupant was Sid Wilkinson, a lodger who rented the small upstairs bedroom at the front of the house. Sid was a quiet chap, an electronics whizz who would ride his push-bike each day to his job at Marconi and occasionally, just occasionally, would be asked by Nana to tell us off when we were too naughty. Just because we were estranged from our parents, that didn't mean that we lived without the security a child gets from a loving home. Both Richard and I were loved very much by Nana, we knew that for certain. Each night at bedtime, because Nana couldn't climb the stairs very easily due to her 'bad legs', she would call out 'I love you more than all the tea in China', which was such a comfort as we walked barefoot across the cold and sticky linoleum floor to our beds. Looking back, I realise now what a wonderful woman our Nana was to look after two boisterous young boys on what must have been a very tight budget. It could not have been easy for her, especially at her age, and, as we only discovered later, suffering the pain of breast cancer. My only regret is that I did not realise exactly how wonderful she was until I was much older and she had long since died from that cancer.

Shortly after my birth my mother and Robin moved less than a mile away to No. 2 Marshfield House, a newly constructed block of maisonettes in Farlington. But within a couple of years Richard and I were back living with Nana as my parents went through a divorce. My mother's career was the catalyst for the break-up of their marriage. She was a successful fashion model and would often model beautiful clothes for department stores such as Knight & Lee in Southsea. She had even won the Miss Southsea beauty contest in the early 1960s. It is understandable that a woman from a tough background who suddenly finds herself a centre of attention and exposed to the finer things in life, simply by using her looks as a model, would see that as an easy route to a better future. It's not so easy to understand that a mother would choose that path at the cost of giving up her children. At this stage in her life, having two young sons was certainly going to hinder that journey. So, for the time being at least, she pursued her career and those aspirations without us.

Having divorced my mother, 'Daddy Robin', as we called to him, would pop into Nana's every Friday night on his way home from work to give us our 50p pocket money, and he would also give Nana money to help towards our upkeep. Richard and I so looked forward to his visit each week. He would bend down and give me a kiss, his rough stubbly chin scratching my face, his blue overalls always dirty and smelling of engine oil. Sadly, after maybe an hour at most, he would be gone again.

The physical similarities shared by my brother Richard and our father Robin grew more obvious the older Richard became. Both were of medium height and stocky build, with dark hair and dark eyes – attributes which were completely at odds with my tall, lanky build, blond hair and blue eyes. For many years during my childhood I sensed that I was somehow different. Even at such a young age I could see a closeness between Richard and his father that didn't exist in the same way between me and Robin. I wasn't exactly troubled by these thoughts but they did occur from time to time, though nothing was ever mentioned. Several decades later it turned out that my concerns were well founded, and by the time I was forty I would discover a completely new set of family members.

Our mother's visits were less frequent, maybe only two or three times a year, but they were much more dramatic than Robin's. In one of my school books there is an insight into one such visit, written when I was aged seven. It reads:

> On Friday I was in bed and there was a knock at the door and Nana opened the door and Mummy came in and woke us up and pulled us out of bed and took us down stairs and put us on the table and put our clothes on and Nana said 'get out' and she went out.

Moments like this, when my mother would unexpectedly appear, were not an uncommon feature of my childhood. They happened with some regularity so, other than being confused, I don't recall being upset by such episodes. Infuriatingly the story in my school book doesn't say what happened next, but she must have left empty-handed on this occasion because it goes on to tell of my visit to the cinema the following day with Nana.

Sometimes my mother was turned away by Nana, other times she would take us away from our home and our everyday lives only to return us to Nana's doorstep like unwanted toys a few days later. My teacher gave me a tick and a gold star for writing that story. A teacher today might be more inclined to call social services.

I attended Solent Road Junior school, which is situated in the shadow of Portsdown Hill, a high chalk ridge which extends a good eight miles from Bedhampton in the east to Portchester in the west and embraces Portsmouth to the south. As a child growing up in Farlington, Portsdown Hill was an enormous, long white mountain which was omnipresent. You could not go out to play without looking up and seeing the imposing white skyline which was lined with Palmerston's Napoleonic Forts, including Fort Southwick, Fort Nelson and, to a child, the amusingly named Fort Widley. For most of my childhood I also firmly believed that the chalk cliffs were home to Stig of the Dump but, despite many an expedition during the summer holidays, I failed ever to locate him or his cave.

Every Monday morning at school we would write a short story about our activities the previous weekend in our 'busy books'. I still have many of those books, and they make entertaining, if slightly uncomfortable, reading – almost two years' worth of weekly diaries written when I was aged six and seven. From reading them, it seems that Nana, Richard and I spent a lot of time at the Co-op and watching television – although in one entry I am at pains to stress that my friend Jimmy had a new colour TV! In general, I seem to have been a happy child and, apart from a feeling of wanting to be part of a 'normal' family, I certainly recall having friends and doing all the things children like to do.

As if my family structure was not complicated enough, one of the things that made me happiest as a young boy was the fact that I had the luxury of my very own 'adopted' family. Not adopted in the true sense of the word, although it was very nearly so. The Pennell family had been our next-door neighbours when my parents lived briefly at Marshfield House. They had offered to formally adopt me when my mother initially suggested the idea to them at the time of her first divorce, when I was just two years old. My mother changed her mind at the very last minute, but the Pennell family continued to offer their love and support to me, and have been every bit my family ever since, right up to the present day. Often there to support Nana when things got too much for her, my happiest childhood memories are of No. 3 Marshfield House and being with my 'Uncle Roy' and 'Auntie Joyce'. Roy and Joyce Pennell, and their three daughters Jenny, Wendy and Val, were the family I craved. Whenever I visited them as a young child, I had such a feeling of security and comfort that I would not have wished to be anywhere else in the world. Not that I was singled out for special attention – it was far better than that, I was just a member of the family, their family, albeit only for the occasional overnight stay or, if I was really lucky, a whole weekend.

Roy was a bus driver for Portsmouth City Council, and the whole Pennell family and I were known by just about every driver and conductor who worked on the buses in the city. Every time I got on a bus in Portsmouth, regardless of where I was or who the driver was, they would say 'Here he is, Roy's boy, no charge for him.' It made me feel so proud. Saturdays were my favourite day. We would catch a bus from the Eastern Road to Charlotte Street market in Portsmouth. Joyce would do her shopping whilst I took in all the sights, sounds and smells of the fruit and veg stalls. We would then head back to Marshfield House, where Joyce would cook us home-made fish and chips for lunch whilst we watched Dickie Davis compere the World of Sport on ITV, and then I'd study Roy as he did his pools coupon, I'd love just watching him.

By all accounts I was a good boy. I certainly don't recall ever being malicious or sly, two traits I hate most in children. I'm not saying that I wasn't naughty, and there's many a time I recall being told off or having my pocket money stopped, but by and large I remember being respectful towards grown-ups. Having a brother with whom I argued continuously was one thing, but having Jenny, Wendy and Val as surrogate sisters was just wonderful – even though I would call them 'auntie'. Just about everyone in those days was an 'auntie' or 'uncle'. Then in their teens, they all treated me like a younger brother and I got to listen to all the latest pop music that they'd play, something that was most notably missing in a house run by our elderly Nana.

Two of Roy's daughters, Jenny and Wendy, were married to matelots, Royal Navy seamen, Tim Edwards and Danny Daniels. Although they were often away serving on ships overseas, when Tim and Danny were on leave they would spend time at home with Roy and Joyce. As the only child in the house at that time, I was spoiled rotten and would hang off their every word – although they wound me up constantly. I was a teenager before I realised that tattoos of naked women did not come out of cornflake packets, and for years I had believed Tim when he told me that you could get drunk on water if you drank enough of it. I would secretly down pints of the stuff and convince myself I was drunk. In another of my 'busy book' entries, dated 2 July 1973, when I was seven years old, I wrote:

> My uncle [Tim] and I went to the pub and I was drunk. I had half a pint of rum, three bottles of coke and nearly half pint of beer.

Maybe the rum bit was slightly exaggerated, but in bold red pen all of that passage has been crossed out by my teacher. So I got a tick and a merit sticker when I wrote about a parental abduction in the middle of the night but I got my work dismissed as rubbish when I wrote a truthful account of a pub trip with my 'Uncle Tim'. How times have changed.

Sadly, both Roy and Tim died some years ago, both of them far too young. Roy was in his sixties, but at least I was with him and

Joyce the moment he passed away. Tim was only in his late forties when he died. He left behind not only his wife Jenny but his three kids too, Carl, Anthony and Carrie. He was a great man, a real man's man, and it was in memory of him that we named our son Timothy when he was born in 2002. Even now, forty years later, nothing gives me greater pleasure than sitting in that same front room at No. 3 Marshfield House having Sunday lunch with the family, all of whom have now grown up and are joined by the third and fourth generations. Sitting there always makes me realise the importance of family, which is brought home even more when I see my son Timothy playing with the same toys I played with, in the same garden I played in and enjoying the unconditional love that I did at No. 3 Marshfield House.

By 1970, my mother was on her second marriage. Her new husband was John Holt, a quiet, intelligent, handsome and successful businessman who would go on to be hugely influential in my later life. Neither Richard nor I had been told she was remarrying, and we were not invited to the wedding. Despite being so young, I think we had the capacity to understand and had a right to know.

One day which stuck in my young memory from that period spent living with Nana was Wednesday 1 December 1971. Pregnant with her third child – but her first with new husband John Holt – my mother had returned to 32 Waterworks Road so she could give birth. John's beautiful big blue Bristol car looked so out of place parked outside Nana's council house. Quite why she had chosen to return to our house to have her baby is not clear to this day, but I remember Richard and me lying awake in our bedroom, listening through the wall to my mother's screams as she went through several hours of labour that night. Then it went quiet for a while until we heard the cries of a baby. A midwife came to our bedroom to tell us that we were allowed to go in and see our mother and our new sister, Lucy. Whilst my mother lay in bed cradling her daughter in her arms, our stepfather, 'Daddy John', was sitting on the end of the bed holding a lump of teak wood in one hand and a chisel in the other, busily carving a dolphin for a figurehead on his new yacht. It was rather a surreal moment, but the dolphins were infinitely more interesting to a five-year-old boy than a crying baby. I lay awake for most of that night trying to figure out where babies came from, a puzzle that was to occupy me for many years to follow.

Within a day of the birth, as quickly as she had arrived, my mother left again, this time taking our new baby sister with her. Once again Richard and I were left behind as my mother, my stepfather and their new daughter headed off to a world of nice clothes and expensive cars, talking of holidays and sailing boats. It would have been easy to feel jealous in some way at being left behind again. But I certainly felt no bitterness, just sadness and loneliness, as though I was being punished for something I had done wrong. I honestly believed that unless I was a good boy, I would never be allowed to live with my mummy. Of course, it was not my fault, I had done nothing wrong, but it felt that way. It was a cruel torment for such a young child and it went on for years. It would be many months before we would see them all again. And it would be nearly another three years before we would be uprooted one last time to start a new life with the Holt family.

3

I had been thinking about sailing around Great Britain in my trimaran dinghy as early as 2004. I'd just heard that one of my best friends had died and I had driven to the place where we had played as kids to have some private time and to gather my thoughts. That afternoon on Lower Swanwick foreshore was like any other weekday, boats hurriedly going about their business on the River Hamble, their wakes lapping at the muddy shoreline, but all I could think about was Simon and the happier times we had spent right here, on this very spot, all those years ago.

Just sitting there, I lost track of time, and it was not long before it started to get dark and I needed to get back home. The subject of 'regrets' came to my mind, and I hoped that Simon had not died with any. I began to wonder what, if any, regrets I would claim when my time was up. Try as I might, I couldn't think of any – well, not any major ones: I was in a settled and contented phase of my life. But there was one thing that I would love to achieve, not so much a regret, more of a 'wouldn't it be great if' ambition, and that was the idea of sailing around Great Britain, on my own. The more I thought about it, the more vivid the idea became. With ideas increasingly racing through my mind, I rushed home to start putting some of my thoughts down onto my computer, worried that I would forget all the things that were popping into my head.

Never one to commit to anything until I have a fair degree of certainty of completing it successfully, over the following six months I slowly put together the bones of a plan without mentioning a word to anyone, not even my wife. My starting point was the basic feasibility of such an attempt. Could I, a man paralysed from the shoulders down, sail my fifteen-foot dinghy around the coast of Great Britain? Just asking myself the question sounded ridiculous to start with, and I allowed myself a wry smile. The first thing I needed to know was exactly how far such a trip was. At the time, not having the right charts available, I used a large-scale road atlas and a pair of compass dividers, set at forty-mile intervals, and walked them around the coastline. For no particular reason, other than it was the direction which seemed most natural, I started walking the dividers from Southampton westwards, towards Lands End, up the Irish Sea and the Welsh coast, across to the Isle of Man, straight up to Scotland, weaving a route between the Western Isles before rounding Cape Wrath at the top, crossing the Pentland Firth and then turning and heading south through the North Sea, down the east coast, crossing the Thames Estuary, before finally coming back along the south coast. With a ballpoint pen, I discretely marked little blue dots on all the pin-pricks made by the compass so Elaine wouldn't see them and ask what I was up to.

'Fifty-one, bloody hell,' I muttered to myself. Fifty-one day-sails at forty miles a day, over 2,000 statute miles. It was only my first, rough stab at a plan. I knew it would never be that straightforward, but at least it gave me an indication of distance and time.

I knew that I could sail up to sixty miles in a day. I had done so twice, once in 1992, the other time in 1997, on each occasion sailing my trimaran dinghy around the Isle of Wight. It was completing these two events which had given me the confidence to even think about such an enormous challenge.

I had learned a huge amount from my previous sailing experiences, not least that with the right preparation and equipment, my body and my boat were capable of enduring a great deal. As far as I was concerned, my biggest worries were getting a pressure sore on my bum from being seated for such a long time, suffering exposure from the relentless sea spray and wind blowing straight into my face, and dehydration from the difficulty of trying to eat and drink at sea whilst the boat is being tossed about. At the end of my first attempt in 1992 I suffered from all of the above but, with lessons learned, I made several changes, and the 1997 attempt was a complete success. I was extremely tired, but none the worse for wear.

On the basis that I could sail up to sixty miles in ten or twelve hours in my little boat, it was logical to conclude that if I were to sail for the same length of time, on consecutive days, I could, weather permitting, sail around Great Britain in about 50 days. When I was much younger I had sailed the oceans many times, so I was fully aware of the dangers I could face – but if I considered each leg simply as a 'day-sail', which I would only undertake when the wind and sea conditions were favourable, it would be a dream come true. After all, it would be summer time, what could go wrong? It would be the holiday of a lifetime. It would be my Personal Everest.

Convincing myself that it was just a bunch of day-sails worked well on my conscious mind, but it wasn't fooling my subconscious . As early as 2005 I was waking in the night with vivid nightmares of drowning, and this before I had told anyone of my idea. I knew that I still had the option to pull the plug and no one would be any the wiser, but for some reason I couldn't let it go and I was loving the excitement of the prospect.

In the document files on my computer, I created a folder called *Personal Everest*. I liked the name, it epitomised what the attempt was all about, it really was my personal Everest, the ultimate challenge for me, both mentally and physically.

On a scrap piece of paper I began to draft a timetable. It was now the spring of 2006, and still I had not discussed my plans with anyone – but I knew that would have to change soon. First and foremost, I had to ask Elaine if she minded me undertaking such an attempt: it was going to mean a huge upheaval. From the start, I was in no doubt that Personal Everest was potentially life-changing, for both of us. It had the potential to become enormous and I needed her understanding and her blessing. Assuming she agreed to me going ahead, the first decision was whether Elaine would be coming with me or not. If she did, it would mean bringing our son Timothy too, since we couldn't possibly leave him behind for two months. Alternatively, she could stay at home with Timothy and I could take a carer with me to look after my personal needs. At this stage, I still didn't know how or where I would sleep each night, but it was the principle of who would be providing my care that I needed to establish. Presuming Elaine and Timothy did come, and because the attempt would have to be during the summer to benefit from the best weather, then it was essential we were back in the first week of September 2007 for Timothy who, being five, would then be obliged to start school. So, working backwards, I would aim to be leaving in May 2007 – which left me just over a year to get to the starting line, and plenty of time to complete the challenge. The time had come to ask Elaine.

Surprisingly, Elaine seemed quite relaxed about it. 'I thought you'd been up to something,' she confessed. Part of me wondered whether she had just resigned herself to the fact that I have these ideas from time to time, and whether she was just going along with them to humour me.

'You don't understand,' I said, worrying that her immediate, unquestioning response needed greater consideration on her part. Perhaps I was hoping she would say no! Now, I really didn't have any excuse.

'Look, you do what you want, but please give me plenty of notice when and where you'll be needing me,' she said. 'Now, what are you having for tea?'

I still didn't think she had fully understood the monster I was about to unleash.

Working for fifteen years in marketing and PR departments for big international firms had given me experience in running successful marketing campaigns and establishing good press relations, and my twenty years or more as a disabled yachtsman had introduced me to some of the most influential journalists in the business.

I set about creating my own marketing plan for my project, with a detailed and timetabled action plan. First up, before I went public, I created a business entity by forming a company called Personal Everest Ltd, and I bought the web domain name *www.personaleverest.com*. I then set about creating the brand. To be honest, I had several attempts at creating a logo but it quickly became wasteful of my time and I wasn't happy with any of the results. Mindful of the marketing mantra, 'drive customers through the website', I decided to do just that, making the website the most prominent aspect of my business cards, headed paper and emails. It was through the website that I would give updates on my progress, and it could contain all the information anyone would need without me having to send out reams of paperwork.

In those early days, pre-launch, the website went through various changes, but with my decision to go public at the Southampton Boat Show in September 2006, it took a lot of work by my friends Richard Trebilcock and Paul Duffield to get it to the standard I wanted. It had to be perfect, and they didn't let me down.

If I was going to launch Personal Everest at the Boat Show, then I needed to be clear about exactly what my plans were. Journalists, particularly yachting journalists, are not easily fooled, and I would need to be as clear and as confident as I could be about exactly what, and how, I intended to execute this idea of mine.

I bought a copy of an Admiralty chart showing the whole of Great Britain, and I re-worked my original route, this time in greater detail. I still arrived at a similar number of stops, about fifty, and the nautical mileage for a complete circumnavigation was about 1,800 miles. Of those fifty stopovers, there were probably no more than two or three that I had visited previously, and certainly the ones I knew had no disabled accommodation within a mile or so of the harbour – so how on earth I would manage for accommodation at these destinations was anybody's guess. At one point, I even considered paying someone to do a recce of all the proposed ports of call in advance of my trip, all fifty of them, but with destinations subject to change because of weather it would have been a completely futile exercise. With no way of knowing what wheelchair-accessible accommodation would be like at each destination, there was only one alternative, and that was to get a wheelchair-accessible motorhome. Never in my life had I been in any motorhome, let alone slept in one for fifty nights, and with no idea where to rent or buy a specialised wheelchair-accessible one, or whether I could even cope in one, I just wrote it down on my wanted list: 'one wheelchair-accessible motorhome'. The other important piece of hardware that I was going to need was my own personal lifeboat. Just like the fast RIBs used to support me around the Isle of Wight, I needed one to stay alongside me to keep me fed and watered and to help me in the unlikely event of ever finding myself in any trouble. Item two on the wanted list: 'big RIB'.

I was also going to need a crew. Elaine would be the driver of my motorhome, but I would need people in the RIB, at least two properly trained crew, ideally three, and they too would need somewhere to sleep. Initial thoughts were that there would be a mother-ship, maybe a large yacht or catamaran that would shadow me and the RIB, providing accommodation for the crew and somewhere to brew up hot drinks and make hot meals at sea. The mother-ship would also need at least two crew.

The plan wasn't perfect, and I knew it would be subject to change, but my equipment list was the best guess I could come up with at the time and, without anyone yet to bounce ideas off, it would at least give some idea of the cost. What became immediately clear was that such an attempt could not happen with just a few companies giving me equipment or benefit in kind. I was going to need hard cash. I was going to have to find a sponsor.

Confident that I could now field any questions with a degree of competence, I started to compile my press list, my list of journalists in the yachting press, the local TV stations, radio stations and mainstream press. Within two days, with some extra digging around on the web and old directories that I had lying around, I had a really good clean list of more than sixty names. It's one thing to write about other people, but you cannot send out press releases about yourself in the first person. 'I am a brilliant sailor and I'm going to sail around Great Britain' could be construed, at best, as somewhat arrogant. But at this time I could not afford to pay anyone to look after my publicity for me: everything I did, I did on my own. So to overcome this small but important hurdle I created a false identity, Ernie Read, a nom de plume which I used to sign off press releases. He even had his own email address that I created for him. And if journalists called for him and left messages on my answer machine, I would return the call saying that he had passed on the message. It was a useful device, allowing me to work my magic and create this monster that was Personal Everest without accusation of 'blowing my own trumpet'. If the campaign was to succeed, then it was important to give, and to maintain, an air of confidence; no journalist was going to run a 'might be' story.

With the outline of my plan in my mind, a wish list prepared of everything I was going to need, and a marketing strategy ready to be rolled out at the Boat Show, I wanted to run the idea past a friend of mine, himself a successful businessman, to see what he thought of the idea and to see if the figures stacked up.

I had first met Peter Harrison in 1998 at the Royal Corinthian Yacht Club on the Isle of Wight. I was a trustee of a national sailing charity called RYA Sailability at the time, and that evening we were holding a posh, black-tie fundraising dinner. Our guest of honour, Princess Anne, was due within the hour and I was sitting on my own in the main dining room, which was beautifully dressed with tables ready laid to receive their guests. I was quietly practising my welcoming speech when a large man, clad in bright yellow oilskins and sailing boots, tramped through the room and across the parquet dance floor dragging an oversized wet kitbag behind him.

'Er, can I help you?' I asked, incredulous, as this fellow stopped to look at the Sailability publicity boards that had been erected around the room. I had just had a pint of Guinness to calm my nerves and was in a relatively calm mood, otherwise, with the stress of the evening ahead, I might have been less hospitable.

'What's all this about, then?' he enquired abruptly.

I gave him the briefest of potted histories of the charity, conscious of time and aware that 300 people were about to take their seats.

I could instantly tell that he was a kindly chap, he just had that look about him. He wanted to know about me, why I was disabled, why was I involved in the charity and what the dinner that evening was in aid of. But the first of the guests had started to come through to the dining room and, as I made my excuses to leave, he said that he would like to help the charity.

'My name is Peter Harrison,' he said. 'I run a company called Chernikeeff. You wouldn't have heard of it, but I'm going to be selling it soon, and when I do perhaps I could help Sailability? I don't have any business cards on me but please look me up through the yacht club, they'll give you my details.'

I thanked him and, as he shuffled out of the door, dragging his bag behind him, my mind quickly returned to rehearsing my speech.

About six months later I was in a local newsagents when I noticed the *Financial Times*. There was a picture of Peter on the front page and the headline news that he had sold a share in his company for £200 million. I hadn't made contact with him following that dinner in Cowes, and it would seem a little crass to start chasing the poor fellow now, even if it was to support the charity.

So it was with some surprise that I took a call from Peter a week later.

'You never called me,' he said. 'I told you to call me when I had sold my company and I would see what I could do.'

Now feeling embarrassed that it was him calling me, especially having just sold his company for so much money, I thought he may have had a change of heart – but not so.

'Can we meet to discuss further my offer to help Sailability?'

Blimey, I wasn't sure what to expect, but I recognised that he was serious about his support.

We did meet, and less than a year later I shared a stage with Peter and Princess Anne to mark the launch of the Peter Harrison Foundation, which he kick-started with a gift of £12 million pounds to aid disability sport in the UK. The Princess Royal was there on behalf of Sailability to accept the first grant from Peter's trust. It was an amazing gesture on his part, and I thought I was the only one who understood exactly how the chain of events had unfolded. But that day, on the stage, Peter was kind enough to recount the story in front of the assembled dignitaries.

'It was this man,' he said, pointing at me, 'that first introduced me to Sailability, and it was listening to his story that inspired me to set up the Peter Harrison Foundation.'

I was deeply moved, not only by his surprise announcement but also by his generosity in making it in front of all those people. So it was only natural that when I wanted a professional to cast an eye over my Personal Everest project plan, it was Peter that I turned to first.

I had expected a gruelling interrogation of my figures and a detailed quizzing of my project plan, and Peter did not let me down. He identified several areas where I needed to sharpen up my prospectus, not least the figures, which he said had not taken into account any contingency. What I hadn't expected was that Peter would underwrite the cost of my motorhome. It represented a third of my overall budget, and he offered to underwrite the cost of purchase so that if I raised the funds to pay for it I would pay him back, and if not it would be sold at the end of the event and the money returned to him.

I was taken aback by his offer. It was completely unexpected and extremely generous. Countless times in my life I had sat in board rooms and committee meetings negotiating money on behalf of Sailability, but never had I done so for myself, and certainly not on this scale. And now, out of the blue, with the motorhome funded, I had got off to a cracking start.

'At least now,' explained Peter, 'when you try and find a sponsor, they will see that you have already got support, and that will help you leverage the money you need.'

On the drive home that evening I could feel butterflies in my stomach. It was only the first of many steps, but it was a big one and, in a stroke, it resolved the whole business of nightly accommodation. I still had to source such a vehicle, which wasn't going to be easy, but I could worry about that another day.

Buoyed up by Peter's offer, I approached another friend, Paul Strzelecki, who owned the yachting and fashion clothing company Henri Lloyd. Paul and I had first met in the early 1990s and the company always took the trouble to find out what my specific requirements were as a disabled yachtsman and helped me select what was best for me. Over the years, as clothing technology improved, Paul had continued to keep me clothed in the latest sailing gear. I knew it would be a bit of an impertinence writing to him as a friend, and, to be honest, I would have worn Henri Lloyd clothing even if he had said no, but I thought I would write and ask for them to sponsor all of my clothing needs, for me and the crew. Luckily for me, I got a pretty quick reply in the affirmative. I now had two really big names behind me, which added to the credibility of me and my project – and 'Ernie Read' was sure to mention both in our launch-day press release.

With the 2006 Southampton Boat Show only a matter a weeks away, my plan to use it as a launch pad for Personal Everest took a major blow.

At the beginning of the year I had applied for a free pitch at the Show where I could display details of my project and exhibit my trimaran dinghy *Billy*. It was in *Billy* that I had twice sailed around the Isle of Wight and, although a bit battered and bruised, it would be in *Billy* that I would be sailing around Great Britain if I didn't find enough sponsorship to buy a new boat.

I had it all planned. I had even been out sailing in *Billy* several times during the summer of 2006 being filmed by my friend Brian Stanislas, a professional cameraman who provided his services for free. With 'sponsor required' and 'your name here' emblazoned across *Billy*'s sail and main hull, I spent hours sailing back and forth in Portsmouth Harbour, Southampton Water and the Solent being filmed by Brian and hoping to be seen by a potential sponsor. Finally, we had all the broadcast footage we needed for the TV stations at the grand announcement at the Boat Show. So to receive the letter telling me that free stands could only be provided to registered charities, which I was not, came as a real blow, and I simply did not have the £700 to spend on a stand. I knew that without a presence at the Show I might as well forget the whole project.

But the guys at National Boat Shows, who run the Southampton show, were not quite as heartless as I first thought. When I phoned them to explain the situation, they agreed to revisit the application but couldn't make any promises.

With only a fortnight until the Show, and with my dreams of a high-impact launch looking doomed, I took a call from the organisers.

'Geoff, we've looked again at your application. I'm sorry, but we have no choice but to adhere to our policy, we simply can't give you free space, nor can we improve on the cost.'

My heart sank.

'Do you know the guys at New Forest Sailability?' the voice on the other end of the phone asked.

'Yes, why?' I replied. I knew them well, an active and friendly disabled sailing group based on an old gravel pit just outside

Ringwood. I had visited and sailed there several times before.

'Well, they have applied and have been granted one of the free charity stands at the Show. I can see on the computer that they have already submitted their stand layout, which is big enough for one boat. We were just wondering, if we were to offer them a double-size stand –'

'Thank you, thank you,' I blurted. He didn't need to elaborate, I knew what he meant. Finishing our conversation, I immediately phoned my friend Eric Blyth, chairman of New Forest Sailability, and explained the situation. Subject to getting approval from his committee, he could see no reason why I could not share the stand. We were there for different reasons, and our exhibits would complement each other. The launch was back on again.

By the time doors opened to the Show on Friday 15 September 2006, with help from Elaine and friends, *Billy* was assembled, polished and proudly displayed on the stand I shared with New Forest Sailability. I had printed a variety of publicity leaflets and display boards, and we even had matching navy blue polo shirts with the web address printed across the shoulders to give the finishing touch.

I had three very clear objectives at the Show. The first was to get as much press coverage as possible. On day one, Press Day, I, or should I say Ernie Read, blitzed the journalists with photographs, background information on me and the project, DVD footage of me sailing and a headline-grabbing press release which stated simply, 'Disabled sailor to set the Everest of sailing records'. It certainly got their attention. I was busy from the outset but, for me, the biggest and most important broadcaster to run with the story was the local BBC television station. That same day, between marine journalists and the local newspapers, the BBC cameras arrived and filmed an interview. It was short and sweet and I would have to wait a couple of days before it was broadcast, but I made it clear that I was looking for a sponsor.

And that was my second priority, to find someone prepared to risk their money on helping me achieve my dream. Of course, it was never going to work like that. Working for years with Sailability, I knew that the days of chairmen writing company cheques to support their favoured cause were long gone. Nowadays it was all about giving something in return, and my promise to them would be to work with their clients and staff and, of course, get them as much good publicity as I could. If I could at least get to the starting line, I would be able to give my sponsor a massive, and prolonged, exposure in the media. I was now selling myself, selling my sailing credentials and selling my good name, in order to make the boast of completing the challenge and delivering on that promise. I was staking everything, my reputation and my honour, on seeing this through successfully.

I had written to many companies. Sixty-five businesses in total – some familiar names in yachting sponsorship, some not so familiar – got personal letters from me enclosing my business partnership proposal, asking them if they would like to be involved. Not one of them ever asked me 'how much?', and some, even those where I had personal contacts, did not even give me the courtesy of a reply. I never thought it would be easy, and my search for funding was still at an early stage, but every rejection or unanswered letter was demoralising and, like it or not, there would be a deadline. If sponsorship money had not been secured by then, the attempt would have to be called off. At this moment in time, I had not decided exactly when that date would be, but my search for funding could not be open-ended.

My third objective in attending the Show was to meet the public, to talk to them and gauge public opinion, and to collect potential offers of help. With my notepad on my lap, I spent the week handing out my leaflets, giving people my business cards and directing them to my website. In return I harvested their details and documented any offers of help they might make. I was so busy, I barely had time too eat, and I loved every minute of it. Just about everyone was supportive of the idea, and I had offers of everything from free Arbroath smokies in Arbroath to a night's accommodation in a hotel in Falmouth. It started to feel real, and it made everything to come seem so exciting. There were of course naysayers, and some who went as far as to say, even to my face, that they thought I was a 'liability' and the attempt was doomed to failure. It was one thing being called 'mad', though even that became irritating after a while, but quite another for someone who didn't know me or my capabilities to suggest I was a 'liability'. But then, an hour or so later, when I was stopped by a lady called Marie from Northern Ireland and asked for my autograph, my first ever, and her husband gave me £100 towards the project, I realised that Personal Everest was going to mean different things to different people, and I certainly wasn't going to please all of them.

It was a glorious week in September and the sun shone nearly every day. Sharing a stand with the New Forest Sailability team meant that there were always plenty of like-minded people to talk to. They had established a rota of volunteers to man their part of the stand and to raise money for their local group. Collecting money from the public is a tough job at the best of times and, with so much competition at boat shows, I felt a bit sorry for them. Their average takings were less than £10 a day until one of their number, Mike Golden, was on duty. He took more than £150 in one day on his own. It was like watching a legalised mugger at work. He was great with people, put them at their ease, a really jolly man. We got on really well and we spoke at length about my plans. Mike explained that, being recently widowed, he enjoyed volunteering at the club and had plenty of spare time on his hands. If I was looking for crew, he'd love to come along and, so long as his expenses were covered, he would do anything that was required for as long as it took.

It was only day three of the Show, I still had another week of exhibiting, and already I had achieved more than I could have hoped for. But there was more to come.

On day four, Monday 18 September, Fiona Pankhurst, the Marketing Manager for Raymarine, a leading marine electronics firm, had agreed to see me following a chance conversation we had had over the weekend. Fiona was keen to hear about my project and asked some pretty tough questions. A sailor herself, there was no way she was going to commit to anything without being persuaded that she was dealing with someone capable of delivering on his promise. She made it clear to me that they would not be in a position to give money, but I must have said what she wanted to hear because, at the end of our chat, she told me that Raymarine would be willing to support me. This was fantastic news. Both my boat and the RIB were going to need a variety of sophisticated electronics and I had already approached other companies but none had shown the slightest interest. Now, after a chance meeting and being given the opportunity to explain my detailed plans in person, I had one of the world's largest marine electronics firms behind me.

Back on the stand that afternoon, and going slightly dizzy from not eating much, I was trying my best to chuck a sandwich down my neck between visitors. I had half-hidden myself in the tent-like structure where we stored boxes and other show paraphernalia so I wasn't disturbed. I could hear Mandy, my friend who was helping on the stand, talking to a passer-by. She tapped me on the shoulder.

'I'm sorry to interrupt your lunch, Geoff, but there's a man here who says he might be able to help you. Would you speak to him?'

Quickly trying to lick the half-chewed sandwich off my teeth, I had a swill of warm Coke and reversed my chair out from among the boxes.

'Hi there, I'm Geoff. Have you heard about my project?'

'Not really,' he replied, 'only what your friend has been telling me. Sounds intriguing, and it's possibly something I might be able to help you with.'

I'd had quite a few offers of indeterminate help from several people already and, assuming this was like the rest, and not wanting to commit to anything this early in my campaign, I asked if he had a card and said I would get back to him.

'My name is Ian Clover,' he said as he handed me his card. 'I run my own sailing school on the Isle of Wight. It sounds the sort of thing I might be interested in. If you get stuck, give me a call.'

I thanked him and stapled his card to the book of notes I'd been collecting. Unknown to me at the time, I'd just met my future project manager.

The following night, BBC South broadcast my eagerly awaited interview. I got just over three minutes on the main 6.30 p.m. news magazine, plus several shorter pieces on their lunchtime and late-night bulletins. Even Sally Taylor, the station's anchorlady, made a point of saying that I was looking for a sponsor. I could not have asked for more.

Rather naively, I hurried into the Show on Wednesday morning expecting a rush of enquiries about sponsorship. The TV appearance had certainly raised public awareness, and for the rest of the Show I was getting dozens of people each day saying they had seen and heard about my plans, but sadly no offers of sponsorship.

On the penultimate day of exhibiting, I had a visit from a chap called Nigel Craig. I'd known Nigel for several years when he worked for a local law firm in Southampton and I was working in marketing for a firm of accountants. Our paths had crossed several times at business seminars and, having seen the piece on television, he had purposely made a point of looking for me at the Show. He was just on his way home when he tracked me down on my stand.

'Hi Geoff, I saw you on the TV the other night. Did it help find you a sponsor?'

'Unfortunately not, but at least I can use the footage to show potential sponsors that there is media interest. So what are you doing these days?'

'Still working, but for a bigger law firm now. In fact, I sit on a local business committee called the Trident Group. It's a bunch of marine-related professional services firms – lawyers, accountants and so on. We are having our annual dinner next month, it's a black-tie do at the Royal Marines Museum in Portsmouth, there's a guest speaker. It's usually a good night, fancy coming? You never know who you might meet.'

'Yeah, sure, I'd love to come. Thanks for the offer.'

At the time, I was making myself available for anything and everything. As far as I was concerned, the more people I could talk to the better.

By the last Sunday of the Show, some ten days of talking myself to the point of losing my voice, I was really pleased with everything I had achieved, not least finding potential members of crew. I had a notebook stuffed full of leads to follow up, both businesses and individual offers of help, I had a promise of electronics, I had all of my clothing needs sorted, I even had a special helmet promised to me by Gecko, one of the exhibitors at the Show, which would be essential for keeping my head warm and protected from the sea spray – it had been a gruelling but productive ten days.

But with the Show now over, the hard work began. Weighing up everything I had learned from the past ten days, I set myself a deadline, after which I would pull the plug on the idea. It was a harsh acceptance, but I could not afford to incur huge personal debts simply to follow a dream. It was important to me, but not that important. All of the talking and all of the hype would mean nothing unless I got to the start line, and that was only going to happen with a sponsor. In order to give myself enough time to plan and execute the plan properly, the deadline I set myself for finding a sponsor was 15 December 2006. I had three months to find the money.

4

I don't remember the exact date in 1974, but I do recall the day that my mother and 'Daddy John' arrived at Nana's house out of the blue, with brand-new bicycles for Richard and myself. Mine was a purple racing bike with dropped handlebars and Richard's was a cool racing green. We had been playing football in the street, but were both completely overjoyed with our new bikes and were soon riding them up and down Waterworks Road showing them off to all our friends. After a few minutes, my mother took us to one side and explained that if we wanted to keep the bicycles, both of us had to get in the car straightaway. She told us that she would collect our things from the house, and this time we would be going to live with her permanently.

Dutifully, we climbed into the car and watched as she disappeared into the front door of number 32. About ten minutes later she reappeared clutching several bags containing all of our belongings. The bicycles were hastily shoved into the boot of the car and she climbed in.

'Just drive,' she said to my stepfather John, and we sped off.

I'll never know the exact circumstances surrounding that day, nor what was said between my mother and her foster-mother in the house, but I remember looking back and waving to Nana out of the rear window of the car. I watched her standing on the doorstep waving with both arms, disappearing out of view as we turned out of the road. It would be another five years before we saw our Nana again but, as an eight-year-old boy, I must admit that I wasn't thinking of how distraught my Nana must have felt, or even of how much I would miss the woman who had brought me up so far. I was just absolutely delighted to know that we were going to live with my mum and our new family.

Our new home was Wisteria Cottage, a Victorian villa once owned by Sir Thomas Lipton, in the Hampshire hamlet of Lower Swanwick. Compared to No. 32 Waterworks Road, this was a completely different world. In our new home Richard and I shared a bedroom at the front of the cottage, overlooking the River Hamble and a large boatyard and marina complex called Moody's which housed many hundreds of wonderful sailing yachts and big, expensive-looking motorboats. We had a lovely large garden to play in and – the ultimate luxury – we even had a black-and-white television in our bedroom.

The concept of a marina was totally alien to me, yet it was a completely magical, exciting and entertaining place. I would sit in my bedroom window for hours and just look out at the view. I could see right down the river for miles and miles, even as far as Fawley oil refinery on the other side of Southampton Water in the distance. I would see boats of all shapes and sizes chugging up and down the river, and I would wonder what part of the world they were going to or where they had been. I would watch the big Renner boat-hoist as it lifted enormous yachts out of the water and positioned them around the boat park on flimsy-looking wooden supports, amazed at how they didn't topple right over. And at night time, as I curled up under my quilt in the top bunk-bed, I could hear nothing but the chink-chink-chink of the rigging as it clattered against the masts of the yachts outside. It was like an orchestra, with literally scores of boats clattering away all night at various pitches. It also gave a great indication of the weather: when it was quiet, you knew that there was no wind, but when a gale blew the chinking was so frenetic that it became a high-pitched screeching noise as the wind screamed through the rigging, fascinating and scary at the same time, but desperately annoying when trying to sleep!

Moving to a new area meant finding a new school, and in the first few months I went to a couple of local primaries before finally being placed in 1974 at Charlton House, a Roman

Catholic private boys school, the junior school of the larger St Mary's College in Bitterne, near Southampton. This was also when I took on my new surname of Holt. Although my mother and John had obtained legal custody of me and Richard from my Nana, I was still, in the eyes of the law, Geoffrey Hoad. But, of my own volition I chose to use the surname Holt when I started at Charlton because I was proud to use the name of my new stepfather. It also gave me an identity that I had been lacking beforehand. This was, after all, a new start in life.

Despite being offered the option of going to private school, Richard chose to attend the local comprehensive and elected to keep the surname Hoad. I don't recall being given a say in which school I went to, but I certainly wasn't complaining. The brown blazer with gold braid, brown shorts, and brown and gold tie, all topped off with a brown and gold cap, may have attracted the odd shout of abuse from local state school kids but it felt smart and I was proud to wear it. And the school motto, *Semper Paratus* ('always prepared'), was to prove useful throughout my life.

I completed two years at Charlton before moving up to St Mary's College, where I stayed a further five years until I was sixteen. School fees were not cheap and I have my mother and John to thank for sticking with it, especially later on as their financial situation got harder. Having said all that, however, I would hate anyone to think that I enjoyed school. On the contrary, I absolutely loathed it, something that wasn't helped by my hour-long journey to and from school each day. It seemed to me that lessons were taught mechanically, without any room for emotion or sentiment and, almost without exception, I always felt one step behind the rest of my classmates. When I really applied myself I could learn, and I did get good grades, but I always wondered what was the point in wasting our time and our parents' money teaching us things we had no interest in and would never need in later life. To make matters worse, the overt religious teachings by the Brothers of Christian Instruction, who owned and ran the school, revealed a hypocrisy in religion that has stayed with me until this day. On one hand we were lectured on morality and sin, yet one of the Brothers, one of our teachers, had got a sixteen-year-old girl from our sister-school pregnant and was forced to leave the Brotherhood. As you can imagine, he immediately acquired a heroic status among the boy pupils, although needless to say the ensuing 'Save Brother Hastey' campaign was doomed to failure.

I am indebted to the school, however, for providing me with some of my best lifelong friends. One of my closest friends during this period of my life was Simon Lawton. Simon was a year older than me and his dad was the PE teacher at St Mary's, a fantastic guy but perhaps the only PE teacher I ever knew who smoked forty cigarettes a day. The Lawtons were a kind family, originally from Lancashire, who lived no more than five minutes' walk away from our house. Sometimes I would get a lift to school with Simon in Mr Lawton's big brown Ford Zephyr, packed in on the back seat with him and his three brothers, but our paths rarely crossed during school time. But once we'd got home and had our tea, we spent almost every minute of every evening and weekend together. Of course we weren't always angels and often got into all sorts of trouble, but it felt like we were the kings of Lower Swanwick. We were known and respected by just about all the kids in the area and we knew every single nook and cranny of our manor.

I'd read *Swallows and Amazons* when I was twelve, and I remember thinking that Lower Swanwick was my very own Wild Cat Island. It was a paradise for any child to grow up in, with everything right on the doorstep. There was the River Hamble with its miles of foreshore, ideal for exploring, fishing and messing about in boats. There were also acres of forests up and down the river, ideal for making camps and exploring, and even a derelict former brickworks, all within minutes of our house.

From innocent pastimes such as building dens under the railway bridge which runs across the River Hamble, to sleeping overnight in bus-shelters drunk on cider or countless hours spent playing Space Invaders in the Jolly Sailor pub, listening repeatedly to 'All Right Now' by Free on the jukebox, smoking endless cigarettes, we did everything together. Simon was without doubt my best mate.

Looking back, I'm surprised at how little time I actually spent at home in Wisteria Cottage. I was always out and about with Simon exploring some new area of the river. I realise now that I was actually given a huge amount of freedom by my parents – no bad thing from a young lad's point of view. Even better, I was rarely questioned on my whereabouts or what I'd been up to, which is probably just as well. Despite a few close shaves with the law for trespassing at the old brickworks and making home-made rockets with gunpowder that we extricated from John's old marine flares, we were actually completely harmless teenagers and kept ourselves to ourselves.

I had another incentive not to get caught doing something I shouldn't. No matter how content and happy I was now that we all lived together, neither Richard nor I were ever in any doubt that we were only guests at Wisteria Cottage. Should we ever misbehave, even once, then we could be returned to Portsmouth to live with our Nana. Perhaps that's the reason why I spent so much time out and away from the house, so there was less likelihood of getting into trouble at home. Of course I missed my Nana, but even as a young boy I could see the advantages of living at Wisteria Cottage far outweighed living with an elderly lady.

Some of the strictest rules laid down by my mum and John concerned food. As a boy I seem to have been permanently hungry, and would often sneak into the kitchen to make myself a sandwich or take some biscuits. It wasn't that we weren't well fed – quite the opposite, there was always plenty of food on the table at mealtimes – it's just that I had an insatiable appetite. Even though I was as skinny as a rake, I was always hungry. To solve the problem of our constant eating, John and my mother attached a padlock to the kitchen door so we couldn't get in to pilfer food. Perhaps I could have understood if we had been short of money, but this was not the case, and the food cupboards were always bursting. The temptation was too great, and Richard and I quickly figured out how to take the door off its sliding runners then, working as a team with one of us on lookout and the other raiding the pantry, we would steal enough food to stifle our hunger until dinner.

John was a successful businessman, and was managing director of the family-run builders' merchants, Holt Southey's, with offices in Portsmouth and Southampton. In the first few years that we lived with him, he always worked very hard and we led a privileged lifestyle compared to what we had previously known. He always had the latest cars, and I particularly remember the Lancia Fulvia sports car that he bought in 1974, shortly followed by a lovely Alfa Romeo. Even before he had met my mother, John had a passion for yachting and he owned a succession of yachts, all given the name *Gulliver*, the most famous of which was *Gulliver G*, which was eventually bought by yachtswoman Clare Francis. To go with the high-rolling lifestyle, John also bought my mother a beautiful full-length white mink coat, so we certainly didn't seem to be short of money.

I was about ten years old and had been living with the family for a couple of years before I really to got to know John. Up until this point, our sister Lucy had been very much the focal point of the family, and having two boisterous stepsons suddenly turn up must have created a few difficulties for our stepfather. He was much older than my mother, her elder by twenty-one years, but was still a good-looking man, often compared by my friends to Clint Eastwood. He was a good man too, both kind and gentle, characteristics which my mother later cited as weaknesses. I'm not sure what he was like as a businessman, but he was very good with his hands and highly creative. He had an enormous workshop in the garden where I would often find him sharpening his chisels or carefully working on a new design in wood. Once I started to show an interest in boats he would occasionally give me his time and share some of his skills with me. Having had a daughter from a previous marriage, and then Lucy with my mother, perhaps I was the son he never had. John took great enjoyment out of helping me to make wooden models of boats and planes, he showed me how to fly kites, how to use his wood-working tools and, perhaps the most special treat, he taught me to sail.

Often at weekends or during school holidays the whole family would go away on the family yacht. Sometimes it would only be to the Isle of Wight or Beaulieu, but other times we ventured as far afield as the West Country, Ireland and even France. While the rest of the family stayed below reading books or lounged on deck sunbathing, I was always asking John questions about how things worked on the boat or why the sails were set in a certain way. I was fascinated by the elements, and I was as keen to learn as he was to teach. My enthusiasm was often rewarded by being allowed to take the wheel of the yacht, where I would try my absolute hardest to follow the course he would tell me to steer – not always easy for a young boy struggling to see over the wheel. In the evenings, moored up in some river, we would sit around in the saloon and play games or read. I was a little bookworm and would read all of the sailing books in John's collection. My favourites were those by a sailor called Robin Knox-Johnston describing his adventures sailing around the world on the yacht *Suhali* – to a small boy this was heroic stuff, and I devoured it. Sat there in the flickering dim light of the oil lamps, I would read until my eyes hurt, the smell of teakwood, damp cushions and paraffin filling the air. I loved all of those sailing trips apart from just one – when I caught bucket-loads of mackerel and was forced to spend many hours scrubbing fish blood, guts and scales out of *Gulliver*'s beautiful teak decks.

Although life had become much easier for me during my early teens, it wasn't the case for my elder brother Richard. No matter what he did or how hard he tried, he was always in trou-ble. Mind you, much of it was of his own making. On his six-teenth birthday, Richard was bought a brand new 50 cc Suzuki motorcycle with all the protective gear that he needed. Just three hours after taking possession of it, Richard had somehow got the bike stuck on the mud of the River Hamble, where it had to be rescued before it completely sank and was a virtual write-off. But he saved his best party piece for when my mother, John, myself and Lucy went to France for the weekend. We returned home to find several things in the house not quite as they had been three days earlier. Upon closer inspection, we noticed that all the valuable silverware was missing, the chimney had been crammed full of empty beer cans, and the beautiful camellia tree in the garden now sported hundreds of cigarette butts stuck on the ends of twigs. But Richard's *pièce de résistance*, using kettles and pans of boiling water, had been to turn my mother's beloved pine kitchen into a steam-room and sauna, which caused the entire pine-clad ceiling to warp and buckle. It also later transpired that the grass and mud embedded in the casters of the antique pine kitchen table were from the garden, where the table had been used as a go-kart on the lawn. According to local folklore, disappointed that he did not have enough guests for the party he was hosting, Richard went to two local pubs at closing time to announce a party at Wisteria Cottage, and minutes later had to contend with scores of drunks ransacking our lovely home. To me it was all mildly amusing, until I noticed that my entire Status Quo record collection had been stolen.

Still the best of friends, by the time we were in our early teens Simon and I were venturing further afield. Armed with pocket money and proceeds from a short-lived mouse-breeding enterprise of mine, we would catch the train from Bursledon back to Portsmouth to see my Nana and the Pennell family. Apart from being a fun way to spend a Saturday, it was also good to see my Nana and Roy and Joyce, but we never stayed for long and, because of the tension that continued to exist between my mother and Nana, I never mentioned our trips to Portsmouth to my mum for fear that she might stop me going again. To be honest, I doubt that would have been her reaction but it was my secret and I liked it that way. I also didn't want to upset my mum and I thought she might feel a sense of betrayal if she found out.

By the time I was about fourteen, the time Simon and I spent hanging out together as long-haired 'rockers' was coming to an end. Even from a young age, Simon had an obvious fondness for alcohol which I could not really understand. It was one thing to get drunk on cheap cider listening to Deep Purple on my cassette recorder at Bursledon Rec on a Saturday night, but quite another to be quaffing barley wine most nights when we met up. Having grown up and shared so much together, we were always going to remain the best of friends. But he became a different person when drinking, and it was upsetting to see him like that – so I increasingly preferred to spend less time with him.

For some years at school, I'd been sitting next to a boy called Sean. Although we were classmates and he lived quite close to me, Sean Cusack was perhaps the most *über*-cool guy at school and all the other major players in the playground wanted to hang out with him, so it never crossed my mind that he would be interested in being friends with me. If you are old enough to remember Sting playing Ace Face in *Quadrophenia*, then you'll know the look. Whilst I would be out playing with Simon on the River Hamble, my old ripped jeans and T-shirts covered in mud, Sean was either working at a local café or in town spending his earnings on the latest trendy clothes. Sean's mum and dad worked very hard running various businesses and they had a lifestyle to match, with a big house, flash cars, continental holidays and so on. That work ethic had rubbed off on Sean too, so it was unusual to see him just hanging about the local streets. But on one such rare occasion we bumped into each other and got chatting, and from that point onwards became good friends. However, to feel less conspicuous amongst Sean's circle of trendy friends, my long rocker's hair had to go. In the end it happened more by accident than design. For some inexplicable reason, I decided to dye my long blond hair with a black hairspray dye. To complete the look, I even took the trouble to colour in my eyebrows. To be honest, it didn't entirely suit my fair complexion so I retreated to the bathroom to wash it off. Several washes later, my hair now a terrifying shade of bright pink, I realised that I was never going to solve the problem with washing alone. So I made my way to Sean's house, wearing a woolly hat in the height of summer, where his mum, a hairdresser, had no choice but to cut it all off. To this day I have short hair – and his mother still calls me Pinky.

With hindsight, it's easy to spot a key moment that affects everything that follows. And, as far as the Holt family goes, that key moment was when John decided to give up his career in 1978 to buy a 45-foot cement hull and build a boat from scratch in our back garden. Of course they couldn't have known it at the time, but that decision, which he and my mother made together, was to cost them their beloved home at Wisteria Cottage, the boat itself and, ultimately, their marriage. But for the time being, this was a really cool thing to have in my back garden. The whole of Swanwick Lane was blocked off by the police for a day as one of the biggest cranes in the country turned up to lift the huge grey, whale-like concrete hull over tall trees and into an enormous sunken pit that John had dug in the back garden. For days, weeks, months and even years, every day saw John out in the garden slowly, ever so slowly, building the yacht. It was an enormous undertaking. In the dark evenings, if he was not in the boat working by torchlight, he was in the kitchen, plans strewn across the kitchen table, doing complex calculations. To bend the enormous lengths of teak wood for the ribs of the boat and the deck, he fabricated an enormous steam tube. In a more successful version of Richard's ill-fated sauna, John used electric kettles and pans of hot water to steam the wood until he could quickly pull it out and peg it into shape in the back garden so, when cooled, it did so to the right curvature.

Whether it was out of sheer determination to see the project through, or whether they had passed the financial point of no return, my parents sold the lovely Wisteria Cottage a few years later and downsized the family to a semidetached urban house in nearby Warsash. *Lord Gulliver*, as the yacht was now called, was moved in her unfinished state to a boatyard further down the river. But within a year or so the house in Warsash was also sold to raise funds to finish the build and we were all moved onto the boat itself at Universal boatyard, right on the river's edge. Despite my younger Swallows and Amazons fantasies, actually living on a half-built concrete and wooden 45-foot yacht, eating and sleeping aboard but washing, showering and using the toilet facilities in the adjacent marina, was pretty tough on us all. Getting to school now entailed either rowing a small dinghy a mile up river or negotiating a very muddy and very tidal footpath just to get to the train station. The entire journey had to be repeated at the end of each day, regardless of the weather, and that winter of 1981/2 seemed to be particularly miserable, which made keeping my school uniform clean and my shoes free from mud almost impossible.

One day in the autumn of 1981 my mother called Richard and me into the kitchen to tell us that Nana had died. We knew she had been poorly with breast cancer, and now it had finally killed her. My mother had taken Richard to see her in hospital shortly before she died but, because my mother thought I was too young to deal with the effect of seeing her so poorly, I was not allowed to go. There were barely any people at her funeral at Portchester crematorium, only my mother, John and a few of Nana's friends, so I was never even given the opportunity to say goodbye or to thank her for everything she had done for me. Immediately after the cremation, Richard and I were collected and taken by car back to Nana's house, the house where we had grown up, and my mother spent the afternoon clearing all of Nana's personal effects before the house was finally handed back to the council. It was deeply traumatic, but I suffered the pain in silence, frightened of showing any emotion for this woman whom my mother so clearly disliked. It was my first encounter with death, and it just so happened to be someone I loved dearly. Even though I was fifteen years old, I couldn't comprehend the concept of death: how someone could just stop living and would never come back, especially someone who had played such a major part in my own life. Whenever I had a spare moment, I would recall all of the wonderful times we spent together and I began to realise what a terrific sacrifice she had made to bring us up. I was upset and angry that I never really had the chance to tell her how much I appreciated that. As young boys she had told us she loved us every night as we climbed the stairs to bed, but as I grew older and had moved away, I hadn't told her how much I loved her and how much I appreciated her care and love, and I deeply regret that.

By now my school years were coming to an end, and I simply could not wait. I went to see a careers counsellor and expressed a wish to become a navigation officer in the Royal Navy, and an appointment was duly made with the Naval recruiting division. The previous year, aged fifteen, I had passed my mathematics and English O levels with flying colours, and I was destined to take a further nine O levels in my final year, including advanced mathematics and English literature, after which point I expected to be free of school, lessons and exams forever. So when I met with the Royal Naval careers officer, and he announced that they would be delighted to take me but to come back when I had the appropriate A levels, a very big penny dropped. Incredibly, at no point in my years at school had anyone ever indicated that I would need A levels for certain jobs. I had just always assumed that going on to college was for people who weren't able to get a job. I know that sounds naive in the extreme, but that's how little my school equipped us for life.

I had always seen sixteen as the headline age, when I would once and for all be rid of school and everything it stood for – so to be told a few months before I was due to leave school that I would have to endure a further two years at the place floored me. I was dumbstruck.

Outside school, Sean and I had been spending more and more time together. We had a lot in common, including our choice of friends, our tastes in music and our ideas about earning money, and we were always thinking of new and innovative ways to make our fortunes. During our last Easter holidays as schoolboys, in 1982, we spent hours considering our futures. Sean had been offered a job cleaning cars on a local car lot, which he saw as an opportunity to learn about the car trade. For my part, the captain of a yacht based on the River Hamble had offered me a job as first mate in the Mediterranean. Sean and I talked over the pros and cons of what we were going to do. Fortunately both of us had parents who said that the decision was to be ours, and they would support whatever we chose to do.

The first day back at school for the summer term, Sean and I sat at our desks, our O-level exams just a matter of weeks away, chatting about whether we had made our decision. The thought of another two years of education was preying heavily on my mind and, in the difficult employment climate of the early 1980s, the stark reality of not working was too much to bear. Sean had made up his mind too.

'Holt! Cusack!' suddenly bellowed our form teacher, Mr Forster, 'stop talking, the pair of you.'

That was enough to make up our minds. 'What are we doing here?' I asked Sean. 'Let's just go.'

And with that, we opened our desks, grabbed our few belongings and walked out of the school. We knew that this was for real, and there would be no going back. With much trepidation we headed home as fresh-faced sixteen-year-old boys, with our school years firmly behind us and a whole new world ahead of us.

5

Following the Southampton Boat Show in September 2006, Elaine began to see the first signs of the changes to come in our everyday lives, not least my need to shut myself away to try and get some peace and quiet to progress my plans. I was increasingly busy on my computer, writing emails, doing research on the internet or writing letters, just about every day of the week. And if I wasn't in the house locked away in my office or busy on the telephone trying to further some aspect of my challenge, then I was out having meetings with potential suppliers. Family life was seriously disrupted, and I became increasingly frustrated at demands on my time from Elaine and Timothy. It was unfair on them, I knew it, but this was exactly how I envisaged the project developing, and it was exactly how I had explained the situation to Elaine from the outset. I was upset that I was missing quality time with them both, but I had to sacrifice that to try and achieve the bigger objective.

Certain aspects of my character began to show themselves to those around me, and not all of them characteristics to be proud of. Most obvious was the 'control freak' in me – my desire to retain ownership and control of every element of the project I had created. I was doing everything on my own, from running the PR to managing the website, and from trying to find a sponsor to writing risk assessments, but it was fast becoming unmanageable and I knew it. I remain undecided as to whether being a 'control freak' is a good or bad thing. It certainly meant that everything was being done to the high standards I set myself, but, with an ever-increasing workload and with only so many hours in a day, I was aware that sooner or later I would need to start delegating some of those responsibilities. It wouldn't be easy. Personal Everest was my baby – I had conceived the idea and nurtured it to this stage – but luckily I was at least aware enough of my own shortcomings to recognise that I needed help.

Not sure where to turn, I picked up the notebook that I had used during the Boat Show, studied the various cryptic handwritten messages I had scrawled in the book and looked at all the business cards that I had stapled to the pages. Whenever I opened the book, one business card kept attracting my attention, that of Ian Clover. It read quite simply 'Ian Clover, Yachtmaster (Ocean) Instructor'. Acting on intuition, I sent Ian a quick email thanking him for his visit to my stand and asking if he was still interested in being involved in some way.

Within minutes my phone rang.

'Hi Geoff, it's Ian. Yes, I think I'd like to be involved. What stage are you at?'

I felt immediately at ease speaking with him, and being able to tell somebody absolutely everything was a huge relief. I gave him the full nine yards, warts and all – what stage I was at with planning, support, money, absolutely everything.

'Well, just let me know what you'd like help with and I'll see what I can do,' he said reassuringly.

I couldn't quite believe what Ian was suggesting. A successful, highly qualified sailing instructor, running his own sailing school, was offering to put all of that on hold, for me, up to and including a trip that would last at least fifty days, for free.

It was now mid October 2006. I knew that sooner or later I had to start thinking seriously about my support crew, and now was as good a time as any. Taking the bull by the horns, I asked Ian to take a look at my plan, which until now no one had seen, and to give me his thoughts.

'Fine, no problem. Email me what you've got so far and I'll take a look. Perhaps I could come over next week and go through things in more detail.'

Even though Ian understood clearly that I had no guarantees

of funding, and that I had set myself a deadline of 15 December – some two months hence – to find a sponsor, he was still prepared to help me. After putting the phone down and emailing him the various documents, I felt as though a huge weight had been lifted off my shoulders. For the first time I had shared some of the burden. If he could deliver on his promise, it would free me up to pursue the pressing matter of finding the money.

Only an hour or so after my conversation with Ian I took another call, this time from my old friend Nigel Craig, who had tracked me down at the Boat Show.

'Geoff, do you remember that Trident Group dinner I mentioned being held at the Royal Marines Museum in Portsmouth? Well, the guest speaker has been confirmed as Dee Caffari. It's a black-tie affair. Do you still want to come along? It's next week.'

Time was slipping away fast and, despite writing yet more letters to potential supporters, I was still no nearer to finding a sponsor. To be honest, I felt that I could have made better use of my time than go to another dinner. But with a weight already having been taken off my shoulders that day by Ian, and with the prospect of listening to Dee Caffari, who had not long since entered the record books by sailing single-handed the 'wrong way' round the world, I agreed.

'Yeah, sure, I'd love to come. See you next week,' I said.

True to his word, Ian arrived at my house for the very first time the following week, laden with bits of paper and files. He and my mongrel dog Max became instant friends – always a good sign – and Ian didn't seem at all worried that he was soon covered in Max's brown hairs. We sat in my front room, Ian with Max sprawled across his lap, and we talked for several hours, breaking only for Elaine to replenish our supply of drinks and biscuits. For my part, I used the opportunity to clarify my past

sailing experience and explain why I had arrived at various decisions concerning my choice of equipment to use, the route to
be sailed, timetable and so on. We then effectively unpicked the
entire plan and started again from scratch. The overall objective,
to sail around Great Britain, remained the same, but through
discussion we arrived at a far more watertight project plan. The
most critical change was to the list of essential equipment. By
the end of the afternoon, we had agreed that, in addition to my
Challenger trimaran dinghy, we would need a fast rescue boat.
This should be a 22-foot inboard diesel-powered RIB, which
would give good fuel economy and good seagoing capabilities
as well as being the ideal safety boat. We decided to forgo the
idea of a mother-ship, and in its place there would be a total of
three vehicles: my wheelchair-accessible motorhome, a rented
motorhome for the crew to sleep in, and a fully fitted Land Rover
to cope with the difficult launching and recovering sites that we
were likely to encounter. With a driver for each of the three vehicles and a minimum of two crew in the RIB, we were going to
need at least another four members of crew.

As if my head were not spinning enough at that stage, Ian
then produced two printed lists he had prepared, one jobs-to-do
list and one kit list. The jobs list extended to three sides of A4
paper, but this paled into insignificance beside the kit list, pages
and pages of it. Buckets, ropes, first aid kits, batteries – it was
endless. And he had kindly added it all up for me, an estimate of
nearly £20,000 – and that did not include the cost of buying the
RIB, buying the Land Rover, renting the crew motorhome, food
and expenses for eight people for nearly two months.

'Holy shit!' I couldn't help myself exclaiming.

'Look, we have only one objective, and that is for you to sail
around Great Britain. It will be my responsibility to ensure you
do that safely, and in my opinion we are going to need everything
I've itemised,' he said.

I half suspected that by presenting me with these two huge
lists, Ian was just testing my resolve. But I certainly was not

going to challenge him on the one thing in which he excelled above all else, and that was safety. I had no doubt that his lists, both of them, were complete and pertinent, but interestingly it was he who was showing signs of optimism, not me. For the first time, I was the one who was taken aback by the huge amount of work to be done and the vast list of items to be sourced. I was certain Personal Everest could be achieved with less groundwork, less kit and less stress, but did I want it to be? The answer was 'no'. I wanted it done Ian's way, and if someone was prepared to give up such a huge part of his life to help me achieve an ambition, particularly someone as qualified as Ian, then I owed it to him to respect his way of doing things. One thing was for sure – Ian's way was belt and two braces, and I would be in the safest of hands, even if it would mean having to find even more money and even more time to acquire all the items we were going to need.

'What a nice guy,' said Elaine as Ian left late that afternoon. 'Now, be quick, you are at this dinner tonight in Portsmouth and I've just collected your DJ from the cleaners.'

I had forgotten all about the dinner. Sitting in my office, a pile of paperwork from Ian spread out on my desk and a backlog of emails and letters to get started on, it was a close-run decision whether to go to the dinner or to stay at home, not made any easier by the heavy rain and full-on gale now blowing outside.

'Go on, just go, it will do you good to take your mind off things for a while,' encouraged Elaine.

I don't recall much of the dinner apart from feeling damp and dishevelled for most of it. The time it had taken to get from my van to the museum entrance on that foul, dark and stormy night on Southsea seafront was plenty long enough for the pouring rain to thoroughly soak me and just about ruin my smart black dinner suit. Despite polite conversation with the gents around me whilst we ate in the magnificent surroundings of the regimental dining room, my mind was preoccupied with the need to find a sponsor. I was now just weeks away from my deadline of

15 December, and no closer to finding the money. It was becoming an obsession and making me feel ill.

After dessert, as Dee Caffari took to the podium, I backed up and allowed myself half an hour of indulgence and escapism from my worries to listen to her talk. She was attractive and articulate, and it was a joy to listen to Dee recount her amazing achievement of sailing solo around the world against the prevailing winds, the first woman to do so. I always enjoy hearing stories of overcoming adversity, and Dee's story was no exception. I was particularly interested to hear how her story was inextricably linked to the support she received from her sponsor, Aviva, and it was good to hear about such a successful relationship between sailor and sponsor. As she concluded her talk and the round of applause was dying down, my thoughts were just returning to more pressing matters when Walter Cha, chairman of the Trident Group and managing partner of local law firm Blake Lapthorn Tarlo Lyons, stood up to give his vote of thanks. I was about to make my excuses and make a discreet early exit when I heard him say, 'Dee, just two last questions. How did you go about finding your sponsor, and how much did it cost?'

Hearing those words was like being electrocuted. I sat bolt upright, turned and looked straight at Walter, who was standing at the far end of the table. They were 'buying questions' if ever I've heard them.

'Aha, you like what you've just heard, and I can see the way your mind is working,' I said quietly to myself. Obviously I wasn't the only person in the room to pick up on the whole sailing/sponsorship theme which came out of Dee's story.

I have no idea what replies Dee gave to his questions. I was out of the door and on my way home like a flash. Arriving home at about midnight, I went straight to my office, turned on my computer, loaded up my sponsorship proposal document and did what research I could on Blake Lapthorn Tarlo Lyons through their website. By 2.00 a.m. I had updated and personalised my proposal document for them and went to bed to grab a few hours' sleep. Early the next morning, I had printed off and bound the document, driven to their Portsmouth offices, where I knew Walter worked, and hand-delivered the proposal to their receptionist, all by 9.00 a.m. All I could do now was drive home and wait.

And I didn't have to wait long. At 3.00 p.m. that same afternoon I took a call.

'Hi Geoff, it's Walter Cha. Thanks for your sponsorship document, which I've had a quick read through. Would you like to come into the office next week and have a chat?'

It was far too early to get my hopes up but I had a gut feeling about this one. I knew of the firm for several reasons, not least because they had acted as executors when my stepfather John Holt had died. I had also used their services when I was pursuing a personal injury claim against my previous employers in the Caribbean and, when I was a trustee of Sailability, we had engaged the services of their specialist charity division. But it had never crossed my mind that a firm of lawyers, perhaps the most risk-averse group of people you could think of, would entertain the prospect of sponsoring a quadriplegic to sail around Great Britain.

As time ticked away, and with no sponsorship agreement in place, Ian and I had no choice but to continue to refine the plan and work on a timetabled strategy. I had decided that a May 2007 start would be best, and that was barely six months away. If we were to sit around doing nothing but waiting for a sponsor, even if I were to find one by my deadline of 15 December 2006, then we would not have enough time to complete everything that needed to be done. We knew that if I didn't find a sponsor, all of our work would have been in vain, but we could not let ourselves think like that – so we pressed on regardless.

Acutely aware of the London Boat Show looming in the first week of January 2007, and aware that businesses would before long be winding down for the Christmas and New Year holiday, I desperately wanted to be able to use the London Boat Show to announce my sponsor. I chose not to take a stand there, despite the success of attending the Southampton Show. Firstly, it was too far to think about travelling each day: a six-hour round trip on trains is difficult at the best of times, but in a wheelchair it is fraught with potential difficulties at every step. And secondly, if I hadn't got a sponsor by January 2007 it would be too late anyway: there was no way a project of this magnitude could be cobbled together in such a short timeframe. Apart from the money, I still had to source my crew and it would be unfair to commit anyone to their support when I didn't even know if the project would get to the start line. And only when I had the money could I source the RIB, the Land Rover and everything else on our kit list. It was a frustrating time, like the calm before the storm, and the strain was getting to me.

Apart from many sleepless nights, I was also suffering from signs of stress. On 2 December 2006 I was on a train on my way to London to give a talk to a disabled sailing group when the pressure started to catch up with me. At first I felt queasy, then cold and light-headed, before my eyes glazed over and all I could hear was my heart pounding in my ears. I was really worried that I might be suffering a heart attack, and summoned up enough strength to ask to be taken off the train at Woking station, where paramedics were called to treat me on the platform. Luckily, having been wired up to a heart monitor, I was diagnosed as suffering only an anxiety attack, but it was very frightening and something I'd never encountered before. I didn't realise it at the time, but it may also have been a side-effect of a stone that had been growing at an alarming rate in my bladder and, only two days after my anxiety attack on the train, I had emergency surgery to have the stone removed at Salisbury Hospital. Worried that Ian and any potential sponsors might be unduly concerned, I chose to keep the surgery a secret. This was not easy, with such a heavy workload, but I got away with it.

After several meetings with Blake Lapthorn Tarlo Lyons to discuss ways in which they could capitalise on their sponsorship, and many anxious weeks of waiting, I still did not know if they were to sponsor me. I had made no bones about my deadline, Friday 15 December 2006, and made it clear that I was not prepared to extend it for any reason. Deadline day eventually arrived, and still I had no commitment from them. No email, no phone call. I could not chase them again. I had done so many times – I had done everything I could possibly do.

The weekend of 16/17 December was thoroughly miserable. Blake Lapthorn Tarlo Lyons hadn't said 'no' but the deadline had passed and I wasn't going to start moving the goalposts I had set myself simply to suit my wishful thinking. Where would it end? A good friend of mine, an experienced yachtswoman, had advised me some months earlier, 'Under no circumstances cross the start line whilst still holding invoices.' In other words, find your sponsor and get the bills paid before setting off. Blake Lapthorn Tarlo Lyons knew the deadline, and it had passed. If I was to be truthful to myself, then on Monday morning I would call Ian and start preparing a press release for the London Boat Show explaining that my Personal Everest was over. No one could blame me for not trying. It would be extremely frustrating, but I had done my best. I had given it my best shot, and hopefully people would understand.

Some weeks earlier, in the hope of finding a sponsor, I had written to Buckingham Palace asking if the Princess Royal would be prepared to announce the launch of my Personal Everest project in March 2007. I had long ago decided that I wanted to use my trip as a means to raise awareness of disabled sailing in the UK and, in particular, for a charity called RYA Sailability. As a past chairman and trustee of the charity myself for nearly seven years, I thought it appropriate to ask the Princess to launch my project, as she is also the patron of the charity.

As I sat at my desk on Monday 18 December 2006 considering how best to word the press release announcing the cancellation of my project, Elaine brought through the morning post. Amongst all the usual white and brown envelopes, I spotted the smart cream-coloured envelope with its red E II R frank mark. A letter from Buckingham Palace. I opened it hurriedly.

I had mixed emotions as I read its contents. The Princess had agreed to launch my project on 21 March in London, but now I had to add her to my list of people to call and cancel. It was a tremendous honour for me that she had agreed to come but I had a duty to let her know, sooner rather than later, that I'd called it off. As if it could not get any worse, in the same pile of post was a letter from the organisers of the 2007 RYA Dinghy Show to be held in Alexandra Palace, London, in early March. They too had written with good news, or so it should have been. They wanted to offer me a place in the main entrance foyer to the show to exhibit my boat and my project. No amount of money would be able to buy such a prominent position, and with more than 20,000 visitors expected at the Show, it was a once in a lifetime opportunity. Now they too would have to be notified of my decision. It felt as if my world was crashing down around my ears. I sat at my desk, head in my hands, simply drained of all emotion, completely and utterly exhausted. I was tired of being so outwardly positive on one hand, giving the impression to the world of a project on track to success, whilst privately living through the hell of uncertainty and the imminent acknowledgement that I had been defeated. I sat there, motionless, for what seemed like hours but was probably no more than twenty minutes. And then the phone rang.

'Hi Geoff, it's Walter. Sorry not to get back to you on Friday but I was busy with client work. I'm phoning to say that we'd be delighted to go ahead on the terms we agreed.'

At first I was slightly stunned. 'Oh, right, thank you Walter. Thank you very much indeed.'

As it started to sink in, I could feel a grin form on my lips which quickly grew and stretched from ear to ear. Whilst talking to him, I tried to stop smiling to myself but I couldn't. I was so excited, I even forgot to tell him the news about the Princess and the Dinghy Show.

As I put the phone down, I let out a tremendous whoop of excitement.

'What's wrong? Are you OK?' asked Elaine as she came running into my office, worried that she had heard me calling for help.

'That was Walter Cha. They are going to sponsor me. Oh my god, Elaine, it's going to happen. I can't believe it, it's going to happen, I've got the money.'

Still shaking and grinning like the village idiot, I phoned Ian immediately with the good news. He was delighted for me but quickly brought me back down to earth by calmly stating, 'and now the hard work really begins.'

6

Morag Mhor was a big, 70-foot-long, navy blue motor-sailing ketch. She was owned by the British Aluminium Company, more famous for Bacofoil than this, their innovative, all-aluminium company yacht. Built in the 1950s, she was a particularly ugly boat with an enormous white caravan-like structure plonked on her deck, ruining the quite graceful lines of her hull. But despite her quirky looks, she oozed character and had the charm of an elderly lady. She was moored on the River Hamble just alongside the boatyard where, as a family, we were still encamped aboard the uncompleted *Lord Gulliver*.

I met with her captain, Brian Jelly, during the Easter holidays of 1982, and he explained what would be expected from me as first mate. Brian was a huge man, rather portly with lots of white facial hair and a somewhat scary demeanour. The owners had ordered that the boat be taken to the Mediterranean for the summer. She would be based in Palma de Mallorca, where she would be used by senior BACO management and clients for charter. There were to be only two crew, Brian as skipper and me for just about everything else. And for this, I was to be paid the princely sum of £13 a week – but at least all of my food and board would be covered. Having decided to take the job, I walked out of school on the first day of the summer term, packed my belongings, moved aboard, and at 5.00 p.m. on Wednesday 28 April 1982 we set out for the Med.

I quickly discovered that making an ocean-going passage on what was effectively a commercial vessel was very different from day-sailing as a child on *Gulliver*. Brian was a no-nonsense guy, and even though I was only sixteen years old I was spared no quarter. If I didn't know something, for example understanding the detail of an Admiralty chart, he would teach me. But if he told me once, he did not expect to have to tell me again. I was in my element. He explained everything patiently and effectively, and I soaked it up like a sponge. Looking back now at my log book, I was detailing our latitude and longitude coordinates, identifying flashing sequences of lighthouses, learning and understanding the concept of dead reckoning, speaking to port authorities on the VHF and even learning how to take sun sightings with a sextant and calculating our position, all in the days before satellite navigation – not bad for a sixteen-year-old.

Within a few hours of leaving from Bursledon on the River Hamble, I did something which could have scuppered the entire voyage, and with it my job. It was night by the time we'd sailed to the western end of the Solent and were clear of the Needles, and as we headed southwest out across the English Channel, Brian sent me down below for a few hours' sleep because I was due back on watch at midnight. Once in my cabin, I opened a porthole so I could have sneaky cigarette and blow the smoke out of the window, naively thinking that I was going to spend the next six months keeping my habit a secret from Brian. Once finished, I closed the porthole and went to the galley for a drink of water.

'Have you been smoking?' asked Brian.

I thought for a minute before answering. I might have lied to my parents, but this was different. He had obviously smelt the smoke. But what would his response be to the truth? Might he order me off the boat at our next stop? I looked him in the eye and stood up straight before replying.

'Yes,' I said confidently, as though I cared not about his response. But I did care, a lot.

'So you opened the porthole to blow the smoke out? You bloody idiot,' he barked. 'We are at sea, the boat could have sunk. Don't you dare do it again. If you want to smoke, do it on deck.'

Inside, I heaved a huge sigh of relief. At the very least I had been expecting a lecture on smoking. Then Brian asked how many cigarettes I had. I pulled my crumpled pack of ten out of my back pocket, now down to just nine to last me until our next landfall. He laughed. 'Right,' he said, 'Come with me.' And took me to the saloon, where he lifted one of the seating cushions.

'I think we are now in international waters,' he declared, and there under the seat was the ship's bonded store, a large grey box with wire around it and a big red wax seal, secured only a day earlier by Customs & Excise. He broke open the seal and inside, next to bottles of gin and whisky, there were dozens and dozens of cartons, each containing 200 cigarettes. 'Help yourself,' he said, 'but remember, don't smoke inside the boat.'

I learned several valuable lessons that night – lessons about safety and, most importantly, lessons about Brian.

Our first landfall was Gibraltar. We arrived in the marina in the dead of night so I didn't realise just how close we were to the airport runway. I found out sure enough at five o'clock the next morning. The Falklands War had started a few weeks earlier and Gibraltar was used as a refuelling point by many of the fighter jets making their way down to the South Atlantic. When I was woken by an RAF jet engine a few hundred yards away it frightened the life out of me. I honestly thought the boat had exploded.

A week or so later we arrived in Mallorca and established our base at the Real Club Nautico in Palma. Straightaway my introduction to preparing a boat for charter began. Brian worked me relentlessly. We would wake early and have breakfast before immediately starting work, stopping briefly for a lunchtime sandwich before continuing until it became too dark to see. The most arduous job was rubbing down and completely repainting the ship, including both sides of her 70-foot hull. Aluminium and sea water are not good bedfellows, so keeping on top of the corrosion was an uphill job, which included painting her hull with a special blue aluminium paint. The air temperature was in the high thirties Celsius but still he insisted I kept going. It took about ten days to complete the work, and it was the hardest physical thing I had done in my life. There were times, when I was rubbing the paint down with sandpaper, that I felt a real hatred towards Brian. It felt like I was being bullied. I was lonely, I missed my friends, and I felt that I had no one to turn to. At the time, I really thought he was being unfair on me, but I had no one to fight my corner. Interestingly, though, not once did I ever consider giving up. I guess deep down I wasn't prepared to be beaten.

But once the hard work was complete, the real fun began. Charter guests started to arrive for week-long holidays, and Brian and I were the perfect hosts. With the hard graft soon a distant memory, we spent our days taking guests to beautiful harbours and secluded beaches in all parts of the Balearics. If we weren't sailing, then we were taking them windsurfing or going ashore on shopping trips. Weighing anchor, pulling up sails, making cocktails and preparing food for guests became the daily routine. And when we had no guests, Brian and I would take *Morag Mhor* on our own sightseeing tour of the islands, including Menorca and Ibiza. They were good times. Even in the early 1980s we tried to avoid hot spots like Palma Nova and Magaluf, which were a heaving mass of bodies on the beach – as we sailed past, you could smell the warm wafts of coconut-scented suntan lotion on the breeze. But despite its reputation, Mallorca offers some of the most beautiful harbours and coastline in the world, and we explored just about all of them that summer.

Sadly the season was over as quickly as it had begun, and it was time to sail home. By mid September we were back on the River Hamble. On returning home, I could see a real change in myself. In less than six months I had matured enormously in my confidence, my knowledge and my social skills, and that maturity was most evident when meeting up again with old friends who were either at college or still living at home with their parents. But, even having spent all that time with Brian, and despite him being one of the most influential figures of my life, I never really got to know him. He was a very private and a very proud man.

I got back to find that, although not quite complete, *Lord Gulliver* was now on the water and moored in a prime location in the middle of the River Hamble, adjacent to the Jolly Sailor pub, made famous in the 1980s drama series *Howards' Way*. With her shiny black hull, *Lord Gulliver* was a wonderful sight and a real credit to all the hard work John had put into her. I moved back on board with my mother, John and Lucy whilst I reviewed my options.

Whilst out with my school friend Sean one night in a local pub, I bumped into another old friend called Gareth Williams. Sailing on his father's yacht *Challenger*, Gareth had only recently got back from competing in the 1981 Whitbread Round the World Race, what is now known as the Volvo Ocean Race. Only seventeen at the time, he was the youngest crew member to compete in the race. Now his father, Les Williams, had plans to sail the enormous 80-foot *Challenger* out to the Caribbean and operate her as a charter yacht. Compared with *Morag Mhor* – which could at best be described as an old workhorse – *Challenger* was a thoroughbred racehorse. At the time she was at the absolute cutting edge of ocean racing technology, a magnificent and striking yacht with winches the diameter of oil drums, a steering wheel six feet across – but with few creature comforts below decks. Whereas *Morag Mhor* was made of aluminium, *Challenger* was made of fibreglass, so her hull did not need painting. However, having just sailed 27,000 miles around the world, the blue gelcoat which covered her fibreglass hull was very faded and the only way to restore her colour was to rub both sides of her entire 80-foot length with fine sandpaper. In need of money but hugely aware of how miserable the work was, having endured rubbing down the hull of *Morag Mhor*, I reluctantly offered my services. It was no less physically demanding than before, but at least I had the company of Gareth, who helped me.

When we'd finished, Les put a proposition to me. In lieu of payment, he suggested I join the crew for the trip across the Atlantic to the Caribbean. It was by then late October 1982 and, with the cold of winter setting in, the thought of going to the Caribbean was too good an opportunity to pass by. I wasn't even sure what would happen to me once I got there, but I didn't give it a moment's thought.

In mid November we set off from the River Hamble with a crew of seven including Les, Gareth and Frenchman Jacques Redon, then husband of yachtswoman Clare Francis. I was quick to discover the two main differences between a motor-sailing yacht like *Morag Mhor* and a maxi racing yacht. Firstly, *Challenger* rarely motored anywhere. Although she had an engine, which rarely worked anyway, it was nearly always far quicker to sail. Secondly, I was to learn the hard way about the immense loads and strains on the rigging and ropes of a world-class racing yacht. On one occasion I was releasing the spinnaker halyard in order to lower the sail, but I had only put a couple of turns around the winch to control its descent. This might have been sufficient on a smaller yacht, but there were tons and tons of pressure on *Challenger*'s spinnaker halyard, and it nearly took my hand clean off as I released it – I was lucky to get away with no more than severe rope burns. With her sails correctly set, it was not uncommon for *Challenger* to clock up speeds in excess of 20 knots, and with a sail locker jam-packed with sails for every wind strength, Les was forever instructing exhausting sail changes, lugging the heavy sodden bags onto deck, in order to get the best out of her.

Almost as soon as we departed from Hamble, the weather turned extremely bad, with forecasts of storm force 10 in the Bay of Biscay, so we sought refuge in Alderney in the Channel Islands until the weather abated. It took two days for the weather to improve, just long enough to get barred from the Diver's pub for 'inappropriate behaviour'. I never found out the exact nature of my offence, but it apparently involved some lewd comments made to members of the women's darts team.

On Saturday 27 November we slipped our lines from the quayside in Alderney and set sail for St Lucia. Over the following twenty-three days, my log records my first transatlantic crossing, most notably the slow but noticeable increase in temperature, my wonderment at the enormity of the Atlantic Ocean, the brightness of the night stars, and sightings of flying fish, dolphins and whales. We worked a watch system of four hours on deck, four hours off, so I was with Gareth on each watch. I quickly got into the routine of life on board, sharing the cleaning and cooking duties whilst always maintaining boat speed and, if that meant changing a sail six times in the middle of the night in the pouring rain, even when you were supposedly getting some rest, then that is what you did. It was my first taste of sailing a yacht hard, and it was clear that Les knew how to get the best out of her. Jacques filled his days below completely rebuilding her interior and fitting her out as a charter yacht, a hard enough exercise in harbour, but attempting to do so at sea seemed bizarre. When we finally arrived in harbour, the resulting ill-fitting partitions and cupboards confirmed my concerns.

I was the first to sight land. I was standing up high on the pulpit at the very front of the boat, straining to see. We knew we were close but I really wanted to be the first to see a Caribbean island. Then, suddenly, there it was. I could just about make out the hazy grey outline of a large island. St Lucia – I'd completed my first transatlantic. We went straight to Castries, the main harbour, to stock up on fuel, water and supplies before sailing to the far end of the island to meet Les's wife Janet and her daughter, Fiona, who had arrived the same day at the airport. It all seemed slightly surreal, having sailed 3,000 miles across the ocean in three weeks, to be immediately joined by friends who had left the UK just eight hours earlier, but it was great to see them again.

Janet arrived with news from my mother. In my absence, my parents had befriended an American couple who had just bought a brand new 57-foot yacht called *Rampant*. The boat was moored on the River Hamble and was in the process of completing her sea trials. The owner wanted her sailed out to the US Virgin Islands in the Caribbean as soon as possible and had asked that I fly home to join the boat to help sail her across. This suited me perfectly. My return flight was booked for 11.00 p.m. on Christmas Eve, departing Antigua for London.

Satisfied that, for the time being at least, I had an ongoing career, I took some time to relax and enjoy the beauty of the islands. That night, we anchored in Marigot Bay in St Lucia. Surrounded by the tall volcanic Piton mountains, the steamy lush vegetation and the pure white, powdery sand beaches, this was the closest I had ever to come to paradise and it was everything I had imagined. I sat in *Challenger*'s vast cockpit, eating a sweet lady's-finger banana picked off an enormous bunch which hung from the boom, just taking it all in, my senses working overtime. The sound of exotic birds in the rainforest, the gentle lapping of the waves on the beach – it was breathtakingly beautiful. In my log I wrote 'What a place – paradise!'

The next morning we set sail for Martinique, where we stayed for one night before heading up to Antigua. We arrived in English Harbour, Antigua, at 7.00 a.m. on 22 December. It was strange. St Lucia was a genuinely unspoiled paradise but Antigua, only a few islands to the north, had a completely different feel. It still had an exoticness without feeling tropical. But the sense of history was palpable. The appropriately named Nelson's Dockyard is exactly that. It is a wonderful place, completely untouched, as though Nelson had only just left but forgot to shut the gates. All around, you are surrounded by remnants of a colonial past and can almost smell the Britishness of the place. If seeing it from sea level isn't enough, a short trip to Shirley Heights, an old garrison which overlooks the harbour, reveals without doubt one of the top views in the world. It is simply jaw-droppingly beautiful.

That strange cultural mix of West Indian and English was highlighted on the afternoon of Christmas Eve, when I sat on *Challenger*'s deck watching a local Antiguan Rasta with dreadlocks down to his waist, dressed as Father Christmas, being rowed around the harbour in a small dinghy by a young boy. In the tropical heat and relentless sunshine, Santa shouted out his ho-ho-ho's to all the passing yachts, while another young lad was throwing tiny bits of ripped-up paper over him to imitate snowfall.

'Merry Christmas! Would you like champagne?'

I awoke with a jolt. Where was I? It took a few moments to gather my thoughts. It suddenly dawned on me from the droning noise that I must be on an aeroplane, but this was the first time I had ever been on a plane in my life so it wasn't immediately obvious. I pulled the blanket off and looked out of an adjacent window. The sun was shining brightly and all I could see below was a thick blanket of white cloud. I looked at my watch. It said 8.00 a.m. I was completely disorientated.

The stewardess spoke to me again. 'Merry Christmas! Would you like champagne?'

Merry Christmas? Champagne? It all seemed totally surreal. I thanked her but declined the drink. The plane was virtually empty. Somehow all three of the middle seats had been reclined and I had fallen asleep across them wearing only my shorts and an old T-shirt with a blanket pulled over me. Ever so slowly, I began to remember the night before, waiting at the airport whilst Jacques plied me rum cocktails. No wonder I was so disorientated.

With no trains or coaches running on Christmas Day, I hitchhiked back to Hamble from Heathrow airport only to find my parents had sailed to the Isle of Wight for the holiday. Luckily for me, my old school friend Sean had anticipated my return and his mum had kept a Christmas dinner warm for me in the oven.

My first priority was to check out my new vessel. Unlike my previous two yachts, *Rampant* was a luxurious charter yacht, purpose-built for the job. Her owner, Fred Taussig, was a wealthy American from St Louis, Missouri, and he and his wife Louise had spared no expense in fitting every conceivable luxury, even a washing machine and tumble-dryer, which was most uncommon in such a relatively small boat. Not only was I employed as first mate, but I was to be paid a decent wage too, and the job was mine for as long as I wanted.

To earn some extra money in order to replenish their now depleted savings, John and my mother had agreed to help deliver *Rampant* to the Canary Islands, at which point Fred, his wife Louise and a couple of friends would join us for the Atlantic crossing. Acting as delivery skipper as far as the Canaries was a man by the name of Andy Brooks.

We left the Hamble on Tuesday 11 January 1983, for what was to become my second Atlantic crossing. We got as far as Dartmouth before teething troubles with the new boat forced us to take shelter and make emergency repairs. Two days later, on 13 January, we set sail again with even worse results, as explained in my log:

> 13 January. Left Dart marina at 0730. At 0800 streamed Walker log. 0910 off Start Point. Log reading 9.0 knots, course 230 degrees, wind NW 5, wind increasing. Steering jammed due to failed cotter pin. Faulty engine alarm. Mum smacked her face up on a winch and got bad concussion so at 1610, turned back. Wind now force 7. at 0315 on the 14th, back alongside Dart Marina.

My mother was prone to seasickness and, in anticipation of bad weather, had used an anti-seasickness patch behind her ear which had made her drowsy. Combined with her drowsiness, the rough seas had caused her to lose her balance and she fell across the cockpit, striking her head on the winch, which, it later turned out, detached a retina in her eye. She decided to leave the boat the following day, but before leaving she came to my cabin and told me it was her intention to divorce my stepfather John. She didn't give me any explanation, nor did I seek any, but I do recall telling her to do whatever made her happy. And with that she left the boat and was driven back home to Hamble by Andy

Brooks. He had also chosen to leave, apparently because of the continual delays. John, however, chose to stay. With hindsight, clearly my parents had been having difficulties in their marriage for some time, so quite what they hoped to achieve by sailing the Atlantic on *Rampant* I will never know.

Andy Brooks was quickly replaced by another delivery skipper who would go as far as the Canaries, whilst my mother's crewing position was taken by a man only a few years older than me, a local Plymouth guy called Richard Purssell. We spent another week or so ironing out a whole succession of teething problems on the boat before finally setting sail for the Canary Islands on 2 February. Once on our way, we had a great sail down to Gran Canaria, arriving ten days later.

Owners Fred and Louise Taussig were waiting for us on the dockside. There had been some doubt whether Fred would be fit enough to make the trip, as he was in his late seventies and had just undergone a hip replacement. His wife and their two friends were not much younger, so the prospect of sailing the Atlantic Ocean with this geriatric crew had great potential for disaster. The delivery crew disembarked in Gran Canaria and flew home, but Richard Purssell was persuaded to remain on board with the intention that both he and I would stay on as permanent crew once we got to the Caribbean. In the short time we had known each other, we discovered that we had a lot in common. He was good fun and had just enough maturity about him to remind me from time to time that I was the junior member of the partnership, which included letting me know the difference between a time to party and a time to work.

Once again my stepfather John chose to stay on the boat for the transatlantic, even though he had every opportunity to leave. I wondered if it was because he was afraid to go back and confront the problems which waited for him at home, but I prefer to think it was his way of finally standing up for himself and demonstrating that he couldn't care less. Whatever his thinking, he was clearly troubled and often preoccupied on the trip.

To those who have never accomplished a transatlantic crossing, the thought of it might seem quite daunting. Although every ocean crossing is a big achievement, if you set off at a certain time of the year and cross between the nearest of two points – the Canary Islands and the Caribbean – then the enormity and danger of the trip is actually much greater in one's imagination than in reality. Using the trade winds, which nearly always blow from east to west, and the Atlantic currents which flow the same way, even without any sails or an engine, a yacht could probably drift across in a couple of months. So, with sails, most boats get across comfortably within a few weeks and without too many dramas.

But what should have been a relaxing sail across the Atlantic turned out to be a pretty tough trip. Not because of the weather – on the contrary, we had perfect sailing conditions – but because of continual concerns for the health and safety of our four septuagenarian passengers. They were pleasant enough, but Richard and I were on different watches so I missed having someone I could relate to. I guess they didn't really understand me either, so a number of factors conspired to make me feel, for the first time, slightly homesick. I celebrated my seventeenth birthday mid-Atlantic, and my diary records how I felt that day:

> It's my birthday today. I should be in England, be taking driving lessons, be with family and friends but no, I'm stuck in the middle of the Atlantic with a bunch of uncaring bastards who think they know it all.

Clearly I was having a bad day.

Once we had arrived in St Thomas in the US Virgin Islands, it was time to say goodbye to Fred and his guests, who flew back to the States. John also flew home within a couple of days and I remember shaking his hand and wishing him luck, hoping for his sake that he could resolve whatever problems awaited him.

By the end of the week it was just Richard and myself, skipper and first mate of a beautiful, luxurious charter yacht, earning good wages. And with the boat moored in a prime location in Charlotte Amalie harbour, it was time to party. My favourite haunt was the Greenhouse, a bar on the edge of the harbour where I spent most nights and befriended the resident band called the Prime Ribs, who were living in a rented villa just outside town. We spent a lot of down-time there, just hanging out and swimming in their pool. With such a new boat, there were very few jobs to do, and with an absentee owner there was a lot of time spent doing nothing.

Very occasionally Richard and I would take *Rampant* out for a sail without the owner's instruction. One such occasion was when the female drummer of the Prime Ribs, Joanna Polama, decided to marry a guy from neighbouring island of St John. Immediately after the band had finished a set one evening, at 1.00 a.m., we loaded the entire band on board and set sail for St John in the dead of night, arriving at 3.30 a.m. so we could all get ashore and climb the highest point on the island – where, at dawn, with the sun rising over the islands, she was married. I'm not sure if Fred would have approved of such a use for his beloved boat, but who could resist such a request.

Over the next few months, Fred and his guests would periodically turn up for a week's charter and we would venture down island, as far as Martinique, but it was fairly uneventful stuff and I was slowly getting a bit bored with the monotony. With poor telecommunication on the islands, I only received the odd fragment of news from England by post. In one letter my mother informed me that she was now living with Andy Brooks, the delivery skipper, and that my sister Lucy was living with them. I don't recall being particularly bothered either way. I was obviously pleased that my mother was happy, and I would support her unconditionally, whatever she chose to do. In the short time I had sailed with him on *Rampant*, I had not really got to know Andy Brooks but he seemed a perfectly decent bloke. I certainly hadn't ever given any thought to him becoming my new stepfather.

By June 1983 the season was now well and truly over in

the Caribbean, and Fred planned to have *Rampant* sailed up to the Eastern seaboard of the USA to Massachusetts. Missing my friends and family back in the UK, I chose to call it a day and head back home. I had no idea where I would go or what I would do when I got there but, at the age of seventeen, I trusted myself enough to know it was the right decision.

7

By the end of the London Boat Show in January 2007, the Personal Everest project had made huge advances. The announcement that lawyers Blake Lapthorn Tarlo Lyons were to be the project sponsor had not only given the project huge credibility – more importantly, it meant that it was actually going to happen. And that meant a revival of interest from the press, which brought with it renewed pressures. Although I joked about having an alter ego, Ernie Read, act as my press officer in the early stages of the campaign, I was simply not able to devote the time or energy to PR that it now required. With my own background in marketing, I knew that the success of the project depended on it being properly promoted. In fact, this was my number one priority. There was only one option, and once again it meant entrusting my 'baby' to someone else.

Susan Preston-Davis and I had known each other for nearly fifteen years. Susan was press officer for Henri Lloyd, and then in the mid 1990s had been press officer for the Time & Tide project, the first all-disabled crew to sail around the world as part of Chay Blyth's BT Global Challenge. Initially I had had misgivings about the project, based around the nature of the crews' disabilities and the way disability was being used to raise money and promote Time & Tide. I recalled an earlier project called Dolphin & Youth, which had been promoted on the back of disability, where crew members had conditions such as dyslexia and asthma – both impairments, but hardly enough to constitute a disabled crew. And to raise more than £1 million of public money in this way had upset a lot of people, myself included. In the circumstances, it was natural that I should have concerns about Time & Tide, but they were to prove unfounded. As I got to know the crew, each with their own disability, I could see that theirs was a genuine challenge, and they completed a massive achievement by finishing the race. Susan had kept in touch with me since Time & Tide, and on top of that we lived in neighbouring villages, so it was Susan that I approached to look after PR for the Personal Everest project. Luckily for me, she agreed to do so at an otherwise busy time for her, and at very generous rates. It still meant a substantial hole in my budget – but I knew Susan was the right person for the job, and it was the right decision.

Delegating the PR to Susan gave me a huge sense of relief. From day one she was off – and before I knew it there were newspapers, magazines, radio and TV stations all over the country running the story. Plenty of publicity was one of the key commitments that I had given to my sponsor, so it felt good to be delivering on that promise.

A day after taking that call from Walter Cha back in December in 2006 confirming their intent to sponsor, I placed an order for a brand new Challenger dinghy to replace my beloved *Billy*. Although *Billy* had been with me for so long and had already helped me achieve many ambitions, she was an old boat, heavy and outdated, and would take too much time, effort and money to bring up to a standard capable of enduring a sail of 1,500 miles.

Many people had asked why I chose the Challenger to attempt the trip in the first place, Ian being the latest and perhaps the person who most needed convincing. Apart from an emotional attachment and a loyalty I have felt since first sitting in one in 1991, I knew in my heart that it was the only suitable boat. Personal Everest would mean visiting at least fifty destinations, and that would entail at least fifty launches and fifty recoveries. Each morning, the boat would have to be pulled out of the water on its trailer so I could be lifted into it from my wheelchair, and then at the end of the day pulled out of the water again so I could be lifted back into the wheelchair. It therefore needed to be suitable for pulling up a slipway on its trailer, and most slipways are just about wide enough for a Challenger. With only a fraction of the destinations on our route having marina facilities, the boat also needed to be able to be pulled over sand or rocks where there was no slipway. In addition, I needed a boat that could be dismantled and put on a road trailer to be towed behind a vehicle if necessary. But, above all, I had to be able to sail it. With no balance, no finger movement, and barely any arm movement, I needed something I could sit in for long periods and actually steer and sail on my own. The Challenger is low to the water and can be cramped and damned uncomfortable, but it works for me. There simply is no other boat capable of the job.

So, with the prospect of a new Challenger in the pipeline, and aware of how much publicity this would mean for the Challenger class, I involved two good friends of mine so they could use my expedition to help promote their own causes. The first was Richard Johnson, chairman of the Challenger Class Association. Our paths had crossed many times over the years, both through Sailability and when I was sailing *Billy* competitively. Instrumental in driving forward the class association, Richard was excited about the publicity to be gained from the project. The other was David Newton, whose son Dan had been a national UK Challenger champion – a charming, charismatic young man, and one of the best sailors ever to race a Challenger. Tragically Dan died from cancer aged only twenty years, but it was his dying wish that the Challenger class became a Paralympic class boat. His father David set up the Dan's Dream charity in memory of his son and to make his son's wish a reality. So it was logical that I should want to involve both Richard and David. Dan's Dream even contributed one-third of the cost of the new boat, as did the makers of the Challenger, White Formula, so for an outlay of £2,000 on my part and the promise to pass the boat back to the charity at the end of the project, I looked forward to the arrival of a shiny new boat in February 2007.

Ian and I continued to meet regularly, and we talked several times each day on the phone. The more I met him, the more I was impressed by his quiet, unflustered professionalism. Knowing how much pressure I had felt relieved of when I first asked him to help, and remembering that same feeling of relief when I asked Susan Preston-Davis to manage my PR, over a period of several weeks I arrived at a momentous decision, one that very much affected me personally. I decided to ask Ian if he would be happy for me to pass over responsibility for what I affectionately called 'all the wet bits' of the project. This covered everything from ensuring that all the boats were suitably equipped to on-water safety, and from boat maintenance to passage-planning our route around the country.

This was a difficult decision for me. As a yachtsman, I know how to navigate, I know how to plan a passage, how to read an Admiralty chart and understand tidal curves, so to even think about passing that over to someone else was a big thing for me to do. But without doubt the hardest aspect was to hand over to Ian the daily decision on whether we sailed or not. Even though I am perfectly capable of making those decisions, if I was going to make Ian my project manager, then I owed him the respect of forgoing that decision. Believe me, even contemplating such a decision was very hard for me, as it would be for anyone who had conceived an expedition like this. But I knew it was for the best. I knew Ian wanted to be part of a successful voyage and would not unnecessarily delay sailing, nor would he knowingly put me in any danger. So if we agreed to sail on a given day, it would, in his view, be safe, and if he decided that we would not sail, it would in his view not be safe. Early on I had identified that this could be a stumbling block at some stage on the journey. I suspected there might be times ahead when the extent of the power that I had given to Ian might become a problem, especially recognising the 'control freak' within me – but I would just have to deal with it if and when it arose.

I think Ian understood that this was a difficult decision for me, but we both understood, regardless of him having overall responsibility whilst at sea, that a boat can only have one skipper, and that I would always be skipper of my boat. Much to my relief, he agreed to accept the responsibility. And it worked. I felt another layer of pressure lift.

Our crew-search net was spread far and wide and, with little or no success, it became increasingly a concern for Ian and me. We even put up adverts in sailing schools and pubs. I followed up a few leads from the Southampton Boat Show, without much joy, but it was the friend-of-a-friend network that was to work best. I had met Mike 'Spike' Spencer a couple of times at the Southampton Boat Show six months earlier. Spike was a volunteer member at New Forest Sailability and was friends with Mike Golden, who had already volunteered his services to the Personal Everest project. At the time, Spike was coming to the end of a career with the MOD, working in a technical capacity proofreading aircraft operation manuals, having previously been a helicopter pilot and commando in the Fleet Air Arm. Spike had some extended leave owed to him and, although he could not come for the whole of the trip, he was available for much of the lead-time and for several weeks after the start. Spike brought with him not only a good understanding of disabled sailing, but also a quite brilliant engineering mind. It was clear from the start that his various skills would make him invaluable, both in helping to look after the engines and electronics and in the practical problem solving that would undoubtedly occur en route.

In early February, Ian took a call from a friend of his who runs a powerboat training school. They knew about my project and our search for crew so they passed on the name of a chap who had recently attended one of their training sessions. His name was Andy Cockayne. I dropped Andy a quick introductory email, and with forty-eight hours he was sitting in my front room being interviewed by myself and Ian. We needn't have worried, though – Max had already given him the OK before Ian and I had time to agree that he would make a great member of the crew. Andy's background was at senior director level of a fashion eyewear company. Not immediately the credentials we were seeking, but he had a sharp business mind, an obvious love of the sea, competent skills driving a RIB and, luckily for us, was taking a sabbatical and was prepared to help out in whatever way we wanted for the next few months. He also claimed to be a good cook and pretty handy with a camera, both of which could be useful.

Apart from still needing one further full-time crew and a possible replacement for Spike if we were not back by the time he had to leave in mid July, we had cracked the crew problem in a matter of days, and so it slipped down the to-do list.

Ian had recommended the purchase of a Pacific 22 RIB some months earlier as part of our revised plan to incorporate a fast support vessel for me. Our search had shown that these robust ex-military RIBs were few and far between, and not particularly cheap. And the ones which were available were either mechanically suspect or needed new rubber tubes, both an extra expense to rectify. Our search was made all the more difficult by the pressures of time: it was essential we got our hands on a RIB as soon as possible to begin making the modifications and installing the huge range of electronics which had now arrived from Raymarine. Finally the decision was made, and after a brief sea trial I wrote the largest cheque to date from the Personal Everest bank account. We had to compromise and, although not a complete heap of junk, it was not far from it. But I was reassured by Ian that it would get us around the country, despite the cloud of steam and grey smoke which followed it wherever it went, puffing and wheezing like some knackered old steam locomotive.

On the positive side, finally having something to do gave Ian and Spike the greatest of pleasure. They were like the proverbial 'pigs in shit'. I would get a call once a day from them, cursing about some other problem they had encountered with the RIB, but they would always end the conversation with 'don't worry, we'll fix it'. I was never in any doubt of that, and as long as they were busy on the Isle of Wight in Ian's workshop there was less chance of them adding to my jobs list or the equipment list.

One huge job that was becoming increasingly urgent was actually piecing together the passage plan, identifying each of the intended fifty destinations and detailing absolutely everything we needed to know about every one of them. On the surface, a fairly modest task, but it was anything but modest, it was an Everest in its own right. And this is where our new crew member Andy made himself invaluable.

Ian, Andy and I had already spent nearly three days sat around a desk using various data sources including Admiralty charts, a nautical almanac, a publication called *Boat Launch*, a road atlas of the UK and the internet, to start identifying each proposed destination. The starting point was that they had to be about forty miles apart, give or take ten miles, the distance I could most likely sail in a day based on past experience. Ideally they needed to provide slipway access at all states of the tide so we could launch and recover my boat at any time of day, and there needed to be good vehicular access for the road crew. It quickly became apparent, even in highly populated areas like the south coast of England, that this was not going to be straightforward – and we had not even started to consider the destinations in more remote parts of the country.

For every proposed destination, we assessed distance to travel both by sea and by road, then accessibility in the harbour for both my Challenger dinghy and the RIB, which had a draft of one metre. We studied the detail of each port on the relevant Admiralty chart and then checked to see what additional information we could glean for the same port from the nautical almanac. *Boat Launch*, a directory of slipways in the UK, was then used to see what, if any, slipway existed in the harbour, its length, width and whether it could be used at any state of the tide. To support our findings, we would then use an internet-based mapping system which gave detailed satellite photographs of each destination. All of this information was entered into a spreadsheet created by Andy that we affectionately called the 'Personal Everest Bible'. This he did for each and every one of our fifty proposed destinations. Once that was complete, he then overlaid it with yet more information such as the name of local Sailability groups, local RNLI contacts, various offers of help that I had been collecting by email and through talking to people at boat shows.

With these details including latitude and longitude of each destination, phone numbers for contacts, tidal data, shore-side facilities and even emergency ports of refuge in case of an incident at sea, it was a task of monumental proportions and one that took Andy several weeks to complete. But far from being a static document, it was forever evolving as new information had to be added. It would be a hugely important document to have, and was intended to ensure that the expedition itself was well planned and as painless as possible.

The calm before the storm was now a distant memory, as activity reached a frenetic pace. To add to the workload for Ian and Spike, we acquired our Land Rover, and that too needed work doing to make it both an expedition vehicle and a home – after all, it was where Ian would be sleeping. But both the RIB and the Land Rover required two major pieces of engineering work. On the RIB we had to construct a large stainless steel framework which would run the length of the boat at a height of six feet to house the radar, VHF antenna and somewhere to store a spare inflatable dinghy. The Land Rover needed an extending crane-like structure fitted to its roof so that, if we ever encountered situations where there were no slipways and no other means of getting me in or out of my boat, I could at least be craned out. At first it seemed quite a ludicrous idea – not least the time and effort it would take to design and make such a thing – and was there ever likely to be a situation when it would be needed? Planning for every eventuality, Ian persuaded me that it would be better to be safe than sorry, although I wasn't convinced. Luckily for us, the Vice-Commodore of the Royal Southern Yacht Club in Hamble, the club which had made me an honorary member for the purposes of the trip, was an engineer and ran his own engineering works. John Beardsley offered to do all of the work for us free of charge on both the RIB and the Land Rover. The only downside was that his company was in Leeds, some 250 miles away. Grateful for such a generous offer, I accepted and Ian drove the Land Rover and towed the RIB to Leeds, where he left them for several weeks while the work was carried out.

Meanwhile, in late February 2007, my brand new Challenger boat was delivered to my house. Still wrapped in polythene and neatly packed on a trailer, I went outside to take a look. It seemed odd seeing her for the first time. Here she was, the boat in which I was going to sail around Great Britain. At only fifteen feet long, she looked so tiny and frail, droplets of rainwater from a passing shower dripping down her anaemic, plain white hull. I'd already decided on a name. For several weeks I'd been wrestling with various options; with nearly 300 similar trimaran Challenger boats in the UK, most names using a play on the words *tri* or *challenge* had been used over the years. But I wanted a name to suit me, and the name I chose was *Freethinker*. And the reason it appealed to me so much is because it worked on two levels. The obvious one is that it reflects my character and the sort of person I am, and that's the assumption most people jump to. But equally important to me is the irreligious connection. When I Googled the term *freethinker*, it fitted perfectly with my outlook on life and religion, but without using what are unfortunately confrontational and aggressive sounding terms like 'atheism' or 'agnosticism'. And with the term 'Humanism' often misconstrued by those who don't understand its true meaning as something slightly 'hippyish', I felt the term *freethinker* was a much more gentle, and certainly a more subtle, way to make a statement about my beliefs.

Before the raindrops had a chance to dry, she was towed away to a local graphics company who had worked hard with me to come up with an eye-catching design. From the outset, I didn't want a boat covered in a mishmash of different companies' logos. With Blake Lapthorn Tarlo Lyons the sponsor, and with

Freethinker
'Challenger' class trimaran

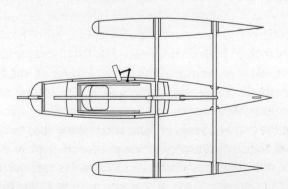

three main official suppliers, the design created by Grapefruit Graphics was simple but had huge visual impact. And the decision to give the bow of each of the three hulls a wrapping in my sponsors' corporate purple colours was inspired.

Despite now having three major pieces of kit, the Land Rover, the RIB and *Freethinker*, my driveway was surprisingly empty with all three away having work done. There were still two major pieces of equipment to source: my specially adapted motorhome and a rented motorhome for the crew. After hours on the telephone and scouring the internet, I finally managed to source the only new wheelchair-accessible vehicle in the country and, with Peter Harrison underwriting the cost, it was to be delivered in April, only a few weeks before our intended departure. I thought finding the crew motorhome would be easier, especially negotiating a long-term hire agreement, but I was wrong. With up to four adult crew needing to sleep in it, and each expecting their own bed, I had to try and find a seven-berth motorhome, as only that would give the four separate beds that they needed. When I did eventually find some motorhomes that fitted the bill, finding one which was available for a ten-week block booking, assuming we would be home by the end of July, was not easy. Finally I found such a vehicle, but even with a discounted weekly rental charge of £500 the cost came to £5,000, another huge outlay.

The first major promotional deadline to loom on the horizon was the Dinghy Show at Alexandra Palace in London on 3 and 4 March 2007. With only a day to spare, *Freethinker* was collected from the graphic designers and taken straight to London for the show. For the first time, she was put together, piece by piece, first the structural cross-beams and then the two outer hulls, and slowly she took shape. It was magnificent to see her come to life before my eyes. Before it was put into place, I located the new Royal Southern Yacht Club burgee into the top of the mast, and then it was lifted and secured into position. A crisp, brand new white Dacron sail provided by Hyde sails was hoisted with a huge screen-printed sponsor's logo emblazoned right across the sail, once again in corporate purple. With *Freethinker* now fully assembled, I wheeled backwards to the entrance door, where the public would be rushing through early the next morning, to see what she looked like. Positioned there, under the main glass atrium of Alexandra Palace, a beam of sunlight streaming down onto her like a spotlight, *Freethinker* looked magnificent, absolutely stunning. But I had one last job to do. I asked a friend of mine to do the honours, and John Harris-Burland applied the sticky transfer print of her name to the transom, written in purple script: *Freethinker*. She was complete.

Even before the doors opened, there was a huge amount of interest from everyone that passed by. Not having had time to add all of the electronics, we still had much to do, but for now it was enough to get people's attention – and *Freethinker* did that perfectly. I lost count of the number of press interviews I did with radio stations, yachting magazines and TV, and even Ellen MacArthur, herself a keen multihull sailor, stopped by to have a chat and wish me luck.

Perhaps the most fortuitous meeting to occur that weekend, although I wasn't to know it at the time, and he would later refer to it as synchronicity, was with a chap called Mike Gallon. Our paths had crossed several years earlier when I was a trustee of RYA Sailability. Mike was a Rotarian and had set up a group named the Rotary/Sailability Collaboration Project. It was, in brief, a mechanism to get Rotary clubs around the UK to learn more about sailing for disabled people and, where appropriate, for clubs to raise money and buy specially adapted boats for disabled people to sail. A simple and straightforward idea, it was incredibly effective, and many Rotary-funded boats were in existence as a result of his initiative. I was aware of Mike's campaign but was never directly involved. It was whilst having a chat with me at the Dinghy Show that Mike first raised the idea of somehow linking my trip with his Rotary project. My knowledge of Rotary was pretty modest at this stage, knowing only that my father-in-law had at some time in the past been president of the Bristol club. Apart from that, I knew very little. When Mike told me that there were some 1,800 clubs and nearly 60,000 members in the UK, I recall my ears twitching. Like Mike, I could see ways that such a relationship could be mutually beneficial to both of us.

'I can't promise,' said Mike, 'but next month, in April, the annual national Rotary conference is being held in Bournemouth. I've got a stand there to promote the Rotary/Sailability Collaboration project. What would you think about bringing *Freethinker* and setting her up there? There'll be a couple of thousand delegates and you may well get some offers of help.'

On the advice of my sponsors and my press officer, we had now agreed a firm departure date of Monday 14 May, so fitting in any extra commitments at this late stage went against my better judgement. I had already turned down several other requests for exactly the same reason. To commit to the Bournemouth conference would take three days out of my rapidly diminishing diary. On top of that was the inconvenience of getting *Freethinker* to the Bournemouth International Centre, rigging her and then going through all the hassle again to get her back home afterwards.

Mike could sense my uncertainty. 'I can't promise, Geoff, but I'm sure you'll find it worth the inconvenience.'

'OK,' I said. 'If you can fix it, let me know.'

With the Dinghy Show over, the next pressing commitment was the launch of my project in London by the Princess Royal on 21 March. To this point, I'd been so preoccupied with the Dinghy Show and with other jobs that I'd not given it much thought. But perhaps also because Susan Preston-Davis and Adam Saturley, our day-to-day contact at my sponsors, had been so effective at organising all the details, I had been shielded from much of the work that was involved. Between them they did all of the liaising with the Palace and the security services which, due to an increase in the terror alert at the time, was extremely detailed and time-consuming. A total of eighty guests had been invited, which included everyone who had helped the project and also members of the press. Every single person had to be checked by the security services and the venue at Surrey Docks Watersports Centre given full security clearance.

In the week before the launch, and with the RIB and the Land Rover still in Leeds, Spike and Ian set to work installing all the electronics in *Freethinker*. With a GPS chartplotter, a VHF and a depth sounder, powering them all was critical – but it was still with much horror that I saw the deck of my beloved new boat being chopped about to make room for a battery, and holes being drilled in the hull to feed the electrical cables. In addition to all of the important navigational electronics from Raymarine, I had another discreet but hugely important piece of kit on my boat. At first I looked on it mainly as a gimmick, but it's no overstatement to say that it was to help keep my whole project alive – and that was a special tracking device called a Track 200D manufactured by a company called Marinetrack. Unlike normal sat nav systems, which tell you where you are, this beamed back the location data so that it could be fed to my website and viewed under the *Where's Geoff?* button. With a predetermined transmission set for every thirty minutes, it would track my position, anywhere on my trip, so people could follow my progress from the comfort of their home computers.

With all of the electronics installed and my new custom-built seat recently arrived from the Department of Medical Engineering in Salisbury, there was time for a last quick polish for *Freethinker* before making our way to London for the Royal launch the following day.

Wednesday 21 March was a sunny spring day but with a bitterly cold northerly wind whistling around Surrey Docks on the Thames. We were kept waiting outside in the cold until the sniffer dogs had done their thing, at which point the venue became a 'sterile area' and only those on the guest list and sub-sequently subjected to a search were permitted to enter. It was a sad reminder of the times we live in but it was an inconvenience worth enduring in the circumstances. Jonathan Lloyd-Jones, senior partner of Blake Lapthorn Tarlo Lyons, shared the stage with myself and the Princess. It was over all too quickly. After we had inspected the boat and made our speeches, Princess Anne worked the room, meeting every single one of the invited guests, and then she left. As we shook hands and she turned to get into her car, she raised her sunglasses and said those words which were to haunt me only a few weeks later: 'There's no going back now, you know!'

By the beginning of April, only six weeks before departure day, the RIB and the Land Rover finally arrived back from Leeds, complete with their modifications. This was fast becoming every schoolboy's dream: it was like Tonka Toys, but for real. The Land Rover looked awesome, with its huge grizzly tyres, electronic winch on the bull-bars, and now a six-foot telescopic extending gantry bolted to the roof – it looked like a battering ram or something out of the *A Team*. But there was still much work to be done on both machines, particularly installing all of the electronics, so the RIB and the Land Rover disappeared back to the Isle of Wight with Ian and Spike and several thousands of pounds' worth of chandlery to be installed, kindly donated by local chandler Bill Foulkes from Aladdin's Cave. Although not completely empty, it did now mean that our 'kit list' had been dramatically reduced, leaving only non-essentials that we could worry about if money allowed.

Meanwhile, with *Freethinker* still not having been on the water and me not having sailed since August the previous year, the time for training was running out fast. In an effort to improve my health for the trip, I had been trying to eat more sensibly and took to wearing weighted armbands to try and strengthen my weak arms, but it was more a token gesture really. Getting physi-cally fit was a luxury for which there was no spare time; it didn't even feature on my to-do list. But I was sensible enough to real-ise that I should at least make time to get *Freethinker* out on the water for a test sail, and to try out the RIB.

We did finally set a date for her first sail, 16 April – only four weeks before our intended departure, but not before I had exhib-ited at the Rotary Conference.

Mike Gallon had gone away from the Dinghy Show and worked his magic by getting permission for *Freethinker* to be exhibited at the Rotary Conference, which would run from Friday 13 to Sunday 15 April. Perhaps understanding the poten-tial greater than me at the time, Mike was extremely excited by the prospect. But it wasn't long before I too recognised what an opportunity this could be. Having set the boat up on the Thursday afternoon, I was back at the Bournemouth International Centre by 9.00 a.m. on the Friday morning. For the next three days, from 9.00 a.m. to teatime each day, I had Rotarians queuing up at my stand to learn more. My faithful hard-backed notebook that I had used at the Southampton Boat Show six months earlier was soon bursting with names, addresses, phone numbers and offers of help from Rotarians from all corners of the British Isles. One small delegation I spoke to were from my very own village of Shedfield in Hampshire, and were members of the Hamble Valley Rotary group. We didn't speak for long but their President, David Cheatham, suggested that they came to see me at home to talk about ways in which they might be able to help, and we set a date for the following week. Attending the conference proved to be a tiring but extremely worthwhile experience, and we col-lected a lot of details and useful contacts.

Despite being absolutely shattered, I was enjoying the roller-coaster ride that I was on. At night, I was still waking regularly from the most frightful nightmares, mostly very dark, sinister dreams of suffering at sea, from violent waves, being soaked to the skin and feeling freezing cold or, worse still, drowning. But by day it was a different story. I was running on adrenalin and, although it was a constant feeling of stress, especially with the start date fast approaching, I was thriving on it. It was a great feeling to slowly but surely tick off items on the to-do list. It was quite simply relentless: phone calls, emails, meetings. One minute up, the next down, and the contrast between the terror of the nightmares and the satisfaction gained from achieving the next objective was strangely satisfying. Having such a good team around me helped enormously, not least having so many wise heads to bounce ideas off.

I'm not so sure Andy Cockayne saw it the same way, especially when I returned from the Rotary conference laden with all of the contact details of Rotarians around the country which he then had to overlay onto the already complicated 'bible' data. But having completed it, and then having emailed all of the Rotary contacts I had met at the conference, he started to build up a comprehensive matrix of offers of help for just about every destination on our route. To be clear what we expected from them, we devised a list of required help from Rotarians that included such mundane items as laundry, cooking, child-minding (for Timothy) and, most importantly, help or advice on local amenities. It was difficult to know exactly what we would be needing, but it was right to forewarn them of the sorts of things we were likely to want. What we couldn't do was allow groups or individuals to turn up and expect to have a social evening with us when we had a tight timetable to keep.

April 2007 was glorious, and the weather unseasonably warm. It made the completion of essential jobs that much easier, since we were able to work outdoors, and our house and garden were unrecognisable. Just about every room in the house was full with boxes of clothing, boxes of electronics and countless day-to-day items and chandlery that we would need on the trip, all of which had now started to arrive from suppliers who had promised their support weeks and months earlier. The wheelchair-accessible motorhome had now arrived and was parked on our front lawn, where it received its full graphic-design treatment from the guys at Grapefruit Graphics. With the motorhome, the Land

Rover and *Freethinker* now fully branded and sharing my front lawn with the RIB and the rented seven-berth motorhome, for the first time we had all of the kit together. It was an impressive sight, and one to be proud of considering all of the hard work in reaching this point. There were still some minor electrical and engineering jobs to be done but, by the end of April and with a fortnight to go, we were just about ready.

During April, once again more by luck than judgement, we found our two remaining crew members. Joel Whalley, an ex-Royal Naval submariner, was recommended by a friend, and a young lady called Sarah Outen was recommended through a contact of Ian's. Joel was able to commit to the entire journey, having to be back by the end of July, and Sarah, recently graduated from Oxford University, would be joining us later in the voyage to replace Spike, assuming we had not already finished by then. But with April giving hope of a beautiful and prolonged summer to come, I was confidently predicting a return date of mid July.

Whilst Ian and myself finished off the last of the risk assessments, a dozen or more in total, those crew not qualified with a Sea Survival certificate were dispatched to the UK Sailing Academy in Cowes on the Isle of Wight which, at no expense, put them through the rigorous course. Thankfully they all passed. The following week a group of us, myself included, received training and qualification in acquiring our VHF licences, provided free by Mendez Marine. And with the RIB crew already holding their Level 2 powerboat certificates, the minimum demanded by Ian, our crew were now fully qualified in every aspect that would be required.

With so many businesses and people offering to help, it was difficult to keep track of them all. Illustrated most obviously by the commitment of my crew, all expecting nothing in return for helping me, that same attitude was increasingly prevalent all around me. I would not wish to take any personal credit for it, but it is my belief that people were already, perhaps unwittingly, beginning to realise that Personal Everest was something much larger than just a disabled guy living out a dream. I could see it in my sponsors, in the suppliers, and in everyone who became involved. Even at this early stage there was a personal commitment on their part and a sense of ownership which gave the whole project a more profound sense of purpose. Although I sensed it, I was not exactly aware of just how important this was going to be.

Susan and Adam were now working full-tilt on the departure day of Monday 14 May. On Susan's advice, the date was chosen to maximise the likelihood of press interest, and the time for departure was set at 1.00 p.m. to ensure that guests, particularly those of the sponsor, could have a light lunch before waving me off on my journey. A good friend of mine, Jonathon Savill, a larger-than-life ex-journalist with a somewhat unorthodox, direct approach to public relations, had somehow managed to get national BBC Breakfast TV interested in broadcasting my departure. There would be no guarantees, possibly right up until the day before, but it would be sensational if he could pull it off. In addition, he had persuaded my local BBC station to loan the project a top-of-the-range high-definition digital video camera to record the expedition. The media interest was tremendously exciting. There was so much of it that my friends had long since stopped calling me to say they'd seen me on TV that night or read another newspaper article. After investing so much time and effort in courting the press and giving them everything they wanted, I only hoped there would be no fall from grace.

Keen to get some film footage 'in the can', to use the broadcaster's parlance, and also to sail *Freethinker* for the first time, on Monday 16 April, with no public or press present, we discreetly took *Freethinker* out for her first ever sail. We launched from the

Royal Southern Yacht Club on the River Hamble late morning and I made my way, closely followed by *Everest One*, our newly refurbished support RIB, out into Southampton Water.

From the very first moment that I pulled in the mainsheet and felt her accelerate, I fell in love with her. Not only did she look stunning in her corporate branded livery, but she handled like a dream. The response was instantaneous when I steered her – it was like driving a Formula 1 car compared to *Billy*. With the electronics all fired up, and feeding me real-time information on depth, location, direction of travel and speed, and with my watertight VHF radio safely concealed in my helmet, the microphone positioned in front of my mouth and the easy-to-push big red transmit button on my chest, I felt like a pilot in charge of a fighter jet. It was windy and there was spray flying everywhere, but inside my specialist clothing I was snug and warm, sitting for the first time on my new, customised seat – it was like sitting on air. Never in the sixteen years that I had been sailing as a disabled person did I feel so comfortable, so completely in control and so confident in my ability. As we made our way back to the club, complete strangers out on their boats, and even people working in the marinas that lined the river, were stopping what they were doing, watching, waving and shouting 'good luck'. They had obviously seen or heard about the story in the press, but it was a great feeling, and being part of such a professional team, especially looking so smart in our branded clothing and equipment, made me feel really proud. I allowed myself a huge grin behind the secrecy of my tinted visor.

8

My friend Sean and I met up within days of my return from the Caribbean and decided to take a flat together in Hamble. It was a tiny room, what today we might call a studio apartment. When not in use, both of our beds folded up into the wall to give extra living space, we had a tiny kitchen area behind a flimsy partition, and we shared a communal bathroom which was down a corridor. What we lacked in space, we more than made up for in an uninterrupted view out across the River Hamble. Already semi-domesticated, we even introduced a couple of pets to our new home, a pair of fish we named Rum and Coke. Sadly they died within a couple of weeks but we kept them anyway until the smell got so bad that our girlfriends flushed them down the toilet. We learned the hard way that fish eat neither bacon nor Rice Krispies.

Never one to sit idle, Sean was working hard as a labourer on building sites during the day and doing shifts in a pub in the evening to supplement his income. I too needed to find work, and within a few days I found the perfect job right on my doorstep. I remember clearly knocking on the door of Beth's Restaurant in Hamble. An incredibly beautiful, elegant lady opened the door to the grand Georgian-fronted restaurant and I confidently asked her for a job.

'How old are you?' the lady asked in a lovely soft Irish accent.

'Eighteen,' I lied.

It was so funny. Restaurant owner Beth was trying hard to be a stern employer and was trying to conduct our meeting like a formal business interview, but even then I could see that she was too polite to turn me away. So, clearly having taken advantage of her better nature, I was duly employed as a front-of-house barman. I worked two shifts a day, six days a week, and my role soon became more akin to that of a maitre d', with responsibility for table bookings, ordering of wines and spirits and even unofficial agony uncle to the waitresses, an unpaid role but one which gave me an eye-opening insight into their love lives. The hours were long but, for the time being at least, it was the perfect job. The restaurant was only a matter of yards from my flat, it had stunning views over the River Hamble, the village was the epicentre for parties and gatherings for all of my friends during that summer of 1983 and, as if that were not enough, I was spoiled rotten by the chef, Audrey. At the end of service, whilst the waitresses huddled around a large bowl of left-over salad and bread for their dinner, without fail, Audrey would have prepared me a full gourmet meal which, combined with the dregs of customers' unfinished bottles of wine, made for my very own fine dining experience. How many seventeen-year-old lads have salmon en croute with Dauphinoise potatoes or tournedos steak Rossini personally cooked for them nightly by a wonderful chef, accompanied by a half-bottle of *premier cru* Chassagne Montrachet?

By November 1983 Sean and I had shared a great summer. But, like me, Sean wanted to stretch himself and was looking for a new job. He didn't have to wait long. An English chap named Tony Snell had advertised for an odd-job person to join him in New England to work on his house before going to the Caribbean to help out at his restaurant in Tortola in the British Virgin Islands. I was quick to encourage Sean to take the opportunity, and after a successful meeting with his future boss Sean packed his bags and was gone. It seemed odd. For the first time it was now me stuck in the UK.

During my time back in the UK, I managed to see my mother on several occasions, and visited her and Andy in their rented flat in Southampton. I wasn't overly surprised when she announced that they were to marry but I was slightly taken aback to learn that they planned to move to the Isles of Scilly with my sister, where Andy had accepted a job as assistant harbour master on the island of St Mary's.

Unfortunately the divorce from my mother had compelled John to sell his beloved yacht *Lord Gulliver* in order to pay the divorce settlement. I met him a number of times that summer and there's no question that he was a broken man. He had dearly loved my mother and, over the years, had tolerated any number of provocations and difficulties to try and keep the marriage alive. The decision to build *Lord Gulliver* may have set in motion a chain of events which ultimately led to the situation he now found himself in, but maybe it would have happened anyway. Now he had not only lost his wife and custody of his daughter, but even the boat which he put his life into over so many years had gone.

Working in a fine restaurant taught me a huge amount and, once again, I was quick to learn. On one hand I learned about food – the importance of preparation, understanding ingredients and the cooking process, plus an understanding of fine wines. On the other hand, I learned about being in the people business; dealing with customers and ensuring their needs were satisfied. I guess I already had a head start in both areas, having worked on charter boats, but this was intense, full-on and was a real insight into a very hard-working but rewarding industry.

One of the regular customers at Beth's Restaurant was a disabled lady called Tid Campbell, whom I would help into the restaurant in her wheelchair whenever she came to eat. Although I thought nothing of it at the time, those chance encounters with Tid, bumping her up the steps, were to completely shape my entire life only a few years later.

With Sean now in the Caribbean, we chatted regularly on the phone, I was always keen to hear how he was enjoying being overseas, and it was clear that he was having a great time. By Christmas 1983 he and his employer had moved from the United States to the island of Tortola in the British Virgin Islands.

A musician, comedian and raconteur, Tony Snell had a restaurant called the Last Resort perched on the tiny island of Bellamy Cay in Trellis Bay, on the east end of Tortola, where his uniquely eccentric British entertainment appealed very much to the passing charter yacht trade. Sean also told me that Gareth Williams, the good friend with whom I'd sailed the Atlantic on the yacht *Challenger*, was now in Tortola skippering his very own luxury charter yacht, and the pair of them had met up several times.

The miserable British winter had only just begun and, envious of Sean and Gareth enjoying the sunshine in the Caribbean, I asked Sean whether Tony Snell could make use of any extra help at his restaurant. Sean said he would ask, but even before he had come back to me with an answer I handed in my notice to Beth and the landlord of my flat. Within a couple of days I was on a plane bound for Puerto Rico and arrived in Tortola shortly after.

I remember Sean being a bit surprised when I turned up that morning at the Last Resort. Luckily for me, Tony Snell agreed to me staying a few nights and helping out in the restaurant until I found something more permanent. Although I tried looking, I need not have bothered. Tony recognised that Sean and I worked well together and decided to take me on as well. Between us, we basically ensured that the business ran smoothly, at least as far as the customers were concerned. Our accommodation was no more than a primitive concrete-block construction on the beach with a corrugated iron roof. It was called the Ice House because that is the exact function it served. It had a huge industrial-sized ice maker and two freezers in one room to supply the insatiable requirement of the restaurant for ice for drinks and, the Last Resort's speciality, pina coladas. As ice was produced, so we bagged it and put it in the freezers. Our bedroom was a twin-bedded concrete space and that was it. Frequently we would have to check our beds and clothing for scorpions, and we were often kept awake by coconut rats scurrying across the tin roof. It was hot and dirty, and even the shower had green slime that oozed constantly from the shower head.

The Ice House was literally on the beach in Trellis Bay, overlooking the Last Resort restaurant in the middle of the bay. Tony and his wife Jackie lived on the island itself with their two children, Jessica and Jeremy, and a pet donkey called Chocolate. Each morning Sean and I would row out to the Last Resort in a small dinghy, where our first job would be to clean up from the night before. The most important task was to empty the bins before the heat started to decompose their contents. It was a disgusting job that required two people to make several trips back and forth to the mainland, only about 300 metres away but far enough to get covered in the foul-smelling toxic fishy liquid (which we affectionately called 'bin juice') if we weren't careful. Having restocked the drinks in the bar and made ready the restaurant for the evening service, the rest of the day was spent trying to help rebuild one of Tony's dilapidated boats on the beach before it got too hot to work in the afternoon, at which point we would usually go windsurfing or snorkelling in the bay. From 6.00 p.m., six days a week, we would be on duty collecting customers from their yachts, serving drinks, taking food orders and generally ensuring that everyone had a good time. Being British worked in our favour. The bulk of the guests were American, so on many occasions we would be tipped handsomely because of nothing more than our English accents and charm.

Working for Tony was actually quite hard graft, but we earned very good money. If we had a problem, it was finding enough free time to spend it. Our day off was Sunday, when all the shops were closed, which made it even harder to spend our earnings. But we would often hire two Jeeps for the day – one each – and we would go to the most expensive restaurants on Tortola and enjoy the finest foods and wines. We were still of course only seventeen years old, and our immaturity in some aspects was manifest. For example, there was the time that I concluded my double lobster dinner with brandy and Benedictine cocktails by the restaurant pool of a five-star hotel. Unfortunately the rich foods and alcohol were too much for my system and were duly deposited in the award-winning pool, earning me an immediate ban from that particular establishment. Over the months we spent on Tortola, we drove to just about every corner of the island, exploring all the hidden inlets and sheltered coves, none more stunningly beautiful than Cane Garden Bay. An idyllic sandy beach with turquoise waters, it was my favourite spot on the island, and I could often be found there, relaxing under the shade of a palm tree, looking out across the Caribbean sea, sipping a fruit punch and just thinking about life in general.

Our earnings were further boosted following a chance conversation I had on my way to the island for bin-emptying duties early one morning. The skipper of one of the charter yachts anchored in the bay called me over and asked where the nearest refuse point was ashore, so he could get rid of his two bags of rubbish. I offered to take it, for which he offered me $1 per bag. With his bags of rubbish in my boat and the two dollar bills in my pocket, I was just about to untie my dinghy from his yacht when I thought I'd ask if he needed any ice. I told him it was $2 a bag. He asked for three bags. From that morning onwards, Sean and I got up an hour earlier to motor our dinghy around all the dozens of boats in the bay collecting rubbish and selling ice, which made us upwards of $50 a day, not bad for an hour's work each morning.

As the season moved into Easter 1984, still we worked relentlessly. Occasionally we would meet up with Gareth and the three of us would go out for a sail on the magnificent boat he was skippering, a 60-foot yacht called *Fly*. It was good to relax and unwind away from work with my mates, and the three of us would often take photos and make audio recordings to send back to family and girlfriends back home.

Working in the restaurant, not only did we meet a lot of transient holidaymakers who were chartering boats on a weekly basis, but so too the professional skippers who would call in weekly with their guests to enjoy Tony's unique brand of entertainment. One such charter captain was a man by the name of

Barry Rice. He was skipper of a yacht called *Endless Summer II* and was married to a lady called Rosalind whose parents, coincidentally, had been good friends of my mother and John back in England. Barry explained that for the next charter season (due to run from September 1984) he was in need of a deck-hand and asked if I would I be interested in the job, which would ultimately lead to a skipper's role. Always up for a challenge, I joined the boat on 5 May 1984 for a trial week sailing around the islands with four guests on board from America, which went very well. At the end of the week we parted company on the basis that should he wish to take it further, Barry would contact me, but I wasn't going to get my hopes up.

Only a day after my trial run on *Endless Summer*, Gareth announced that the owner of *Fly* was going to sail her back to Europe, and asked if Sean and I would like to help crew her back across the Atlantic. The season was nearing an end, and the Caribbean out of season is a fairly quiet place because of the risk of hurricanes. After a short discussion, both Sean and I decided to leave, so we gave our notice to Tony and on Sunday 13 May we set off for my third Atlantic crossing. But this crossing was different because we would be heading west to east, sailing up the north American seaboard before bearing east and heading across the notorious north Atlantic. With only four of us on board, Gareth, Sean, myself and the owner, Robert Hurst, it was a tough trip, working a four-hours-on, four-hours-off watch system. The weather got progressively colder the further north we travelled. It was also particularly rough, and we narrowly missed a couple of tropical storms off Bermuda. On one occasion, close to the danger zone for icebergs, a terrific storm battered the boat for several days, eventually snapping the boom in two midway across the Atlantic. After twenty-eight days, we finally made landfall in Benodet, France, from where we flew home.

Once again on the trail of work, Sean applied to another advert he'd seen in the Sunday papers, this time as an estate agent in London. I remember sitting in his parents' front room, incredulous as he lied through his teeth on the phone telling the owner of this fledgling London agency that he was twenty-one years old with three years' experience in estate agency. At his interview he came clean about his age and his CV, but the owner, so impressed with his nerve, offered him a job as a trainee on a two-month trial.

For my part, I dumped my belongings with one of my old school friends, Si O'Callaghan, and set off to Scotland on a survey vessel which was working on a short-term contract with the Admiralty and the Hydrographic Office to survey the Pentland Firth. Having made our way up the east coast of England on this converted lifeboat, we spent several weeks tracking backwards and forwards at fifteen-metre intervals across the notoriously dangerous Pentland Firth. Establishing our exact location using a trisponder system with shore stations in two locations on the northern coastline of Scotland and one in Orkney, and towing a side-scanning sonar behind us, we would follow one track from the Scottish shoreline across the Firth to the Orkney shoreline, before moving only fifteen metres eastwards and reversing our route. Following the exact course would have been difficult in its own right, and keeping to the exact track with 8 knots of cross-current was incredibly tough, but it was fascinating to see the sea bed slowly take shape each night as we downloaded the data. I lost count of how many times we traversed the Firth taking soundings, but it was many hundreds.

One evening in mid August 1984, I had just been watching the northern lights flickering in the sky when I headed into the pub in Burray, Orkney. I bought myself a pint of beer and was walking to a free table when the landlady called out from behind the bar –

'Is there a Geoff Holt in the bar?' she asked. Surprised, I took the call.

'Hello?' I said, amazed that anyone had known my exact whereabouts.

'Hi Geoff, it's Barry Rice,' came the reply. 'Are you still

interested in joining us on *Endless Summer* in Tortola?'

Having decided that the opportunity was too good to miss, I gave my apologies to my skipper and jumped ship in Orkney. On the flight back from Aberdeen to London, my mind was racing. This was my dream job and I knew it. *Endless Summer II* was a 65-foot purpose-built charter yacht and one of the most successful charter brands in the Virgin Islands. Unlike *Rampant* and *Morag Mhor*, this would be full-on chartering, with back-to back weekly turnarounds for up to eight guests per charter for a non-stop, eight-month stretch. It had good prospects too. Barry told me that he would be stepping back from the role of skipper in the near future to concentrate on his other interests, and I considered myself uniquely placed to take over that role. I pulled out my notebook and started to scribble down all of the matters I needed to discuss with Barry. He was back in the UK and we had arranged to meet at Moody's Marina in Lower Swanwick the following day to finalise arrangements.

Once back in Hampshire, my first stop was at my friend Si O'Callaghan's house. I turned up unexpectedly and asked if I could bed down for a couple of nights before heading off to the Caribbean. That night, Si and I sat up late talking. I hadn't realised that, as I spoke excitedly about my forthcoming job, he was secretly hatching a plan of his own. At about 10.00 p.m., he disappeared into the living room and I could hear him talking to his father. About twenty minutes later he reappeared.

'I've got great news,' he said. 'I'm coming with you. Dad said he'd pay for my ticket.'

To be honest, I was pretty surprised. I had no problem with the suggestion but I had no idea why Si would want to come with me, nor what he intended to do once he got there. I quite liked the idea of travelling with a friend, but knew it would create an extra set of difficulties for me as well – not least suddenly asking my new employer if I could take Si with me. I decided to sell Barry the idea that Si would help out with some work on the boat for a few days before leaving to do his own thing.

◄ My mother, with me as a newborn baby, and my brother Richard, 1966

▼ My 'dad', Robin Hoad

▲ With my little sister Lucy, 1976

◄

Hoisting the sails, St Peter Port, Guernsey, 1976

▲ Nana at the piano

My stepfather, John Holt
▼

▲ With Chef Audrey at Beth's Restaurant, 1983

◀ Jolly sailor

At my mother's third wedding, Bristol 1983

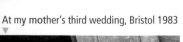

(L–R) Friends Gareth Williams, Sean Cusack and me, Tortola, British Virgin Islands, 1984
▼

▲ At the wheel of the yacht *Challenger* on my first Atlantic crossing, 1982

Sean enjoying breakfast, mid-Atlantic on the yacht *Fly*, 1984
▼

▲ Waiting in the Canary islands, with the yacht *Rampant*, 1983

Celebrating my seventeenth birthday mid-Atlantic on the yacht *Rampant*, 1983

At Heathrow Airport on 4 September 1984, the day before my accident ▼

► Cane Garden Bay, Tortola, BVI, where I broke my neck on 5 September 1984

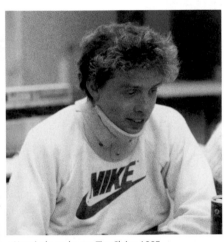

▲ Hospital ward mate Tim Claire, 1985

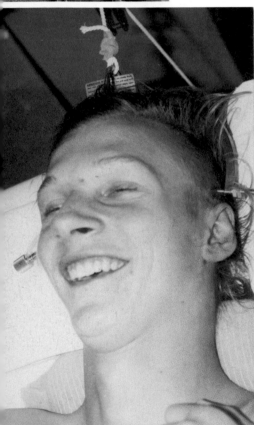

▲ Lying in hospital in Puerto Rico with cranial traction screwed into my skull

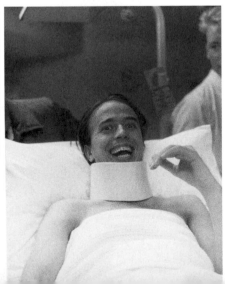

►

Hospital ward mate Dave Howard, 1985

◄ With Elaine on our wedding day, 19 September 1987

► 1991 – my first ever sail in a boat on my own since my accident seven years earlier

DOUGLAS HURNDALL

◄ With Diana 'Tid' Campbell, launching my new trimaran *Billy*, 1992

▲ My real father, Ernie Read

My new brother, Ted Read, with his wife Lorraine ▼

▲ My brother Richard (driver) choosing three wheels instead of three hulls

◄ With Joyce (left) and her daughters (L–R) Jenny, Wendy and Val

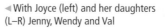

▲ (continued)

► Prime Minister John Major launching a new Sailability site in 1996

▼ Graduation day 2002

▼ With Tim Claire and Dave Howard at Twickenham, 2008

▲ My record-breaking sail round the Isle of Wight, 1997

▲ Competing in the World Disabled Multihull Championships 1997 in Australia, where I won a bronze medal for Great Britain

▲ Sharing the front cover of Sailability's magazine, *Foghorn*, with Ellen MacArthur

◄ Taking my son Timothy for his first ever sail, 2004

▲ HRH the Princess Royal launching my project on 21 March 2007, with my sponsor Jonathan Lloyd-Jones, senior partner at Blake Lapthorn Tarlo Lyons

▶ At the Southampton Boat Show 2007, with sponsor Jonathan Lloyd-Jones (L) and good friend Peter Harrison (R)

The following morning, Saturday, I met with Barry at Moody's Marina. I bought my list with me, and over the next thirty minutes we discussed various matters. First up was Si O'Callaghan. Barry was not overly enthusiastic, but on the basis that Si paid for his own flight, that he would help me get the boat ready for charter and would be gone in a couple of weeks when the first charter guests arrived, Barry agreed that he could stay on the boat. It seemed a perfectly fair arrangement. My salary was agreed at $800 a month plus tips, which was usually 10 per cent of the weekly charter fee divided by the three crew. With charter fees upwards of $6,000 a week, a third share of a 10per cent tip was a great perk, especially when all my food and board was covered too. Having dealt with general housekeeping matters like the list of jobs which needed doing on the boat when I arrived, we rounded off the meeting with two items that I had highlighted on my list. First up was immigration. Barry advised me to complete my entry visa when I arrived in Tortola as a 'tourist', not as an employee, on the basis that it would be a few weeks before I would get my work permit application approved and the tourist visa would remain valid to that point. Finally, I raised the matter of medical insurance cover. Earlier that year, whilst working at the Last Resort, Sean had become quite unwell and I'd been surprised at how much his medical treatment had cost, so I was determined to make sure I was covered. Barry reassured me that, as an employee of Endless Summer Charters, I would be insured against any medical condition. I was happy with that, so with the formalities over we shook hands and Barry said 'Congratulations, good to have you on board' – and with that the contract was sealed.

That same day was Bursledon Regatta day, the highlight of the annual calendar for everyone living in the Swanwick and Bursledon areas, and after my meeting with Barry I headed over the river to the Jolly Sailor pub. This was to be my last weekend in the UK for some time, and anyone who was anyone would be at the Jolly Sailor that day for the Regatta, including all of my friends, so it was the perfect opportunity to say goodbye to them all and watch their envy as I announced yet another trip to the Caribbean. It was a wonderful September's day, the sun shone, all of the boats on the river were dressed overall with their colourful flags reflecting in the water, the river teemed with rowing dinghies and home-made rafts of all descriptions competing in races, whilst the jetty and the shoreline at the Jolly Sailor was heaving with revellers, myself included. Mid-afternoon, I even entered the swimming race, but wearing my jeans and T-shirt and having consumed several pints of 6X real ale, I didn't fare terribly well.

Si O'Callaghan and I travelled to London by coach early on Monday morning. We went straight to Covent Garden, where we picked up our plane tickets before changing what spare cash we had into US dollars and making final checks on our belongings.

We arrived on the island of Puerto Rico late afternoon on Tuesday 4 September 1984, just in time to board the last inter-island plane of the day to Tortola. It was dusk, and as the small six-seater twin-engine aircraft made its way the hundred miles or so at low level, we had a cracking view of the islands silhouetted against the bright orange sunset. By the time we arrived at Beef Island airport in Tortola, it was dark and a lone, rather disinterested, immigration officer leaned forward on his desk and, in no particular hurry, studied our landing card declarations. As instructed by Barry Rice, I had completed mine as a tourist and my passport was stamped accordingly. We luckily got the last taxi on the rank and, as we made our way to Nanny Cay marina to join *Endless Summer II*, I was keen to point out all of the places of interest to Si, for whom this was a whole new experience.

We picked up the keys to *Endless Summer II* from the marina office and, once aboard, were both soon asleep, tired from having been travelling for so many hours.

We woke early that Wednesday morning. After a light breakfast of toast and a mug of coffee on deck looking out across all the yachts in harbour, we started to rub down the woodwork in the saloon with sandpaper in preparation for varnishing it that afternoon. Barry had made an appointment for me to meet with his management office to complete my work permit application at 11.00 a.m. that morning, so at 10.30 we downed tools. I had a quick shower, put on some clean clothes and then drove the company car into the capital, Road Town. The meeting didn't take too long, no more than twenty minutes, and once I had signed the various sets of work-permit papers, I decided to drive Si over the back of the island to the beautiful Cane Garden Bay for lunch. It was my favourite place on the island and I was keen to show him the sights. We parked up and walked barefoot along the golden sand beach, then sat for a while in the shade of a palm tree, smoking a cigarette and just looking out across the bay. It was a hot day and the cool waters looked so inviting, an almost flat-calm sea, waves gently lapping on the shore.

'Come on,' I said. 'We've got to get back to the boat shortly. Fancy a quick swim before lunch?'

With that, I took off my T-shirt, placed it on the sand alongside my cigarettes, lighter, shoes and wallet, and ran down the beach and into the sea.

I kept running, the cool water splashing out in front of me with each stride of my legs, until the water was up to my knees and I could run no further. Then I put both arms above my head and dived forwards into the sea.

9

In the week leading up to 14 May, crew members started to arrive at my house, bringing with them their kit bags and belongings. Elaine and Mike Golden, being the two full-time motorhome drivers, were busy drawing up lists of essential equipment for the motorhomes and making visits to the local cash and carry. It was pointless buying large quantities of food because there was simply not enough storage space in the motorhomes. We were not hiring the vehicles for a simple week's holiday – they were carefully packed with clothing and equipment that would be needed for self-sufficiency for up two months. We would be able to buy food at every destination, so food storage was sacrificed for storage space for charts, buoyancy aids, marine radios, wet-weather gear and other essentials.

By day, supplied with endless cups of tea by Elaine, the guys would finish off small jobs on the RIB and Land Rover, and by night we would talk through various scenarios, determine our responsibilities, and clarify any areas of uncertainty. On Saturday 12 May, all members of the crew, except Ian, had arrived and were sleeping somewhere in our house or in the crew motorhome; you could feel the growing sense of excitement. Ian arrived on the Sunday afternoon, and the job of stowing equipment into all three vehicles commenced. It took more than seven hours to list and stow everything in the motorhomes, into and onto the roof rack of the Land Rover. There was little I could do other than watch so I set about dealing with the last few emails. As it became clear that we had done as much as we could, I began to feel nervous. In the privacy of my office, whilst the others finished off their packing, I recorded the last of my diary-cams before we set off:

> Sunday 13 May 2007. Oh my god. Well, Geoff, this is it. Tomorrow is the
> start of a new chapter in my life. After all the heartache, all the ups, all
> the downs, all the tears, all the laughter, tomorrow is one of the biggest
> days of my life. I'm really scared but I'm really excited too. Whatever
> happens, I hope I do it, I really want this so badly.

I was interrupted by the phone ringing. It was Jonathon Savill.
'Geoff, good news. I've got you national BBC Breakfast TV coming
tomorrow morning. They'll be doing a couple of live links. The
bad news is you've got to be there by 5.30 a.m.'

With a 1.00 p.m. start, we hadn't planned on getting to the
yacht club until 9.00 a.m., but having national coverage was too
good an opportunity to pass up.

'Wow, thanks Jonathon, I'm sure we can make it.'

'Sure you can make it? You ungrateful bastard, you'll damn
well be there if I've got to come around and kick your arse out
of bed at 4.00 a.m. Have you any idea how hard I've worked on
this?'

I laughed. This is what I loved about Jonathon, flashes of
genius interspersed with personal abuse, but he always came up
trumps.

I wheeled to the front door to break the news to the crew, who
were now sat around in the front garden in the fast-diminish-
ing evening May sunshine, discussing their Chinese take-away
choices for dinner.

There was an air of reluctant acceptance of the early start, but
with such a big day ahead it was unlikely any of us would get
much sleep anyway.

'Geoff, can I just borrow your computer to check tomorrow's
weather?' asked Ian.

'Not good news,' he declared, returning a matter of minutes
later. 'The forecast is for a northerly wind, possibly gusting to
18 knots by lunchtime tomorrow afternoon. That's above our
limits, Geoff.'

In our risk assessments, we had set 15 knots as the uppermost
limit of wind speed, equivalent to a force 4 on the Beaufort scale.

Eighteen knots was not significantly higher, but it would take us over that limit.

'All we can do is assess the situation tomorrow,' said Ian. 'If necessary, we either delay the start or we foreshorten the passage and make a token departure. There's no point in worrying about it now. Fingers crossed that it will be OK.'

I could not even begin to contemplate delaying the departure. I had invested so much personal energy in this precise moment. I had become so blinkered, so intently focused on 1.00 p.m. on Monday 14 May, that any change was inconceivable. As I contemplatively picked at my chicken curry and chips, I desperately hoped that the weather forecast was wrong.

Monday 14 May, 0400 hours. I was right about the early start, it hadn't made a blind bit of difference. None of the crew had slept particularly well, and they were now sitting in my living room, bleary-eyed, cradling their morning coffees, barely a word spoken, but all very much aware of the vast significance of the day that lay ahead.

As the last of the sleeping bags and personal belongings were transferred to the motorhomes, Elaine and I made our final checks that the electrics and gas had been turned off before locking the front door to our house. It would be at least two months before we were home again.

With only the first hint of daylight far on the eastern horizon, we could already hear the trees in the garden being blown by a blustery breeze and could see the faint grey outline of clouds rushing across the dark sky above. It looked as though the forecasters were right and we were in for a windy, cool day – such a contrast to the previous month of April. With everyone loaded, the three vehicles made their way the ten miles or so to the Royal Southern Yacht Club in Hamble. It was a case of 'wagons roll' as we travelled in convoy following the lights of the vehicle in front through the winding country lanes, everyone quiet and pensive, how I imagine soldiers feel on their way to war.

By the time we arrived, it was just after 0500 hours and it was now fully light. As Elaine swung the motorhome into the car park, I could see the tall antenna of the BBC satellite truck and a large group of people already gathered, huddled in groups, drinking cups of steaming coffee.

'You ready?' I asked Elaine.

'I think so,' she replied.

'OK, here goes –' and I opened the door of the motorhome to be met with flashes from cameras and a sea of smiling faces.

As the morning went on, so more and more people arrived at the club. Mostly those who had been invited, but also others who lived locally and had seen the broadcasts live on national television and couldn't resist coming to see everything for themselves. The tension was increasing with each hour that passed, it was palpable. As I was pulled from one press interview to the next, I could sense myself getting increasingly nervous. I was feeling a bit dizzy and slightly sick, probably due to the adrenalin that was now pumping through my veins. As excited as I was, I couldn't help but worry about the wind speed: it was showing no signs of abating.

Allowing me to get on with dealing with the press and the publicity, I could see all of my crew quietly and efficiently going about their well-rehearsed routines, rigging my boat, checking and double-checking all of the safety equipment. Occasionally I would catch Ian's eye and signal 'OK?' to him, at which his expression would change to one of concern, and with a roll of his eyes he would indicate the clouds above, moving at great speed across the sky. He and I were both conscious that the wind was above our agreed limits – but every so often it would lessen for a while, giving us a glimmer of hope, before picking up again.

At 1130 hours I went inside the clubhouse to give a short farewell speech, and my sponsor and the Commodore of the club each said a few words to the assembled group. I was surprised and extremely flattered to see that Sir Robin Knox-Johnston, one of my childhood heroes, who had only arrived home from sailing around the world less than forty-eight hours earlier, had taken the trouble to come and see me off. It was the perfect send-off party, and of the hundred or so people who had come, I just about had time to say a quick 'hello' and 'goodbye' to them all.

Forty-five minutes later, I was ushered out of the room and into a private changing area where Elaine helped me into my sailing clothes. We barely spoke as she lifted me into my salopettes and pulled my special semi-dry top with neoprene cuffs and neck over my head. I caught a glimpse of myself in the mirror and I looked as white as a ghost. Outside in the boat park, once I had been lifted into my boat by Ian, Joel and Spike, Elaine made final adjustments to the clasp of my new lifejacket before placing my helmet on my head and fastening the buckle under my chin. At last, with the helmet securely fastened, the noise of all the people around me was muffled and quieter. Despite being surrounded by people shouting 'Good luck Geoff!' and 'Geoff, one last photo!', all I was paying attention to was Ian, talking to me on VHF channel 77 from the RIB, down on the jetty.

'*Freethinker, Freethinker*, this is *Everest One*, over.'

It seemed strange. All these people around me and none of them could hear what I was hearing. They must have thought me rude to ignore their calls for interviews and photos.

'*Everest One, Freethinker*, go ahead.'

'Geoff, it's still very windy down here. I suggest we get you launched, sail out into Southampton Water, see what it's doing out there and make a decision about whether we press on to Lymington then – what do you think?'

'Yep, happy with that. OK, ready when you are. Out.'

With that, Spike and Elaine slowly reversed *Freethinker* down the slipway into the water. One of my crew, Mike Golden, was a member of the Southern Union Chorus, a barbershop harmony group, and twenty of them had come along to sing me off, dressed in magnificent matching bright red shirts, all lining the slipway to sing, at my special request, Louis Armstrong's 'What a wonderful world' – but, being so nervous, I don't recall hearing a note of it. With now only seconds before setting off, out of the corner of my eye I could see all the journalists running down the pontoons, carrying their cameras, to get into their RIBs to follow me out to sea.

With *Freethinker* now afloat, and with my rudder and centreboard lowered and secured, I waited for Ian's OK before departing.

'*Freethinker, Everest One*, ready when you are.'

I turned to Spike, who was holding the stern of my boat, waiting for the command. 'OK Spike, Ian says to go. See you in Lymington.'

As I pulled the mainsheet in, I powered away from the slipway and out into the middle of the river before turning and heading due south into Southampton Water. I glanced down and could see that I was already, with an ebb tide running in my favour, sailing in excess of 10 knots – way above the 6-knot limit on the river. Normally a sailing vessel breaking the speed limit would not be a terrible worry to the Harbour Master, but with a dozen RIBs following me, all doing the same speed and creating a terrific wash, I knew that they would not be best pleased. *Freethinker* was now going so fast I could feel the boat humming as she reached her hull speed. With the wind now directly behind, gusting up to 20 knots, and with a moderately calm sea, controlling *Freethinker* was like ice skating with no brakes.

Despite having given specific instructions at the press briefing for all spectator boats to stay to my port side and to stay behind me at all times, the clamour to get the best photograph and film footage had turned the originally well-controlled flotilla of press boats into maritime mayhem, with me caught in the middle. With so much spray obscuring my view and the cacophony of RIB engine noise all around me, I became slightly disorientated and was relying on my compass to steer a course towards Calshot Spit. Ian's voice soon crackled in my ear.

'Geoff, you are drifting out of the main channel and over the sand bar. You'll need to come to port more, there's not enough depth in there for us if you get into trouble.'

With both hands busy trying to control *Freethinker*, and unable to push the transmit button on my VHF, I nodded my head to acknowledge his transmission and started my turn to port. Seconds later, close to the South Cardinal marker, I saw a RIB cut across me with its big yellow battle flag flying from its stern.

This was supposed to be the most amazing day of my life, and it had started with such high hopes. But as the morning had worn on it had begun to feel more and more out of control. Perhaps it was no surprise that it was to end in disaster. Just lying there, not for the first time in my life, slumped on the surface of the water, holding my breath, powerless to save myself, was not the way I wanted to end my life.

In the short space of time that it took to be thrown into the water, to be saved from drowning and then to make that seemingly endless journey back to the Royal Southern, soaking wet and clinging to Ian on the edge of the RIB, I was so completely and utterly devastated that I wanted to close my eyes and wake up in the hope it was some horrible nightmare. Everything I had dreamed of, everything I had worked so hard for, all the people who had given up so much for me – it was all over in less than ten minutes, fortunately without my death, but not far from it. It was, without question, the lowest moment of my life. I was numb and vomited several times into my mouth, not through swallowing sea water, but through complete and utter humiliation and a feeling of failure.

The only ray of light in a mire of gloom and despondency came when the RIB was back alongside the club pontoon, less than half an hour after leaving. In that short space of time, the mood had changed from hopeful expectancy to sombre melancholy. Too ashamed, I could not bring myself to look at any of the many people lining the pontoon. Without prompting, my son Timothy ran down the pontoon, climbed across the RIB, threw his arms around my neck and, pulling one of my earlobes down with his tiny fingers, whispered in my ear –

'Dad, you're a rubbish sailor.'

IO

Surprisingly the bump to my head was not that hard. In fact, it was more a case of my head being forced forward onto my chest. I had miscalculated the depth, and the weight of my body landed with full force on my head. As my head rolled forward, I felt the vertebra in my neck break, not so much a snapping of bone, more like the crunching of gristle. Although I felt no pain, I knew immediately what had happened.

I lay there in the water like a stunned animal. Fully conscious, face down, unable to move, holding my breath, eyes wide open, staring at the sandy bottom only inches below my face, shafts of daylight piercing the water all around me. I just floated there, slowly rising and falling, with each warm and gentle swell that passed by me lifting and lowering my body. Instinctively I tried to turn myself over but realised that I could not. No matter how hard I tried, I could not make any part of my body move.

My most immediate fear was that I was on the verge of drowning. I tried desperately to save myself but I couldn't. I tried and tried to move my arms, but the instructions from my brain failed to connect with my body. I could see my hands just hanging there in front of me but they would not move – it was like being in a dream where everything is unreal. Luckily I had taken a big breath just before diving in, but as I stared at the sand below I started to panic.

'Oh my god, oh my god, oh my god.' All I could say over and over again in my head was 'Oh my god'. I was frightened, so very frightened.

Time stood still and I seemed to be suspended there, just hanging in the water, for what seemed like forever. After a while, my lungs were burning and the urge to breathe became almost unbearable.

I didn't feel Si's hands on me but I remember being rolled over and seeing Si looking down at me as I spluttered for air.

'Geoff, are you OK?' he asked, the urgency clear in his voice.

I couldn't speak. I tried but my mouth didn't open, my jaws were clenched shut. I looked straight into his eyes in absolute desperation, silently pleading for his help. Thankfully he registered the fear in my face and realised that this was a very serious situation.

'It's OK, don't worry, it's going to be OK,' he said, and very carefully, with help from a bystander, pulled me out of the water and dragged me a few metres up the beach.

All of my senses were on fire. I felt mild electrical shocks all over my body, a high-pitched buzzing in my ears and a strong metallic taste in my mouth. My eyes were so wide open, it felt as though they might pop out of their sockets. I was hot. I was cold. My jaws were locked tightly shut yet my lower jaw was shivering uncontrollably. But above all I was frightened, more terrified than anything I had ever known. Tears rolled down the sides of my face, they tickled my cheeks but I couldn't wipe them away. They were not tears of pain, nor were they tears of self-pity; they were tears of fear, abject fear.

By the time Si had called an ambulance, a small crowd had gathered around me.

'Can you feel this? Can you feel that?' people were asking as they prodded and touched different parts of my body. I couldn't feel a thing, nor could I see their faces, only shadows in my peripheral vision.

'Oh my god, oh my god, oh my god,' I kept repeating in my head. Perhaps it was my body's defence mechanism, trying to shut out reality. I would close my eyes then tell myself to wake up in the hope it was a bad dream. I repeated this several times but it didn't work. This was real. It was a living nightmare.

The ambulance arrived, containing a nurse and a driver. The

ambulance man bent down and, with arms outstretched, began sliding one hand under my neck, the other under my legs to lift me. I caught Si's eye and with all my strength managed a whisper, pleading with him to stop.

'What was that, Geoff?' asked Si. 'Be quiet everybody,' he instructed.

He lowered his ear to my mouth.

'Please, don't let him lift me like that,' I pleaded, 'please Si.' Trying to talk through clenched teeth and with barely any strength in my lungs was so difficult. But I was aware enough to realise that if I was lifted in that way it could make my injury worse.

Si challenged the ambulance man, who in return kicked the sand near my head in a fit of anger, so that much of the sand went into my eyes and mouth. An angry exchange of words followed between Simon and the ambulance driver, while I just lay there on my back, the fierce sun burning my face, terrified.

Eventually, three people helped lift me onto a stretcher and loaded me into the back of the ambulance, my head firmly gripped by the thighs of the nurse in the back of the vehicle. As we climbed the winding road up the hill at great speed, sirens blazing, I lay staring at the white roof of the ambulance, still in abject fear, as a large West Indian nurse gently smoothed my burning brow with her bare hand, humming a gentle lullaby to me.

No more than a few minutes into the journey, the situation took a severe turn for the worse. I remember a screech of brakes and a sudden thump followed by the ambulance leaning at a sharp angle. My body fell off the stretcher and, for the first time, I felt real pain, a shooting pain up my neck into the base of my head. I tried to cry out but was still unable to make a noise. Along with my entire body, my breathing muscles were paralysed, rendering my attempts to cry out futile. The driver appeared at the back door and helped lift me back onto the stretcher, explaining to the nurse that he had swerved to avoid a child on a bicycle. Thankfully I lost consciousness at that point – my body, incapable of enduring any more torture, finally shut down to spare my mind any more suffering.

'Geoffrey, can you hear me? Hello! Geoffrey! Can you hear me?' As I slowly regained consciousness, I opened my eyes to see a doctor leaning over me.

'Geoffrey, you've had an accident. You're going to be OK but you must stay completely still. Can you feel this?'

I had no idea what he was doing. 'No,' I whispered, 'I can't feel anything.' I had woken up and the reality had not changed, but at least now I was in hospital, and felt that I was in expert hands.

I heard so many voices and sensed I was in a room with lots of people, but I could neither see them nor hear what they were saying. All I could do was try to understand what had happened to me. I had no idea, and, for the time being at least, no one was telling me.

Once they realised the severity of my injury, and without the expertise to cope with it, the medical team in Road Town Hospital called upon the US Coast Guard to fly me to a neurological centre at a hospital in Puerto Rico. At dusk, exactly 24 hours after I had flown into Tortola with such high hopes, I was making the return journey, but this time I could see neither the sunset nor the islands. The sides of the helicopter were open so there was a terrific breeze and a loud thump, thump, thump from the engine, just like a scene out of *Apocalypse Now*. The US Coast Guard crew were superb, holding my hand and telling me everything was going to be alright.

By the time we landed at Puerto Rico, it was dark, very hot and humid. I was removed from the helicopter and, covered in blankets and strapped to the stretcher, left to wait on the side of the runway. I waited there for nearly two hours, the smell of aviation fuel thick in my nostrils, making me gag. Incredible as it may seem, with neither money nor a guarantee of it, the medical centre would not agree to my admission. So I was literally left waiting by the airport runway until that money could be found. Fortunately for me, the necessary phone calls were made and eventually, thanks to a financial guarantee by the Royal British Virgin Islands Yacht Club, I was admitted to the Rio Piedras Medical Center.

Despite a great deal happening around me, I was aware of very little. My mind was working overtime, and with so much to try and absorb personally I was shutting out almost everything externally that was going on. Everyone was speaking Spanish, with the one exception of a man wearing a white coat who, in very poor, broken pidgin English, kept trying to translate the stream of dialogue from the various medical staff who surrounded me.

I was taken first to x-ray, where they x-rayed my neck, and then to a room where the sides of my head were shaved with a disposable razor. Still nobody explained what was going to happen and my fear remained unabated. It was more than just being scared; I really was terrified. I was right to be, for the man who was trying to translate for me held up a pair of steel tongs and put them to the sides of his head, gesturing what was about to occur. I was in no doubt what it meant, but I was not prepared for the pain. With my temples shaved, the tongs were placed about two centimetres above each ear, then they were tightened with spanners. With each turn, the needle-sharp points screwed into my skull, and with each turn I felt warm blood flowing behind my ears and head, down to my neck to the point of paralysis – at which point I could feel it no longer. The pain was like no other pain I had ever felt. Not only was there the pain of having steel tongs screwed into my head, without anaesthetic, but in order to ensure a secure enough grip the tension was quite literally compressing my skull. The pressure was unbearable, and once again I screamed in pain – but no sound came out. I was so frightened and so lonely I just wanted it to end.

That night I learnt that the Puerto Rican health service runs along very different lines from the NHS in Britain. Most immediately obvious was the lack of basic bedding on the ward. It was considered normal practice for relatives to supply sheets, blankets and pillows. But I was alone and so I had nothing.

As I lay awake in my bed, I felt cold. Someone found me a blanket but it did little to keep me warm. At one point, late into the night, a young man was rushed into the bed next to me and there was much to-ing and fro-ing by medical staff for over an hour until everything suddenly went quiet. As his body was removed, a woman, who I subsequently discovered was the man's mother, passed me the pillow she had supplied for him, still spattered with his blood stains. I later learnt that he had shot himself in the head with a gun and had died in the bed next to me. Despite being inconsolable over her son's death, his mother had noticed that I had no pillow and bequeathed his to me. With my head carefully lifted and lowered onto the pillow, I finally managed to get some sleep.

Early the next day Simon arrived at my bedside, having flown up from Tortola. He started to tell me what the doctors had been telling him: that I had broken my neck and suffered a spinal cord injury. It still meant nothing to me, I was so overwhelmingly frightened and confused. But the doctors stressed that these were early days and there was a very real likelihood that I would make a full recovery.

The recently applied cranial traction was attached to thirty pounds of weight, suspended over the back of the bed to keep my head and neck straight. That morning, whilst Simon sat at my bedside talking to me, I felt the traction tong on my right side of my head suddenly slip, and the skin on my temple begin to tear. Before I could ask Si to get help, the tong on the left side also dislodged itself and I felt them slowly scratching up my skull, like a nail across a window, slowly ripping the skin as they dragged under the 30 lb weights before they finally fell out completely and crashed to the floor. I could feel the blood pouring down my neck, and I was screaming in agony, but still it was no louder than a whisper. Simon quickly found help, and the last thing I remember before going to sleep was seeing a nurse inject my arm with a syringe full of clear liquid. Then I was at peace.

I awoke nearly two days later to find both Simon and Phil Scott, another Endless Summer employee, at my bedside. It was by now nearly four days since my accident. With no traction in place I now had nothing stabilising my fractured spine, so Si was dispatched by the duty doctor to the local pharmacy to buy me a rigid neck collar. With the collar in place, the staff decided it was safe to sit me up in bed to enable me to eat and drink, but with a broken neck and an ill-fitting collar, my head was just flopping unsupported to one side, causing blinding headaches and nausea.

Phil felt he needed to explain the delays in my admission to hospital and told me that, even though he had a supply of pre-signed Endless Summer company cheques, the American owners (both lawyers) had forbidden him to underwrite the costs of my medical treatment, for fear of it being construed as admitting liability. At the time, this information meant nothing to me. I simply did not care – I had more important things to worry about.

Si and Phil told me that they had made contact with my parents. Unbelievably, I had instructed Si not to contact my mother and worry her unnecessarily, on the basis that I would probably get better. Quite rightly, albeit three days later, Si and Phil had overridden that instruction. A week after the accident, my mother and Andy Brooks arrived at the hospital. As one would expect, there was a lot of hysteria on my mother's part. Trying to put her mind at rest, I made light of my situation, but I was fooling no one but myself.

Incredibly, only a week after the accident, I was being sat up in bed at least three times a day as the nurses attempted to feed me but, unable (and unwilling) to eat their milky foods, I was losing weight fast. Despite being hungry, I simply could not eat most of the food that I was presented with without retching. Apart from cheese, never in my life have I eaten anything dairy, such as milk, butter or eggs, with custard being the food I despised the most. I simply couldn't eat it without being extremely ill, a situation exacerbated at the age of ten when a teacher at St Mary's College, a member of the religious brotherhood, had aggressively held my head back by my hair and forcibly spooned rhubarb and custard into my mouth. Even in hospital, and wasting away through malnutrition, there was no way I could eat all of the milky foods they were putting in front of me. I was admitted to hospital weighing just over eleven stone, which was quite a good weight for my age and my 6 foot 3 inch height. But with every passing day I was shedding pounds and feeling weaker and weaker.

If I was to survive, and if I was to receive the specialist care that I needed, then I had to get back to the UK, and quickly. With my rapidly deteriorating condition, the matter of repatriation was becoming more urgent every day. By then claiming that I was not an employee of Endless Summer Charters, Barry Rice, in what seemed to me the most callous and inhumane act that I have ever been subjected to, refused to fund my repatriation and disassociated himself and the company from me. At that point, my parents approached the British Government for help but, saying that I should not have travelled without proper medical insurance, both Kenneth Clarke MP (then Health Minister) and Tim Renton MP (then Foreign Office Minister with responsibility for consular affairs) refused to accept any liability for my repatriation. Despite daily flights of RAF Hercules aircraft from neighbouring Belize back to the British Isles, the Government refused to take me without an up-front payment of £20,000, money my mother simply did not have. Having been disowned by my employers and, worse still, effectively left to die by my own country, my situation was becoming desperate.

However, there were occasional glimmers of kindness. My mother and Andy Brooks were being accommodated free of charge at the Ramada Inn hotel in San Juan. In an effort to get some nourishment into me, the chef at the hotel would make fresh chicken soup which my mother would bring in for me in a Thermos flask – just about the only nutrition I had during my stay in Puerto Rico. The days kept rolling by, and still I did not fully understand my condition. Whatever was being discussed between the doctors and my mother, it was not finding its way to me. Part of me still believed that I would get better once I was home. Had I not had that belief, then I'm not sure where I would have got my strength from to continue.

With staff shortages at the medical centre, Simon was taught how to wash me without hurting my neck and how to change the dressings on my temples, which had become infected after the traction had fallen out. He was even shown how to catheterise me. Even then I was incredulous that my friend, an eighteen-year-old guy, was having to catheterise me to empty my bladder without even the dignity of a curtain around me or the use of a sterile preparation area. I could feel the discomfort of the procedure but I could not move away from it, like a form of torture. So I just closed my eyes and hummed to myself to escape from the reality of it. In the first few days I had coped because I was in a type of self-preservation mode. Now that I was fully conscious and aware of my surroundings, some of the procedures being performed on me to keep me alive were difficult to come to terms with, so I just shut my mind to them and hummed until they were over. As a survival technique it was pretty basic, but it got me through those early days.

Just as I thought my belief in humanity had disappeared, with both Endless Summer Charters and the British Government disowning me, it was partially restored with the news that the airline British Caledonian had offered to help in the most wonderful way. Rena Court, head of Customer Relations at the airline, had read about my plight in a national newspaper and persuaded her employers to lay on a 'mercy flight' to get me home. The airline volunteered to remove thirteen seats from one of its scheduled airliners to accommodate me lying flat on a special air mattress – this they had to do before leaving the UK to attain a flight-worthiness certificate. In addition, they also provided four extra free seats, two for my parents and two for a private medical doctor and nurse from Wings Medical Group, who had agreed to waive their fees to travel out to Puerto Rico to stabilise my condition before accompanying me on the return flight.

On 22 September 1984, I said my goodbyes to the nurses at the medical centre, the few 'get well' cards that were stuck to the wall above my bed were taken down, I was lifted onto a special low-pressure mattress and we made our way to the airport in an ambulance.

Slightly sedated for the flight, there are only two things I remember vividly about the journey. The first was a searing thirst. I was desperately dehydrated, but to avoid the need to catheterise on the flight I was not allowed to drink. With the dry air from the plane's ventilation system, it was difficult surviving with only the occasional sip of water to wet my mouth. The second thing I remember, as clear as though it were yesterday, was the moment the wheels of the plane touched down on British soil.

'I'm home,' I said quietly to myself, 'I'm home.' The relief was completely overwhelming and I could fight it no longer. I cried my heart out.

I I

By the time we set off again on Sunday 20 May, we had learned valuable lessons about our equipment, not least my lifejacket, and we had made modifications to the boat so that such an event would never happen again. The incident had well and truly brought the crew together in a way I could only have wished for, and I could be in no doubt of the mandate of support that I had received from them and my sponsors. That did not mean for one minute that I was complacent, far from it. The accident had given me the shock of my life and made me realise that this challenge was to be taken extremely seriously. I doubted if I would get any more second chances.

Blog entry, Sunday morning, 20 May 2007:

Blimey, that came as a bit of a surprise, a very pleasant surprise. You often read about expeditions sat around waiting for the mythical 'weather window'. Well, I never thought it would be me, but having assessed and re-assessed our kit and procedures over the past week, we had completed all there was to do by Friday night and our only hurdle left to clear was the weather. It's simply been too windy to go and the outlook has not been much better with a series of lows skimming over the Azores high. Even a look at the Met Office website last night didn't look too promising, so it was with some incredulity and much joy that Ian announced to the crew this morning that he was happy to go.

On the one hand we are delighted, but it has meant a flurry of phone calls to friends and family – all the kit has remained stowed, ready to go at a moments notice, but there is still much to do on any departure day.

I'll sign off now but hopefully update from Lymington later today. What a great day to go sailing.

And it was a great day: bright sunshine, but not too hot and not too breezy. By the time we reached Lymington, our first stop, on the evening of Sunday 20 May, it felt as though I had broken the spell that had been preventing me from leaving and had, at last, started my Personal Everest. It was not a particularly long leg, only fifteen miles or so, but with only a couple of miles to go the wind had died, the tide turned and we were losing daylight fast. Reluctantly, I took a tow from *Everest One* for the last twenty minutes and, as we arrived on the slipway next to the Royal Lymington Yacht Club, I could see a small welcoming committee waiting there in the twilight. It was such a great feeling, having finally started, despite all the hardships, and here we were, making our first landfall. It was a short, but incredibly significant step, and I was pleased that the local press gave my arrival at Lymington as much coverage as they had done my fall from grace a week earlier.

Everything had worked exactly as planned. All three vehicles had made the journey around by road and were safely parked in the Royal Lymington Yacht Club car park. Both motorhomes were connected to mains electricity and we had use of the club's showers and toilets. It was very early days, but having had no time previously to rehearse a full-scale movement of vehicles and crew, there was relief all round that the theory had worked in practice.

The Lymington stop was hugely significant to me for three very different reasons. Firstly, although I had sailed for only about six hours, it was the longest time I had sat on my bum in a boat for nearly ten years. Although I felt no discomfort on the short sail that afternoon, my priority when we got ashore was to retire to the privacy of my motorhome, where Elaine would be able to check my backside for any signs of a pressure sore. They were desperately anxious moments as she lifted me onto the bed, rolled me onto my side and pulled my trousers down. I had always made a point of saying that the one thing likely to scupper my chances on this trip was if I got a pressure sore. There was no way of training to avoid one; I just had to hope that the special seat that had been made for me had done its job. I closed my eyes tight and just repeatedly said to myself, 'Please let it be OK, please let it be OK,' as I waited for Elaine's verdict. Not exactly the best job a wife has to perform for her husband, but Elaine has always known the dangers of a pressure sore, and checking my bum for pink marks had become a routine part of our lives.

'It's fine,' she said. 'In fact, it's less pink than it is when you are sat in your wheelchair all day.'

Oh, I was so happy. Had the diagnosis been less favourable, in an instant it could have been more devastating to my project than falling in the water the week before, but thankfully it was fine. This was of course only day one. There would be at least fifty more voyages, many for much longer periods, and the cumulative effect of successive days in the boat might cause problems later – but, for now at least, it was a terrific relief to know I was OK.

The second reason why the Lymington stop was significant was that it was the first time I had ever slept in a motorhome in my life. Indeed, it was only the second time I had even been in one, the first being the journey to the Royal Southern Yacht Club the previous Monday. And now, once we had de-rigged the boats and been provided with a wonderful three-course dinner in the Royal Lymington Yacht Club, I found myself with Elaine and Timothy in this eighteen-foot by seven-foot box that was to be our home for the next two months.

To this point in time, I had never even lain on the bed, let alone tried sleeping in it. Considering that we were now so far outside our normal comfort zone, away from our lovely house with all the usual creature comforts of home, Elaine was remarkably calm. I had purposefully not interfered with stowing items in the van; she had her own system in place and it was better for me if I just kept quiet and did as I was told. She had somehow managed to squirrel away all of our clothes, all of her kitchen utensils, all of Timothy's paraphernalia and goodness only knows what other bits and pieces – I was mighty impressed. But what surprised me more than anything that first night was just how comfortable my bed was. Elaine had chosen to sleep above the driver's cab with Timothy, allowing me to spread myself across the only other bed at the rear of the vehicle. It was incredibly snug and I was soon fast asleep.

The third reason why the Lymington stopover remains so prominent in my memory is that it was the first time the issue of towing arose, and this became something that was to play on my mind increasingly as the expedition progressed. I was extremely restless that I had been towed by *Everest One* for the final few miles to Lymington. At the time, I had no choice. With light disappearing fast and *Freethinker* going backwards on a foul tide, it was the only option if we were to make landfall before midnight. But when I restarted, I felt that I should be towed back to the point where I first accepted the tow. I spoke about my concerns with Ian, but he didn't seem to share my misgivings.

'You're welcome to go back to the same point if you want, but we've got a long way to go, Geoff. Think about it,' was the only comfort he could offer me.

As it transpired, the following day saw a weather front pass over us so we could not sail anyway – another first for Lymington, our first forced lay-day due to weather. But when we did resume on Tuesday 22 May, on one of our longest legs, a sixty-mile run along the south coast to Portland, we were forced to leave at 0400 hours to catch all of the tide we possibly could in our favour. As I was making my way out to the mouth of the River Lym to start leg two, and still persecuting myself about being towed for only a couple of miles two days earlier, the prospect of going back towards Southampton to the point where I undertook the tow before turning around and recommencing my trip towards

Portland seemed stupid in the extreme. For the time being, I would just have to live with the guilt.

I had several knots of tide under me as I powered through Hurst Narrows, and the sail westwards out through the Needles Channel was awesome. Bathed in the early-morning sunshine, the white chalk cliffs of the Needles took on a pinky-orange glow.

This was our first full day, and an opportunity at last to get into some routine at sea. Our RIB, *Everest One*, was manned by three crew. As project manager, Ian would be in the RIB every day, while Spike, Joel and Andy would each spend two consecutive days in the RIB, followed by a day driving the Land Rover, what we termed road crew, along with Mike and Elaine, who each drove a motorhome.

The RIB crew all wore drysuits, and each day one would be the designated diver, the one person always ready to jump in the water at a moment's notice to rescue me should anything untoward happen. *Everest One* was very striking, with a bright red hull, dark grey tubes and two spare inflatable dinghies strapped to the stainless steel scaffolding-like structure running above the driver's position. She was noisy and smelly, her big inboard diesel engine thumping away continuously, even on tick-over, and I could always hear her and smell her, even if I couldn't see her. She was anything but pretty, looking more akin to a water-borne gypsy caravan than a high-tech support vessel, but she was at least performing her role adequately.

With several cool-boxes packed full with our lunches, snacks and umpteen flasks of drinks, all prepared by Mike in the early hours of the morning, the Lymington to Portland leg was the first opportunity to get a basic understanding of who liked to eat and drink what, and when.

Luckily for us it was not a particularly windy day. For the first three hours I was making a steady 8 knots with the tide underneath me, and there was little or no sea state to worry about.

Watching the boys on the RIB with envy as they consumed hot drinks and snacks, it was time to test the system for myself.

'*Everest One, Freethinker*, could I please have one of your finest hot Bovrils?'

The team sprang into action and had soon filled a sealed Thermos mug with my favourite brew. The problem was of course transferring drinks, food, anything, from the RIB to *Freethinker*. The theory, as yet untested, was for me to maintain speed and direction whilst Ian eased *Everest One* alongside. It was a good theory but it quickly became apparent that my sailing dinghy was more nimble and responsive than the RIB, which was as agile as a sea slug. So the roles were reversed, and it was I who brought *Freethinker* alongside the port side of *Everest One* whilst they maintained speed and direction. With Ian at the wheel, Spike and Joel leaned over the side of the RIB, each grabbing my starboard float and making me fast with ropes. At which point, the Thermos cup was placed in a child's pink shrimping net, the sort with a long bamboo handle, which was extended until it was over me and then inverted, depositing the mug in my lap.

Anxious to press on, and also aware of the damage either craft could inflict on the other whilst attached and being buffeted by waves, I was then released and continued on my course, trying to drink my hot cup of Bovril with one paralysed hand whilst trying to steer with the other. With scalding hot liquid flying everywhere, I imagine that it would have been marginally easier to have done this whilst riding a roller coaster. And with Bovril being very salty anyway, it made little difference when the mug was topped up with sea water from each wave that passed.

Our efforts were a success, although we were lucky that the sea state had been kind. Having finished my drink, the safest way to return my mug to the RIB was not to come alongside *Everest One* again, but simply to jettison the mug back into the sea followed by the cry 'BOB', or 'Bovril Overboard'. The Thermos mug floated perfectly well, and practising the Bovril Overboard drill at least gave the crew something to relieve the monotony of just sitting and keeping a watchful eye over me.

One of my later blog entries summarises the situation perfectly:

> I'm getting a lot of questions about how I eat and drink whilst sailing. Well, it's not easy. For my fresh water, I have a two-litre bladder behind my seat and if you look carefully you'll see the blue tube attached to my left shoulder allowing me to take sips every twenty minutes. However hot Bovril and easy-to-eat foods have to be delivered by the RIB crew. I call them up on my VHF and within a minute the thunder of the RIB engine appears, an eight-foot pole with a net on the end containing my menu choice appears, it gets inverted and the contents deposited on my lap. Eating and drinking at speeds of 10 mph are not easy, especially if your fingers do not work, what little hand movement you have is controlling the rudder and mainsheet and the boat is pitching and yawing over waves. I often arrive with a strange blend of foods and drinks splattered on my clothes and in my cockpit. All of my good eating habits have gone out of the window as I need to get food from lap to mouth. It's simply not feasible to eat pasta salads or cheese salad sandwiches on granary bread with a fruit shake. Pies and chocolate are among the few foods able to cope with a dousing of sea water whilst retaining some semblance of their pre-formed shapes.

By the time we reached Anvil Point on the south Dorset coast, with its imposing lighthouse reflecting brilliant white in the morning sun, we had been at sea for nearly six hours. It was still only 1000 hours and I had another five hours of sailing ahead of me. The tide now turned against us and, even though the wind had picked up and I was actually sailing faster across the water, with a tide moving at 2 knots in the opposite direction I was effectively sailing more slowly, and progress was tedious.

This leg was a huge test on all of the crew and all of the equipment. It was as long as any leg ahead of us, and being thrown into it on only our second day of sailing made it physically and mentally demanding. These were early days and spirits were still very high, with an almost holiday atmosphere amongst the crew.

Everyone was well aware that there was a serious job to do, but we were all getting along like lifelong friends, much to my relief. With so many pieces to the Personal Everest jigsaw, I knew that one of the cornerstones to success would be the morale of the crew, and they had to get along with each other. By midday on only our second day of sailing, so concerned was I about wanting to maintain that happy dynamic, that I recall feeling guilty that the RIB crew might be getting bored just sat in the RIB for so long, and worrying myself that they might be having second thoughts about seeing out their commitment. Maybe irrational thoughts, especially so early on in the voyage, but with so much time to think, my mind was continually racing, not yet having settled into a calmer routine.

The wind was all over the place that day, though mercifully it remained well within our limit of 15 knots. But by the time we were off Lulworth, and with our destination of Portland some miles away on the horizon, the wind continued to decrease and progress was reduced to a snail's pace. I was forced, for the second time, to take a tow from *Everest One*, but this time for safety reasons and only for a matter of minutes. With the wind having dropped and the tide still slowing my progress westwards, I found myself unable to sail clear of the Lulworth gunnery range. This is a large area of sea off the Dorset coast where the armed services fire live artillery rounds from the mainland out to sea. The area is protected by a Royal Naval gunnery range vessel, which is there to keep shipping out of the danger area, by force if necessary. I could just about see the vessel, its grey naval hull camouflaged against the coastline some three miles north of me, but when I saw it steaming towards us at great speed, I knew it had something to do with our presence. As I could only listen on channel 77, I could not hear the VHF radio exchange between Ian and the gunnery protection vessel on their channel, but with live firing in progress they told Ian that I had to move for my own safety, even though I was only a matter of yards within the outer safety zone. It was more a case of them being seen to be doing something than me being in any real danger, but we acquiesced and *Everest One* towed me a couple of miles southwest and away from trouble.

Eleven hours after setting off from Lymington, we were met by Andy, Elaine and Mike on the slipway at the Weymouth and Portland Sailing Academy. It was still only 1500 hours, and on shore the sun was shining brightly. Still wearing all of my sailing kit, it felt very warm, certainly in comparison to the cool sea breeze I had been enduring all day. As *Freethinker* was pulled up the slipway and Elaine unfastened my helmet, I felt a huge wave of exhaustion wash over me, such as I don't ever recall experiencing before. All day I had been so focused on sailing *Freethinker* that I had given little thought to my own condition. Safely ashore, I realised that my arms now felt like lead weights and were aching like hell, the weight of the helmet was causing a shooting pain in my neck and my hands were red raw where I had been wrapping the main sheet around them. But perhaps the thing I noticed most was how sore my face felt; partly due to the sun, but mostly due to the constant salty spray that had been blowing across it all day. Now ashore, as the heat of the sun evaporated the last of the sea water from my face, I could feel the salt crystallising on my forehead, around my cheeks and on top of my eyelids.

Within ten minutes of being ashore, I was back in the motorhome, face down, trousers around the back of my knees for the 'bum inspection'. If there was ever a worry about those damn pressure sores, it would be now after such a marathon sail, confined in my tiny cockpit, sat in my seat for eleven hours.

'You're not going to believe this,' said Elaine.

'Oh no, here we go ...' I thought, thinking the worst.

'Geoff, there's not even a pink mark. It's incredible that your backside should be better than when sat in your wheelchair.'

It was at that point that I really felt I could relax about the pressure-sore problem. It had been a source of worry for months and, now we had actually started the challenge, it was a massive relief to know that it was OK, even after such a long time in the boat.

I remained on the bed and, overcome with exhaustion, quickly fell into a deep sleep for a short while.

A couple of hours later, awake, fed and watered, I sat outside in the warm evening sunshine with the rest of the crew and Ian, who had called a crew briefing to review the day. Apart from some minor technical matters, the news was good and we were all buoyed up that we had managed such a long leg without incident – although Ian put us on notice that an incoming weather system looked likely to mean yet another delay the following day.

I wheeled down to the bottom of the slipway, where the guys were now de-rigging *Freethinker* for the night and drying out their sailing clothes. It was a beautiful evening, and I had the opportunity to admire the venue, soon to become home for the sailing events in the 2012 Olympic Games. All I could see was row upon row of sailing dinghies lining the foreshore and groups of brightly clad children in lifejackets, dotted all over the place, being taught how to sail. In the distance, beyond Portland Harbour wall, lay the town of Weymouth.

Ian's pessimism about the weather was proven correct, and we spent the morning of Wednesday 23 May with unexpected time on our hands. Excessive wind early in the morning had prevented us from making our 0400 start and therefore we had missed our tidal gate at Portland Bill. The prospect of making our next stop, Brixham, a fifty-mile dash across Lyme Bay, was now out of the question. It's a wonderful irony that actually the sun was shining and it was a lovely warm early summer's day, but the wind was just above our limits. The problem actually lay in the direction of the wind, not the speed. To round Portland Bill, the peninsula of land several miles to our south which sticks out, finger-like, into the English Channel, we had to negotiate the notorious Portland Race. Here the currents and tides are compressed and forced around the headland, causing them to flow at greater speed. As they pass over the shallow water at the end of the headland the currents are also pushed upwards, and the result is a large body of unsettled water, stretching for several miles and moving at terrific speed. During spring tides, when they are running at their fastest, and with even a moderate breeze blowing in the opposite direction causing what is known as 'wind over tide', the Race can be a match for the largest commercial ship. It is certainly no place for a fifteen-foot dinghy.

Having a few spare hours did at least give me the opportunity to keep my blog updated. As soon as I had retired to the seclusion of the motorhome, I inserted the special dongle into my laptop computer which gave me access, albeit painfully slow access, to the internet. My homepage automatically logged me onto my Personal Everest website, where first click was always the *Where's Geoff?* button. The Marinetrack device on *Freethinker* was continually transmitting my whereabouts, with pinpoint accuracy, every thirty minutes and it was remarkably encouraging to log on at the end of the day and see the long line of arrows which had tracked my progress that particular day. Close up, it always looked impressive, but as I panned out to view the daily trip in comparison to the whole of the UK, the scale of the challenge that lay ahead was too daunting to fully comprehend.

With our progress checked on the web, next on my list was email. It would often take thirty minutes or more to download all of my messages. By now, they were just about all messages of support, many from people I knew, but a growing number from strangers.

Having read and answered my messages, only then would I start to write my blog. With the luxury of a lay-day in Lymington, and now a few spare hours in Portland, I had plenty of time to write and then upload my latest message, blissfully unaware at this stage if anyone was actually reading it.

Whilst I was busy with my computer and requesting peace and quiet – not easy with an active five-year-old running about – Elaine made her second call of the day to Susan Preston-Davis, her initial one being first thing in the morning with our departure time, and the second giving an abridged version of the day's events, time of arrival, distance travelled, anything in particular of interest and so on. Susan would then write the daily e-bulletin and fire it off to her list of press contacts.

Luckily, by mid-morning on the 23rd the wind had abated and swung around in direction, giving us, by Ian's calculations, enough time to head for West Bay harbour in Lyme Bay, about a thirty-mile run, assuming we could make it around Portland Bill on the turn of the tide when the sea state would be at its calmest at 1500 hours.

I was disappointed not to be making Brixham in one hit, but at least we were keeping on the move and, bang on Ian's prediction, we rounded Portland Bill with an almost flat calm sea. To avoid the worst of the Race I was instructed to keep as close inshore as possible. Having only ever sailed around the Bill in large boats, and always keeping well out to sea to avoid the Race, it seemed very strange indeed sailing so close inshore. I could even see the faces of the people waving at me from the foot of the imposing red and white hooped lighthouse directly above me. I was, according to Ian, at a distance known as the 'biscuit toss' – and I could see why.

Every minute afloat during those first few days was spent learning about our vessels and how we were going to cope with being at sea for such extended periods of time. Even the routine of having a pee. Luckily for me, I'm plumbed into a tube direct from my bladder, through a hole in my abdominal wall to a bag on my leg, so with the addition of a short piece of rubber tubing my leg bag drained directly through the centreboard slot, straight into the sea: I could drink as much as I wanted. For the guys on the RIB it was more of a hassle, as they had to disentangle themselves from their lifejackets and drysuits before hanging on for dear life over the back of the RIB, one-handed, to do their business. From the moment we left Hamble, we flew a big white battle flag every minute we were at sea from the stern of the RIB with our sponsors' name printed in large letters across it. It was huge, some four feet long and three feet high. I can't recall exactly who came up with the euphemism 'visiting the solicitors', but it was certainly very apt – and it was a brave man who used an ungloved hand to roll the flag away at night.

We arrived in West Bay at 2045 hours, and we were fast losing light. I recall hearing our shore crew, Everest Mobile, transmit the message '*Freethinker*, we have a goldfish-bowl situation' as I neared the harbour entrance but I wasn't entirely sure what that meant. But then the penny dropped. The twenty or so silhouettes I could see lining the harbour wall were in fact Rotarians. As pleased as I was to be greeted by well-wishers, it came as something of a surprise that so many should turn out, suited and booted, most accompanied by their good ladies, in near darkness, to welcome me in. Whilst the crew de-rigged the boats, I posed for countless photographs, reluctant to disclose that I was extremely hungry, extremely tired, and not particularly in the mood for happy snappers.

This was only our third stop, but already it was becoming clear that whatever relationship we thought we had with Rotary, if this was a taste of what was to come it would not work. That's no reflection on the kind folk who turned out to wish me well – indeed I was most appreciative – but if we were to be arriving at destinations late and leaving early, what we actually needed was practical help. But now was not the time to think about this. Right now I needed food and sleep.

The longer I spent at sea in *Freethinker*, and the more miles I slowly clocked up, the more time I had to reflect on just how lucky I was to be achieving my ambition of sailing around Great Britain. But having time to think also gave me time to reflect on my sailing career and my accident. The south coast provides good cruising for yachts of all sizes, and I had seen plenty of them over the past few days. On those that passed close by I could see the crew, who would often stand and wave. It was a paradox to me that having once sailed some of the largest and finest yachts in the world, I was now physically incapable of doing so on my own. So the only way I could fulfil my ambition was to sail one of the smallest boats probably to ever attempt the 1,500-mile journey. I worried at times that those people who sailed past me in their thirty-something-footers were thinking to themselves, 'Oh, that's nice, that brave disabled chap is sailing in his little dinghy,'

Brave? I hate that word. So often I have been called brave. Firemen and soldiers are brave, certainly not me. I felt an urge to let them know, to shout out loud that prior to my accident I had been perfectly capable of sailing a much bigger yacht around the country, and I was now sailing a fifteen-foot dinghy because it was my only choice. Indeed, many of the boats I had sailed previously made theirs look as small as my dinghy did in comparison to their boats. Many years earlier, just after my accident, I had felt a similar urge to tell complete strangers that I hadn't always been disabled, as though I were somehow embarrassed by it. Perhaps there was an element of that underlying my feelings about sailing *Freethinker*, but with that sense of embarrassment came also a sense of vulnerability. Not just from the elements and the huge seas that were now rolling in from the north Atlantic, but vulnerability in terms of my sense of being. I had staked everything on this trip, and it was my opportunity to prove to myself and to everyone else my abilities, not my disability.

Luckily for me, my crew were very concerned for my physical wellbeing in these early stages. Having only known the problems I was likely to face from what they had been told or read about in the risk assessments, for example pressure sores, dehydration, exposure and the dreaded autonomic dysreflexia, they we very caring and showed great compassion. Each of them would ensure that after a day at sea it was I who was fed first, it was I who had the first hot drink and it was I who was first into the warmth of the motorhome. Elaine, having lived with me for more than two decades, was less forgiving and more pragmatic about such problems, but by removing all worries from my shoulders and allowing me to concentrate only on the sailing, the crew were giving me the support I needed to see this through. Even though I was physically incapable of helping them de-rig the boats or perform any of the other labour-intensive tasks, there were times, lying in my cosy bunk, when I could hear them at work outside on my behalf, in all sorts of weather, and I would feel guilty. Part of me wanted to get up, to join them, to be one of 'the lads' – but what would it have achieved?

Blog entry, Day 5, Thursday 24 May 2007:

> We left Bridport at 0500 this morning with a stiff northerly breeze blowing off the land behind us. By 0700, looking back towards Lyme Regis and the coastline, it was a lovely sight with the sunshine on the coastal hill fog as it rolled over the cliffs like a waterfall, down into the sea reflecting the pink sun. Once again the breeze died for several hours until two hours before arrival in Brixham, when we were treated to one of the best sails of the trip so far, arriving early afternoon.

It was a good day to be out sailing. The sun shone and there was a steady 15 knots of breeze on my beam as I made my final tack towards the breakwater which signalled the entrance to the harbour. *Freethinker* was flying, and poor old *Everest One* had to splutter and wheeze to keep up with me. Rising steeply above the harbour itself, the houses seemed glued to the hillside and created a colourful backdrop, and with the prominent white Brixham Yacht Club building perched overlooking the water, I threaded my way between the many boats moored in the harbour, towards the slipway and another welcoming committee.

We had been scheduled to arrive in Brixham at least a week earlier, but with my false start on 14 May and subsequent weather delays, we were lucky to find that the club, who had previously offered to help us, were still able to retain that offer.

A month earlier, crewman Andy had compiled our 'bible' for

the trip. In addition to all the data for the fifty destinations en route, we were forced to put dates of arrival alongside each port. We did so reluctantly, aware of the potential difficulties with weather. But when contacting ports like Brixham to notify them of the expedition and the impending descent of the Personal Everest circus upon them, it was understandable that they wanted an idea of when we would be arriving, so we had little choice. Rather ambitiously, we compiled a schedule of all fifty ports, each with a date of arrival. Even more ambitiously, the dates were decided by calculating a routine of three days consecutive sailing, with every fourth day set aside as a lay-day to relax, catch up on jobs and maybe do a bit of sightseeing. Yeah, right. When forewarning them of our arrival, we did make it clear that all dates were 'subject to change', but we had no idea to exactly what extent. And with the weather deteriorating in Brixham so much, we found ourselves stranded there for a week, making a complete mockery of the original itinerary.

Day 8, Sunday 27 May 2007:

> Well, we are still without internet access. As beautiful as Brixham may be, it hasn't got the greatest network coverage for our 3G net cards. We are currently weather-bound again, this time in the dinghy compound of Brixham Yacht Club, who have been wonderful hosts. The reception on arrival here Thursday was great. Members of the BYC and the Brixham Rotary Club were on the slipway to help us in. We have even been given use of their dinghy compound to house our entourage of vehicles. Thursday night was race night and we were treated to dinner in the Club before I was asked to give a brief update on my Challenge and guests subsequently raised money towards the local Sailability group.

It was now late May, and the Brixham I remember from childhood, when we would sail here on my stepfather's yacht, was considerably different. Still very pretty, the main harbour front was now full of tourist shops, fast food outlets and ice cream parlours, and with coach-loads of visitors being bussed in almost hourly, it felt more like a twee theme park.

The Club themselves were great hosts and allowed us to cram our three vehicles, two trailers and *Freethinker* into their dinghy compound without complaint. Whilst it was safe and secure, living in the motorhome behind a seven-foot-high steel fence, with a never-ending stream of tourists walking past us to and from their coaches, we felt at times like animals in a zoo.

There was still a hint of a holiday atmosphere amongst the crew, especially now that they were able to saunter into town in the morning, pick up a daily paper and have a pie and pint at one of the harbour-side pubs, watching the day trippers going about their business. Despite a frustration because of the weather, I too was guilty of feeling the same sense of relaxation and even, dare I say, enjoyment at being ashore. But that all changed with one phone call –

'Geoff, it's Susan. Geoff, I've had the BBC on the phone and they want to know if the rumours are true.'

'What rumours?'

'You've not updated your blog for a few days and obviously, with bad weather, your tracker is not showing any progress either. People are beginning to say you have given up.'

It was a wake-up call if ever I needed one. Internet access was indeed non-existent from our base by the yacht club. The couple of blogs that I had posted, I had written off-line on my laptop computer and then had to get a lift in a car out of town towards Paignton before I had enough reception to upload them to my website. It was such a palaver that I had decided to wait until we reached Salcombe, our next destination, before my next update. But I had not realised until then that in my physical absence it was my cyber-presence through my blog and tracker that was actually keeping my project alive in the minds of those following me. Whilst we were living it for real, they were living it through my website.

Even though it was so near the start of the expedition, it is possible to pinpoint Brixham as the point at which, for me at least, Personal Everest stopped being a jolly, and became more like a job. By the time we came to leave that Devon port, the focus was purely on achieving the original objective as agreed by Ian and myself all those months ago: 'To sail around Great Britain, safely.'

12

The Duke of Cornwall Spinal Unit was a brand new, purpose-built centre that was opened by Prince Charles and Princess Diana in June 1984, only a few months before my arrival in September. Built next to the world-famous Odstock Burns Unit with its characteristic World War II corrugated-iron dome-shaped wards, the Spinal Unit looked quite out of place with its magnificent modern brick design, high up on the plain over-looking the city of Salisbury.

As a brand new unit it only had a small number of patients, and I was the first to arrive by helicopter. Despite a request on medical grounds by John Russell, then senior consultant at the Spinal Unit, that I be flown immediately from Gatwick to Odstock by helicopter, Gatwick's local health authority refused to pick up the cost, declaring that my admission to Odstock 'did not constitute an emergency'. With the only alternative being a ten-hour ambulance journey from Gatwick to Salisbury – travelling at less than 10 miles per hour with a police escort – once again British Caledonian Airways stepped into the breach and covered the cost of the helicopter, mercifully speeding me on my way to proper treatment.

I didn't realise it at the time, but as my stretcher was carefully wheeled from the helipad on that cool, breezy autumn after-noon in through the doors of the Spinal Unit, Odstock was about to become my home for the next ten months. Here I was going relearn everything I ever knew about my body. I was also going to have to learn to readjust my mental attitude towards myself, my friends, my family and, ultimately, the world outside. It was essential that I separated any sentiment and emotion I may have felt from the brutal reality that I was now paralysed. If I was to be capable of surviving life as a quadriplegic, both mentally and physically – no matter how tough it might get – when I left hospital I had to accept my predicament and deal with it. That may sound harsh, cold and clinical, but it was my only option and I knew it. In the weeks and months to come, I would feel as physically helpless and dependent as a baby, yet with the active mind of a young adult. It was never going to be easy, and at times it would be torture.

Upon arrival, I was immediately taken to the eight-bedded ward for new admissions, where I underwent yet more examinations, x-rays and tests. The trick I had learned in Puerto Rico – closing my eyes and humming to myself whilst my body was poked and prodded – helped enormously. John Russell decided that he wanted me back in cranial traction with immediate effect to stabilise the fracture to my spine, but at least this time I was sedated and the area around my temples was anaesthetised. I felt no pain, but it was no less uncomfortable having steel tongs screwed into my skull for the second time in three weeks.

For the first time, I started to hear the terms quadriplegia and tetraplegia being used in reference to me. I learnt that they are exactly the same thing, with *tetra* meaning four in Greek and *quadri* meaning four in Latin. I learned that my accident had fractured the sixth vertebra in my neck and therefore, with all four of my limbs affected, I was quadriplegic. The nerves in my neck had been severed, with the result that apart from some slight arm movement I was completely paralysed from the chest down, both in feeling and in movement.

Once again I found myself lying flat on my back in bed, in traction, staring at the ceiling. My arms were extended at right angles to my body, resting on pillows to keep the tendons straight like a supine crucifixion. Above me, a strategically placed articulated mirror made it possible to see some of my surroundings, and wearing prismatic spectacles set at 90 degrees meant I could at least read newspapers, books and the many get-well cards

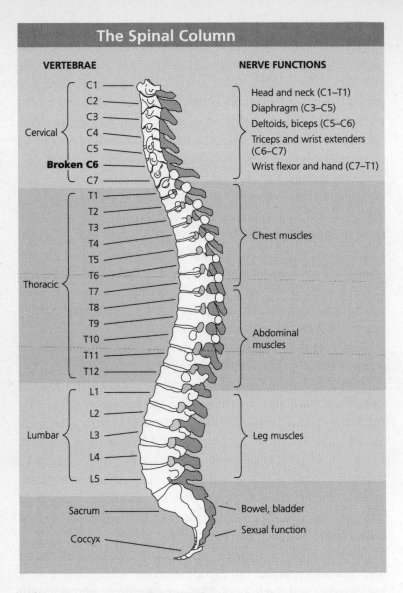

The Spinal Column

VERTEBRAE		NERVE FUNCTIONS
Cervical	C1	Head and neck (C1–T1)
	C2	Diaphragm (C3–C5)
	C3	Deltoids, biceps (C5–C6)
	C4	Triceps and wrist extenders (C6–C7)
	C5	
	Broken C6	Wrist flexor and hand (C7–T1)
	C7	
Thoracic	T1	
	T2	
	T3	Chest muscles
	T4	
	T5	
	T6	
	T7	
	T8	
	T9	
	T10	Abdominal muscles
	T11	
	T12	
Lumbar	L1	
	L2	
	L3	Leg muscles
	L4	
	L5	
	Sacrum	Bowel, bladder
	Coccyx	Sexual function

when they were placed on my chest.

On arrival at hospital, I was appointed a primary and a secondary nurse to look after me. They were supported by a team of staff, all of whom had undergone specialist training to deal with patients with spinal cord injury (SCI). My primary nurse was called Diane and my secondary nurse was called Elaine. I didn't pay a lot of attention to individuals at this stage, although I could hardly not be aware of nurse Elaine Osborn. At barely five feet tall and with frizzy blonde hair, everyone knew when this pint-size bombshell was on duty – at times the ward resembled a *Carry On* film with Elaine like a young Barbara Windsor (but without the boobs). You could always hear her somewhere on the ward, either laughing or causing a commotion.

Dressed in their bright blue trousers, training shoes and smart white tunics, the nurses were there to help with all of my personal needs. Whether it was eating, drinking, going to the toilet, getting dressed or even cleaning my teeth, I was completely reliant on them. As a previously independent, able-bodied person, suddenly being so reliant on other people for my every need was not an easy thing to come to terms with. Even having someone cut up my food and put it in my mouth only highlighted my sense of helplessness.

At first, I accepted that I required medical treatments and personal assistance because I was newly injured and because I knew I needed the help. But, ever so slowly, I started to resent the fact that I could not achieve even the smallest task on my own. I found myself continually asking people 'Could you just ...' do this or 'Could you just ...' do that, and forever having to thank people. A succession of 'pleases' and 'thank-yous'. Not that I have a problem with basic civility – but I started to feel like a nuisance, and there were many occasions when I found I would rather go without something than have to ask. More than two decades later, the same remains true today.

In contrast to my previous laid-back, unstructured and somewhat luxurious way of life living on yachts, my days were now governed by a rigid timetable of personal care, most notably the avoidance of pressure sores. A condition I had never heard of before, it's a term that I have come to dread. Unable to feel my body, I have no idea if I am developing a sore until my skin is checked by someone, and then it can be too late. I would be turned in my hospital bed every four hours, day in, day out, in an attempt to avoid my skin ulcerating on sensitive areas like my backside, my hips and my heels. This routine of pressure relief whilst seated in my wheelchair or whilst lying in bed is still a practice that must be followed every day of my life. If I don't maintain a high degree of vigilance, a pressure sore could form in a matter of hours and, if untreated, could rapidly deteriorate and lead to infection deep inside my body – ultimately they can be life-threatening. The only treatment is complete bed rest until the sore is healed. Even the slightest pink mark on my coccyx often kept me face down on my hospital bed for two or three days, which in turn caused difficulties in breathing, eating, drinking and sleeping. Luckily it only happened a couple of times whilst I was in hospital, but remembering the suffering they caused keeps me ever mindful of the potential danger.

Amongst a long list of new things I had to learn about my body was that my sympathetic nervous system had also been destroyed by my injury. At first this didn't seem particularly important – I had no idea what it was anyway. But the first obvious sign was discovering that I have no ability to sweat or to shiver, so I have no way of regulating my body temperature. I was forever feeling too hot or too cold. I am, in effect, like a reptile and I must continually take into account the temperature of my environment wherever I go or risk seriously damaging my body. But most importantly, I also learned that my body no longer had the ability to control the rise of blood pressure.

There is one condition I fear more than a pressure sore, and that is autonomic dysreflexia (AD). Within a day of admission to hospital, my primary nurse Diane went to great lengths to explain what it was, how to spot the systems and, most importantly, what to do if it occurred. Unable to feel discomfort or pain because of my paralysis, and with my sympathetic nervous system out of action, if any part of my body below my neck is subjected to a source of pain, no messages alerting me to that pain can reach my brain. In other words, I can not feel when I am being hurt by something. Before my accident I would instinctively move away from something that was hurting me but now, unable to feel it, my body reacts by raising my blood pressure. With no sympathetic nervous system to stop it going up, and with a rise of only 10 per cent above normal being enough to bring about a stroke or heart failure, AD attacks can be fatal.

Diane had explained everything I needed to know about pressure sores and autonomic dysreflexia, so I had an idea something might be wrong when, one afternoon about two weeks after my admission, my forehead started to feel a bit clammy. With my head still pinned to the bed in traction, I looked in the mirror above me and saw that my face had become quite flushed. I also had the beginnings of a piercing headache above each eye. Within minutes, the headache had become quite severe and I was feeling extremely uncomfortable and sick. The duty nurse took my blood pressure and, realising that there had been a sharp increase, immediately raised the alarm. The source of the problem turned out to be incredibly simple. I just had a full bladder, but I needed to be catheterised urgently. In the few minutes that it took to prepare to catheterise me, my blood pressure rose critically high and my body felt like it was going to explode, the pain was so intense, and I felt a massive weight on my chest. I was given a drug called nifedipine to lower my blood pressure but, once I had been catheterised, as suddenly as it had started, my headache was gone and my blood pressure was back to normal. The fact that something as simple as needing a pee could put my life in jeopardy brought home to me exactly how fine the line was that I was going to be treading for the rest of my life.

Those early days were very tiring. Once awake, after my bedding was changed, breakfast served and medications taken, I had daily treatment from my physiotherapist and various medical procedures performed whilst I was still lying in bed. Then the visitors would begin – an almost endless procession of family and friends, and even the local Round Table group set up a visiting rota to ensure I had company at least twice a week. Whilst I appreciated the efforts visitors would go to in order to see me – after all, Odstock is not an easy place to get to, and many would have round trips in excess of fifty miles – I rarely had time to myself. And because friends and family knew that I would not be going anywhere, they would nearly always arrive unannounced. Although I was lying down, it was the talking which tired me out so much. A visitor's first visit was always the most exhausting. I had to explain about the accident and my injury over and over again, trying my hardest to make light of the situation to put them at ease, as the last thing I wanted was people crying at my bedside. I was starting to feel like public property, and I was beginning to resent never having any private time, alone, for myself.

The first visit of my sister Lucy was without doubt the hardest of all to deal with emotionally. It was one thing putting on a brave face for my mates or trying to make light of the situation with more distant relatives, but Lucy had always been my little sister and I felt protective towards her. I wouldn't say she idolised me, but I was her big brother and I really wanted to protect her from any distress she would suffer from seeing me lying paralysed in a hospital bed, a catheter tube leading to a bag of urine clamped to the side of the bed and traction screwed into my skull. A few weeks into my stay, my mother had told me Lucy wanted to come and see me. Of course, I could not stop her from wanting to visit: she was thirteen years old and quite capable of making her own decisions. In advance of her visit I had decided the only way I was going to cope was to make light of the situation – but as I heard her footsteps on the hospital floor get nearer, then heard her say, 'Oh Geoff' as she reached my bedside and start crying, I couldn't help myself and the tears rolled down my cheeks as she hugged me. I hated her seeing me like that. I felt so helpless. I couldn't even hug her back. I believed that it would change her view of me as her big strong brother. Thankfully she didn't stay too long, but that first visit was bloody tough. In many ways I would have preferred her not to see me like that, but they were my selfish reasons and it wasn't really my decision to take.

My mother and her husband, Andy Brooks, were provided with accommodation near to the hospital so they spent a lot of time with me on the ward, carrying out many of the nursing chores to save the staff time. I appreciated their concern and their reasons for wanting to be there, but it was not easy for me. If there ever was a time when I needed to be given some space to come to terms with the magnitude of what happened, it was now.

At one point I overheard my mother in the corridor talking to my father Robin Hoad, saying that she felt I would have been better off dead than survive with my disability. Having been given so much independence as a child, even when I most wanted her to look after us, I felt extremely angry that somehow my accident now gave her the right to discuss my right to life behind my back. Maybe it was not intended in the way it came out, maybe it was an unguarded remark by a distraught mother, and I am fairly certain she didn't realise I was listening, but to hear the suggestion that I might be better off dead than spend the rest of my life as a quadriplegic, especially coming from my own mother, was heartbreaking. I might have lost the use of my limbs, but my mind was fully functional, and what I needed most at that time was unconditional love and support, not to feel stigmatised because I was disabled.

At the time, it seems that everyone except me knew that Robin was not my biological father. Obviously now wasn't the time to reveal the truth, but visiting hours would descend into a farce when Robin, my stepfather John Holt and Andy Brooks occasionally all visited at the same time, all calling themselves my 'father' or 'stepfather'. My mother, her husband Andy, Robin and John would talk in the corridor outside my ward. All sorts of bickering would ensue and I would overhear Andy, in the belief my mother was hard done by in the divorce settlement, demanding money from John – along with heated arguments over the custody of John's daughter, Lucy. It was a god-awful mess, and I found myself trying to deal with the emotional complexity of it whilst lying flat on my back with a broken neck. Thankfully there was one constant, and that was the sanity of the Pennell family. Every Sunday, after lunch, Roy, Joyce and never fewer than four other members of the family would visit from Portsmouth, laden with culinary treats, my favourite being Roy's home-made spicy pickled onions. At least when they visited, I knew there would be no squabbling. My mother would not dare to do so in their presence, as Roy, Tim or Danny would not tolerate that, at least not in front of me.

Having spent six weeks in traction, lying flat, the steel tongs were eventually removed and, for the first time since Puerto Rico, I was permitted to sit up in bed. I had by then been moved to the far end of the ward, and the view from my bed was one of the best I could have wished for. I could look out across Salisbury plain and, in the distance, some three or four miles away, was the unmistakable spire of the thirteenth-century Salisbury Cathedral, the tallest spire in England, a truly magnificent sight. And sitting up in bed I could see something else too – my fellow room mates.

As it was still a relatively new unit the wards were not full, but there were three other guys in my ward, all of whom had endured an injury within a few weeks of me, and all of whom were of a similar age to me. Scouser Dave Howard had broken his neck in a car crash, Tim Claire had also broken his neck in a car crash in Lanzarote, and Dave 'Dizzie' Holmes, our resident Mod, had broken his back in a scooter accident. We were a unique mix of four characters, all from hugely different backgrounds, all of whom had suffered life-changing injuries, and that unique bond was to give each of us strength in those difficult first months.

In the few precious hours each day when the four of us were not inundated with visitors, we were able to speak openly and frankly to each other. At first, lying flat on my back, pinned to my bed with traction and unable to see them, I could only differentiate between the guys by their voices. The times we spent chatting helped all of us understand that we were not alone with our problems. As you'd expect from four teenage lads, there was a lot of macho bravado but, no matter how big and brave we wanted to appear, we were all very definitely in the same boat. We often found ourselves discussing personal matters that we wouldn't even have discussed with our best friends before our accidents. As paralysed teenage lads, our two most pressing concerns were continence and sex, both deeply personal issues but hugely important to get to grips with. Not exactly subjects that are easily talked about, but our discussions weren't frivolous. And, in many ways, that made us mature beyond our years.

I peed through a condom into a bag which was strapped to my leg. Not an ideal method but the only one available at the time. It was not uncommon for the condom to burst or to come off completely, and the end result was always urine everywhere, over my trousers, soaking into my seat cushion, and the ubiquitous puddle on the floor. It was a problem the four of us often spoke about, and we could each cite our own examples of it happening to us. I lost count of how often it happened to me in the first month. But whether it happened in hospital, at home, at work or at a function, it was never any less embarrassing. On one occasion some years later, at a friend's wedding, it happened three times in as many hours, ruining two pairs of trousers and leaving a trail of urine from Elaine's car seat to the aisle in the church and even the reception at the hotel. I stank and was sure everyone could smell me. I hated that so much, I wanted to curl up and die – but it would be ten years after leaving hospital before I had an operation to put a tube directly through my abdomen into my bladder which removed the need for condoms altogether.

Though I was paralysed, my body still looked the same and testosterone was still coursing through my veins. Even though in many ways I felt emasculated because of my disability, I was certainly no less attracted to the opposite sex than I had been previously. But the rules had now changed enormously. All personal dignity had long since been taken away from me by the intrusion of medical procedures. Just about every member of nursing staff had seen me naked and had stuck tubes into every orifice in my body. I felt completely dehumanised by the process and it had taken away something incredibly personal from me. So any relationship with a girl, let alone any sexual relationship, could not occur without them having an understanding of exactly what that would entail. It felt so unfair. There could be no spontaneity any more, no normal relationship where both parties retain their privacy, their dignity and the façade they wanted their partner to see. Assuming I could find anyone to fancy me now I was in a wheelchair, how would I then explain that I'll need help to be lifted, help to be undressed, and 'oh yes, and by the way, I wear a condom in case I piss myself'? Not exactly romantic.

We may have been quoted facts and figures by the doctors, or read about various aspects of spinal cord injury in magazines, but there was no substitute for discussing these things with your peers. Fortunately, the machismo that we each tried to portray inadvertently got us through some of the most difficult days. When we heard recently injured patients in other wards crying at their predicament, we would openly mock them. I'm certain we all realised just how unfair this was, but it was our own survival mechanism, and it meant we would never dare show any sign of weakness ourselves for fear that we would end up on the receiving end. If you had a problem, then you either boxed it up and buried it deep in your mind, or you dealt with it privately.

Some weeks into my stay, John Russell came to my bedside, pulled the curtains around my cubicle and said the most difficult words he ever had to say as a spinal consultant –

'Geoffrey, there's no easy way to tell you this, and I'm sorry, but you are never going to walk again.'

I heard his words clearly enough but I don't recall showing any expression on my face. Inside it felt as though my bubble of hope had just been popped. Coming from John, an expert in these things, his words carried weight, but I was still young and arrogant enough to believe that he could be wrong.

One of our group of four, I don't recall who, had been told that it was possible to make a full recovery from SCI if you showed signs of improvement up to ten weeks post injury. Secretly, every day, I would try and wiggle my toes or move my fingers, aware that time was slipping away fast. As the invisible ten-week deadline of hope passed, the next rumour to circulate was that it was still possible to make a full recovery up to six months post injury. They might seem almost pathetic, little crumbs of optimism, and maybe each of us knew they were just that, but they were just enough to give a glimmer of hope. But as time marched on and each deadline passed without any improvement in my condition, so I got more and more used to fact that I would be living with my disability for life.

Unlike the time when I broke my leg as a child and went home a week or so later, this time I was likely to be in hospital for many months, initially being treated for my injury and then going through a long period of rehabilitation. Being there for so long, the Spinal Unit was to become like my home, which also meant that the relationship between staff and patients was unlike that in other hospital departments.

Many of the nursing staff quickly became good friends, and with so many of them working shifts it was like living in our very own soap opera, with them sharing stories on a daily basis of their love lives and news of the big world outside. But having the trust and confidence of the staff also meant that the four of us could exploit their every weakness to our advantage. For weeks we had held a private game amongst ourselves to see how late we could get a member of the nursing team to make us a toasted cheese sandwich. The rules were quite clear: none of us could ruin the chances of another, and the cheese toastie had to actually be completely eaten to count. Dave was well ahead, having secured several cheesy snacks shortly after the 10.00 p.m. curfew imposed on toasties by the ward sister, who was getting frustrated at constant late-night food preparation. One night, after the televisions had been turned off and the lights turned out, the four of us stayed up chatting for an hour or so.

'What time is it, Dave?' I asked, knowing he could see the clock above the nurses' station from his position.

'Half twelve,' he replied.

If I could pull this off, I'd win by a mile.

'OK, get this,' I said, 'Everyone be quiet ... Nurse!' I called, in a slightly pathetic voice, just loud enough to be heard by the night shift. 'Nurse!'

One of our favourites, a pretty young redheaded nurse called Emma, came to the ward, her torch guiding her to my bedside.

'What's wrong?' she whispered, thinking the rest of the patients were asleep.

I could barely see her in the darkness. 'I don't know,' I said. 'I'm having a tough time coming to terms with things,' I sniffed.

She took hold of my hand. 'What sort of things?' she asked.

'I'm sorry, I can't talk about it Emma, it's too painful. I can't sleep and I can't get these horrible thoughts out of my head. I've tried everything but nothing is working.'

'Would you like a drink of water or a biscuit?' she asked.

'Would it be OK to have a piece or toast, or maybe a cheese toastie?' I asked. I was biting my lower lip so hard, trying not to laugh.

At the words 'cheese toastie' there came a snort of stifled laughter from Tim's direction, quickly followed by a fake snore. Thankfully she didn't hear it.

'Of course,' she said, and scuttled out of the ward towards the kitchen.

'You bastard,' whispered Dave as she disappeared. 'Have you no shame?'

'Shhh, she's coming back,' I retorted.

Not only did she cook it for me, but the poor girl fed it to me too, piece by piece. Between mouthfuls I was fighting the urge to laugh so much that I could barely eat it. After the last mouthful, she must have wondered why I announced, 'Oh, that was wonderful, thank you Emma.' But of course it heralded that I had won the contest – drawing much amusement and cheers from my three mates.

She didn't see the funny side, and I don't blame her. It was many weeks before any of us were to enjoy a cheese toastie again, and about as long again before Emma spoke to me. It was a very mean thing to do but it brought home to us how we could turn a situation to our advantage because of our disability.

With my traction removed, the next major hurdle was getting up and into my wheelchair. The night before I was due to try for the first time, I was quite anxious. Tim, Dave and Dizzie had all had their turns in recent days and I recall their excitement at finally being out of bed, but it was disconcerting nonetheless. When the moment came, it was all over quite quickly. I was lifted into the wheelchair from my bed with one nurse taking my legs, another taking my torso. Once seated, I immediately felt unbalanced; it felt as though my head wasn't connected to my body at all and it was just balanced on a swaying pole over which I had no control. Even with a nurse standing behind me, holding my shoulders to stop me toppling forward, not being able to feel my chest, I had no balance whatsoever – it was an incredibly odd feeling. I was wheeled in front of a full-length mirror and, for the first time in months, saw myself, now sat in a wheelchair. It was a fairly shocking sight, not least because I had lost so much weight. I looked gaunt, thin, grey. My long blonde hair was now a straggly tangled mess. I remember thinking, 'Oh my god. This is it Geoff, you'd better get used to it.' Within a couple of minutes I was feeling faint, and everything in front of me seemed to glaze over. By the time I came around, I was back on the bed.

Within a few days I was getting into my chair every day, and each day I was spending longer and longer in the chair until, within two weeks, I was sitting upright for most of the day. Once at this stage, I now had to attend physiotherapy and occupational therapy sessions as part of my daily routine. Although they provided an escape from the ward, it was anything but easy.

My daily visits to the physio department were to keep my joints supple and my muscles toned. As I was only able to partly move my arms, much of the manipulation of my joints was performed by my physiotherapist, Linda. The physical exercise part of the treatment was designed to strengthen my muscles. It involved strapping my arms to weights attached to overhead pulleys and flapping my arms like the wings of an injured bird; it was quite exhausting and must have looked completely stupid, but with such weak arms anyway I never really felt any benefit.

Another purpose of physio was to see what my physical capabilities were and how best to exploit them, to see if I could ever live independently. For many hours, lying on one of those rectangular green foul-smelling rubber gym mats, just like the ones you see at school, with Linda encouraging me every inch of the way, I tried to get to the first stage of raising myself into a seated position from lying on my back. After many painful and frustrating hours I eventually succeeded – but it was a near-pointless skill unless I could next lift my backside off the floor. Despite days and weeks of practice, I simply could not lift myself. My ultimate goal was to become independent – but that could only be achieved if I could 'transfer' myself, in other words, use my arm strength to lift my backside enough to move myself from my wheelchair to a bed, a toilet or car, for example. My injury had also paralysed my triceps muscles, so I had almost no ability to lift myself. Hating to be beaten, I would sit in my wheelchair alongside a bench and, using my wrists, try to apply enough downward pressure with my arms to get my bum off the seat, but it was futile. I tried so hard that I was beginning to damage my wrists and my fingers. Accepting that I was unable to transfer myself, the realisation slowly dawned on me that I was never going to be independent; I was going to spend every day of my life reliant on someone else to lift me. That was tough to come to terms with, and I'm not sure I fully understood the enormity of it. But it hit home hard enough to cause a few sleepless nights.

Another problem was that, despite eating large quantities of hospital food, I continued to lose weight at an alarming rate. I was monitored quite closely, and at one stage my weight fell to just over seven stone. To be honest, I felt OK, but I was obviously becoming malnourished. The hospital's solution was simply to order me three times the amount of food, but three times the quantity of crap-quality food is not the same as one portion of decent food and they never seemed to grasp that point. Luckily, my food intake was supplemented to some extent by treats brought in by my visitors, but no matter how much I ate I simply could not put on weight. At one point I was even forced to see a psychiatrist. I didn't understand the reason at first, but then it dawned on me when he started asking questions about my state of mind. I discovered that I was being secretly monitored to check my food intake and to see if I was being sick afterwards. I was absolutely livid and felt that the nursing staff had betrayed me. Without even talking to me about it, senior staff seemed to have decided that I had an eating disorder. I was so angry, as nothing could have been further from the truth. But once I was aware that I was being watched, after meal times I would go to a bathroom and deliberately dribble yogurt on my chin as though I had been sick and then push my wheelchair past the nurses' station to wind them up. My games backfired, and I was forced to see another psychiatrist. It would be nearly fifteen years before I would return to my normal weight, and being so skinny meant that I had to be extra careful about pressure sores, particularly on my backside.

My other daily duty was to attend occupational therapy. Here I would be equipped with the skills I would need to live my life. From how to hold a hair brush to how to put clothes in a washing machine – I was to be taught it all. However, my particular therapist, John, had a more pragmatic approach. On one of my first visits to the department, he explained –

'My job is to teach you how to do everyday duties around the house –' and he went on to reel off a long list of examples.

To which I replied, 'John, let's get one thing straight. If I'm always going to be dependent on other people in order to live, then I'm not ever going to need to load a washing machine and I'm not ever going to need a device to help me put my socks on, so let's cut the crap and focus on the things I'm going to need.'

I thought at first he was about to hit me. Instead, he stood up, opened a cupboard, took out two pint glasses, one with a handle, one without. He filled them both to the top with water and put them on the table in front of me. Pointing to the one with a handle, he said, 'That's called a jug.' Pointing to the one without a handle, he said, 'That's called a sleeve.'

'Now,' he asked, 'Which one can you pick up the easiest?'

I tried both, but the one with the handle was by far the easier.

'Right,' he said, 'next time you're in a pub, you say to the barman, can I have a pint of beer in a pint jug, not a sleeve.'

Now, that was my kind of occupational therapy – and from that point forward we got on famously as John helped me with all sorts of practical things that I was actually going to need.

During one visit, my friend Fiona had suggested that I write to her. She wasn't prepared to accept my excuse that I wouldn't be able to hold a pen and argued, 'I don't care if you have to write a single letter on each sheet of paper, just put them all in order and I'll read them.' At the time it only seemed a minor quip, but the next time I was in OT I asked for a pen and paper. I was presented with a variety of pens, but with no grip in my fingers it was difficult to stop a pen slipping out of my hand. I did not want to use one of the purpose-made leather pen-holders strapped to my hand – that was only going to draw attention to my disability. After much trial and error I finally found a black felt-tip with a thick enough stem which did not slip when I applied pressure. With several sheets of blank paper in front of me, I slowly started writing the alphabet. Sure enough, the letters were very large at first. I could only write two or three per page, and with no fine finger or wrist movement it was difficult coordinating my shoulder and arm to make the letters, but at least they were identifiable. The more I practised, the smaller the letters became. But I hadn't realised that my mother and Andy had been standing behind me, watching.

'That's fantastic,' exclaimed my mother, appearing over my shoulder. 'Well done, it looks great.'

Surprised, I turned on her. 'No it's not! It's bloody awful. Stop patronising me.' And with that I threw down the pen and pushed myself back onto the ward to get away from everything. I was cross at myself for snapping at her, but equally I was fed up with all of my actions being monitored and commented on.

As winter slowly gave way to spring, Dave, Tim, Dizzy and I were moved into a four-bedded side-ward. Newly injured patients were being brought into the unit on an almost weekly basis and we were fast becoming the 'old boys'. Now mobile in our wheelchairs, we could sit in the communal rest areas of the ward, and here I would observe the relatives and friends of the new patients. Out of earshot from their loved ones lying injured on the ward next door, I would hear their discussions and watch their tears as they too lived through the horror of SCI, just as my family had probably done some months earlier. To some of the relatives, our presence, sitting their in our wheelchairs, laughing and joking, must have given hope. To others it most probably confronted them with a reality they did not want to see. And at night, when all the visitors had left and the staff were busy elsewhere, the four of us would quietly slip onto the admissions ward and chat to some of the newly injured guys and girls. Unable to see their faces, we would talk about anything and everything, and they would often say that it was good just to chat to someone without being judged or knowing they were being pitied. But that's where they were wrong – I pitied every single one of them, regardless of their age or injury. Given what I now knew about SCI, I wouldn't have wished it on my worst enemy, and these poor bastards had it all to come.

And I pitied no one more than I did a five-year-old boy called

James. A few days earlier he had jumped onto a settee at home and one of his mother's knitting needles had pierced right through his throat and his neck, immediately paralysing his tiny body in an identical way to me. Every day I would see his distraught parents at his bedside through the glass of his private ward and I would hear their sobbing as they left the ward each night. One evening, after visiting hours, Dave and I were just pushing around the wards chatting when we overheard a nurse say that James had not yet had his evening meal because all the staff were busy with an emergency. Without asking permission, Dave and I managed to sneak James's tea-tray off the trolley, and we made our way into his room. Two teenage quadriplegics trying to feed a five-year-old quadriplegic spaghetti bolognese was not easy, but James was a cheerful chap and found our efforts quite funny. I even managed to hold his orange juice close enough for him to drink it through a straw, and just long enough for him to get a few mouthfuls, before I dropped the plastic cup on the floor. Once he'd finished, we told him a made-up story before saying our goodbyes. As Dave and I turned to leave we noticed half a dozen noses pressed up against the glass window. The nurses had been watching us, and there was barely a dry eye amongst them.

As time marched on, so I found more and more opportunities to go on day trips out of the hospital. I would normally go out with whoever was offering to take me but I increasingly found myself being taken out by my nurse, Elaine Osborn, when she was off duty. At only 5 feet tall, she had perfected an unconventional but extremely effective method of lifting all 6 foot 3 inches of me into her beige Austin Allegro. Although most trips were no further than Salisbury to do some shopping or go to a pub for lunch, at first the prospect of going out filled me with trepidation. Not only was I leaving the security of the Spinal Unit, but I had to face the uncomfortable feeling that everyone in the street was looking at me. I was convinced that people were staring and were judging me or pitying me because I was in a wheelchair. I had an urge to shout out, 'I haven't always been disabled, you know, I was able-bodied until recently' – as if it was important for people to know that I had been like them. Perhaps I was feeling embarrassed. I know that I went to great lengths to make myself look 'normal'. Whilst other patients would wear soft tracksuit trousers because they were less likely to cause pressure sores, I would insist upon wearing jeans. And where others would be wrapped up in tartan rugs to keep them warm, I would wear just a shirt to look less 'disabled' if it seemed trendier. The more frequently I ventured out, the more I came to realise that actually people weren't staring as much as I originally thought, although some parents were put in difficult situations when their children would shout out, 'mummy, why's that man in a wheelchair?'

Those early trips out brought home some stark realities. From getting around to simply getting into shops, restaurants and pubs, I became aware of how much I had taken for granted when I was able to walk. I realised that absolutely everything I now wanted to do had to be thought through in advance. My disability had taken away something I had not realised that I had held so dear: it took away spontaneity. Just as my reliance on others for my personal care meant that I had to forfeit my right to dignity and privacy, I now had to accept that I had also been stripped of the ability to act on impulse. That was gone for ever. My disability was starting to make me feel as though I had lost control over every aspect of my life, even my love life.

After several day trips out, Elaine and I started spending more and more time together, but I quite quickly found myself in an awkward situation of my own making. I had been in a long-term relationship with a girlfriend since I was fourteen. Having grown up together, she had long gotten used to the fact that I would disappear overseas for long periods of time and she was semi-tolerant of my boyish shenanigans. I would often return from sea, a bunch of flowers in one hand and a box of chocolates in the other, and all would be forgiven, at least until the next time. Turning a blind eye to my indiscretions and my teenage exuberance was one thing, but my accident came as quite a blow to her and her family. I was half-expecting that the enormity of my injury and the prospect of a future together would scare away a girl of eighteen, but I was wrong. Rather as I had felt when my sister first visited me, I felt completely emasculated and embarrassed at what I had become and would rather be hated as a callous bastard than go through the pain of seeing her. No matter how much she protested otherwise, I believed that I could never be the person I had been before my accident, so I decided her life would be better without me. Maybe that wasn't my decision to make, but I felt it was the right one. I could not bring myself to face up to my responsibilities or to be honest about my feelings, so I decided to avoid the subject altogether in the hope it would go away.

Elaine was aware of the situation and, to be fair, offered to act as an intermediary if I wanted – but I wasn't sure what I wanted. I was flattered by Elaine's attention and was surprised some weeks later when one of the staff told me that she fancied me. At first I thought it was a joke, but we increasingly found ourselves talking about anything and everything and getting fonder of each other as time went by. Conducting a romance in hospital with my nurse was not exactly easy, nor could it be conventional. On one hand we were trying to keep it secret, on the other trying to be as 'normal' as possible. On Valentine's Day 1985 I sent her a bunch of red roses and had the card signed on my behalf from 'Mr Scilly' in a thinly veiled attempt to hide my identity. Obviously Elaine was aware of every detail of my medical needs, but for me to know that, despite all that, she still fancied me was a terrific boost to my self-esteem. And without the need to explain all the medical stuff, it meant that whatever came next in our future together, there weren't going to be any surprises.

Usually Elaine and I would just go to a pub in the evening, but one night I was carried by some mates up three flights of stairs to have dinner in Elaine's nurses' quarters with a group of friends. Everyone had a great evening, although having to be lifted back down the stairs and sneaked back onto the ward at 2.00 a.m. presented some difficulties and earned some disapproval from the staff on night shift.

Not long after that a curfew for patients was set at midnight and senior management moved Elaine away from me and onto a completely different ward. Although the reason given was that our relationship might cause problems with other patients who might not approve, clearly it was the hospital management who did not approve of our relationship, and it was more of an attempt to prevent us seeing each other. In many ways it made it easier for us, because at least now there could be no allegations of favouritism.

As time drifted on, so I became increasingly bored of hospital. I was still receiving at least one visitor a day but I was finding I had more free time as I became quicker and more efficient at getting through my daily routine. The days were becoming warmer and Dave, Dizzie, Tim and I were the undisputed Lairds of the Odstock Manor, pushing ourselves around the hospital complex, using Dizzie's strength to help us around the difficult bits. As the only paraplegic in the group, he helped us quadriplegics up the various ramps and would use his dexterity to put our money into the vending machines to buy drinks and sweets. In particular I remember one quiet day at about 6.00 p.m. when the staff were busy distributing the evening meals. Tim and Dizzie were in the TV room and Dave and I were in our four-bedded ward chatting. I'm not entirely sure which one of us instigated it, but for some reason we thought it would be funny to see how far we would get pushing Tim's bed out of the ward. The procedure was quite complicated. In order to push it, we each had to position ourselves correctly in our wheelchairs and apply our brakes to stop the force pushing us backwards. We then pushed the bed one arm's length, unlocked our brakes and moved ourselves forward one arm's length before reapplying our brakes and repeating the process.

After ten minutes, we had surprised ourselves on three counts: firstly that we had managed to push the bed out of the ward, down the side corridor and into the dining room; secondly that we had found the strength to do so; and finally, perhaps most surprisingly, that no one had seen us. Buoyed up with our success, we continued our progress through the dining room, out into a main corridor and into the large goods lift. Occasionally hospital porters and visitors passed us but obviously the sight of two quadriplegics pushing an empty hospital bed gave no cause for concern, and we were never challenged. We took the bed down one floor and, by then almost completely exhausted, mustered just enough strength to push it out through the last set of double doors and onto the car park directly below the window of our ward. The whole process had taken about an hour, and when we got back onto the ward, realising that no one seemed to be any the wiser, we pulled the curtain around Tim's now empty bed cubicle. An hour later Tim appeared, calling for a nurse to help him to bed, whilst Dave and I just sat there pretending to read the paper.

'Where's your bed?' enquired the nurse, pulling back the curtain.

'I don't know,' retorted Tim indignantly, as though he was somehow being held responsible. Catching our expressions, I think he sensed that we were involved.

Dave and I let them spend five minutes hunting for his bed before Dave looked out the window and asked, 'What's that in the car park?'

As spring slowly turned into summer, some eight months after my arrival, so the talk turned increasingly to the subject of leaving hospital. Having been so protected, and having felt so safe and secure within the unit, it was slightly uncomfortable to be thinking about leaving. Inside we had 24-hour specialist care to avoid pressure sores and autonomic dysreflexia, to ensure we did not overheat nor get too cold, to help with washing, dressing and going to the toilet; unwittingly we were becoming institutionalised, protected from the dangers of the outside world. Apart from meeting all of our physical requirements, the unit had its own social services advisor, who helped with information about financial benefits and housing. My advisor had been in contact with Southampton City Council about the prospect of finding me an adapted flat, but nothing was likely to become available until October 1985, and the hospital thought I would be ready to leave by mid July. To be honest, I almost couldn't care less; no matter what I said, it seemed that my mother and those responsible on the unit for my out-placement had their own plans for me and, for the time being at least, I was happy to go along with them. It was fast becoming clear that those plans involved me going to live with my mother, Andy and my sister Lucy in their semidetached cottage on St Mary's in the Isles of Scilly.

I had visited the islands earlier that year with Elaine as part of a 'weekend away' scheme to acclimatise patients to life outside the unit. With no other options on the table for a more permanent housing solution, final arrangements were made with the local health authorities and a date was set for me to permanently return to Scilly in July.

Elaine and I had to face up to what would happen to us when I left the hospital. We needed to talk. One evening towards the end of May 1985, I took Elaine to a pub in Salisbury. After a few drinks, I plucked up the courage and asked her if she would be prepared to come with me to the Isles of Scilly. I was under no illusion that it would be an enormously brave step for her, a massive decision which, for the time being at least, would mean forfeiting her career in nursing. Without any hesitation and to my complete surprise she said 'yes'. On a roll, I thought I would ask the next question –

'Will you marry me?' I asked, as I fumbled in my pocket to show her the diamond and platinum engagement ring my mother had given me for the occasion. Indeed it was she who suggested the idea of marriage. I had not wanted to ask Elaine to marry me first in case she then felt pressured to leave work and join me in Scilly. Now I was worried it would seem that it was like a reward for saying 'yes'. No matter in which order I asked it could have been misconstrued, but I needn't have worried. I got a 'yes' on both counts and, at the age of just nineteen, I found myself engaged to be married.

Shortly after, Elaine handed in her notice. Our announcement was not met with universal approval on the Spinal Unit, and I was summoned to a meeting with the senior nursing staff, who advised me that, in their view, a patient/nurse relationship was destined to fail. It was even implied that I was merely taking advantage of Elaine's specialist nursing skills to provide myself with my own dedicated carer. I felt really insulted by that. We were together because we loved each other, for no other reason, despite what others at the time may have thought. My only regret is that I didn't have the maturity at the time to make a formal complaint against such an allegation. But luckily I did have the maturity to trust my instincts and completely ignore their advice.

With Elaine's Austin Allegro laden with our belongings, my life savings of £200 in my pocket and a small farewell party gathered at the rear entrance to the unit, we waved our good-byes early one summer's morning and started the long drive to Penzance, where we were booked on the evening helicopter to St Mary's. I had mixed emotions. Certainly trepidation, but excitement too – my life's journey was moving into the next phase. As we turned out of the hospital, I looked at Elaine and put my hand on her lap.

'You OK?' I asked.

'I hope so,' she answered.

For both of our sakes, I hoped so too.

13

Brixham was the turning point. The weather was so bad during our week's enforced stay that one 45-foot yacht was shipwrecked metres away from our compound. I realised the extent to which the whole project was at the mercy of the weather. From now on, there could be no voluntary lay-days whatsoever. We would have to sail every day that we possibly could.

Blog entry, Day 12, Thursday 31 May 2007:

It's 1030 hours on Thursday 31 May. It's hard to believe we've been in Brixham for a week now, it seems more like a month. I'm writing this sat in the motorhome looking north across Torbay towards Torquay. I can't see Torquay because of the rain, nor can I hear myself think as it pounds the roof of the van. The first of the dozen or so coaches bringing tourists into the town has just arrived and we feel like goldfish surrounded in our iron-fence compound as hundreds of people file past and stare in at us all day. For the past seven nights we've gone to bed in expectation of leaving the following today. This morning, like the previous seven mornings, we've awoken to the disappointment of strong winds, rain, and the utter frustration of spending another day just waiting.

The crew are OK although all of them would be happier were we not sat around here – there are only so many jobs that Ian can think of for us to do.

Yesterday the boat which was wrecked in Sunday's storm was finally lifted out onto the hard, the huge metre-square hole on her port bow testament to the ferocity of the weather. We all felt for her owners as they sat and watched their beloved boat, only just recently restored at great expense, being lifted out by the salvage crane. It must have been heartbreaking for them.

Much to everyone's relief, the opportunity to leave Brixham and continue our journey finally presented itself on Friday 1 June, day 13 of our voyage. My blog for that day reads:

After eight days weather-bound in Brixham, we finally managed to set sail this morning at 1015 hours. As much as we liked Brixham and received wonderful hospitality from the Yacht Club and Rotary, we needed to move on. Rumours were already circulating that the event was over, but anyone who understands sailing and can read a weather report would have seen the problems we faced.

Anyhow, that was then, this is now – another car park, this time in Salcombe. It's been some years since I've been here but it is more like Kensington-on-sea, houses with price tags in excess of £1 million and a car park full of expensive 4 × 4s. In contrast, our encampment is more akin to a bunch of travellers, with foul-weather gear hanging from wing-mirrors and our generator running to give us power. However, the one saving grace is I have access to the internet so after I've finished my blog, I've got 37 emails to reply to ... !

I should say that today's sail was cracking, sadly it was all to windward, all 10 hours of it – just look at my *Where's Geoff?* link to see the evidence – but it was wonderful sailing close in around Berry Head, sailing past the entrance to Dartmouth, rounding Start Point so close you could see people by the lighthouse and then going close into East Prawle bay, it was all stunning coastline.

Morale is high tonight. Andy is cooking one of his trademark dinners, this time a spicy sausage stir fry and, if the forecast is correct, we should be in Plymouth tomorrow.

Andy was a surprise find in our search for crew. On paper he was not an obvious choice, but his business skills were instrumental in preparing our passage plan 'bible', which had become an invaluable reference source. But he was also confident in his handling of the RIB and willing to do whatever was asked of him. Before leaving, we hadn't give much thought or attached much importance to stills photography, so it was lucky for me that Andy not only possessed a decent camera, but knew how to use it. Whenever he was on RIB duty, he would take a great number of photos which, once ashore, we would download onto our respective laptops, and slowly they began to form a comprehensive photographic record of the voyage. To add to his long list of domestic credentials, he was pretty handy in the kitchen too and knew his cumin from his coriander, with a little help from the collection of Jamie Oliver cookbooks that he brought with him.

Cooking was always going to be a difficulty on the trip, and it proved to be so. When ashore, breakfast was easy: I don't eat it, Tim was easily catered for with a bowl of cereal and Elaine would have a piece of toast and a cup of coffee. The four guys sharing the motorhome, Spike, Joel, Mike and Andy, would be joined by Ian, who was sleeping in the Land Rover, and between them they would sort themselves out, usually with porridge and toast. Lunch, the same as when at sea, was mostly sandwiches and soup, normally prepared by Mike. But it was the evening meals which presented the greatest challenge. The only means of cooking was in one of the motorhomes, or often in both of them simultaneously, to accommodate the vast quantities needed for eight people. Neither motorhome had an oven, only a small twin-burner gas hob. Unfortunately the budget did not stretch to takeaways or eating in pubs or restaurants every night and, even if it had it would not have been practical to arrive ashore late at night, de-rig the boats, get changed, then eat out late, dragging along a tired five-year-old. In practice, evening meals were chosen to satisfy the majority, usually recipes that could be cooked in large pots, and the chefs rotated between Elaine and Andy, occasionally Ian, and sometimes a collaboration of all three. To eat at times later than 2100 hours was not uncommon, but the real difficulty was deciding where to eat. We managed several times to seat eight people around the tiny dining table in our motorhome but, more often than not, it was grab your food, and retire to your bunk to eat it in relative comfort. One advantage of cooking was the avoidance of washing up but, to be fair, the others never shirked their duties.

But perhaps Andy's greatest asset was his character. Not that the others were not charismatic, each in his or her own way, but Andy was very witty, gregarious, constantly jovial – the unofficial Personal Everest 'maintainer of spirits'. The project itself and our clear objective was the glue that kept the crew together, united by a common purpose and focused on their own responsibilities. But Andy wore his heart on his sleeve, and his open and frank assessment of people and our situation made him a useful sounding board for me when making decisions, and he was good for the morale of the team too.

Thankfully we managed to clear Salcombe after only one night, and headed for our next destination, Plymouth. My blog entry for Saturday 2 June records the events of the day:

> After a fairly uneventful night in a Salcombe car park, we left about 1030 hours. Little did I realise that I would end my day under tow only five hours later.
>
> As stunning as the scenery is overlooking the entrance to Salcombe, a spring tide at full ebb (going westwards) coupled with the southerly wind created a very localised sea state consisting of very high, very steep swells rolling into the entrance. They were certainly high enough to cause concern, and it was an hour before we could make our course.
>
> A matter of hours later the collar at the base of my mast sheered its rivets and the whole mast dropped into its box, a potentially dangerous situation if it worked its way through the hull. The RIB crew went into emergency procedures and within five minutes the rubber tender was launched and Ian had dropped *Freethinker*'s mainsail, not an easy feat in rolling seas and a good force 3 blowing. To prevent matters from getting worse, Ian remained in the support tender, slung between my main hull and starboard sponson, whilst holding the boom to prevent further damage – then followed a slow tow the final hour into Plymouth. Once ashore, we took the mast out to see the problem: a plastic collar supporting the entire weight of the mast, with only two rivets and a stainless steel wedge glued in place to prevent it slipping, had sheered and slid up the mast about 6 inches – a poor design that could have ripped the side of my hull out had we not acted quicker.

The rig failure happened very quickly and the bang which accompanied it was enough to snap me back into emergency mode. Within seconds I transmitted my message to *Everest One*, and with Andy now at the helm and Joel making *Freethinker* secure alongside, Ian was quickly aboard to drop the mainsail and prevent any pressure from the base of the mast inside ripping open the hull. The severity of the situation and the potential consequences were not lost on Ian and myself: they were a nervous few minutes whilst Ian clambered around my narrow deck and secured the rig. Had the wind been only a knot or two stronger, or the sea state slightly more bumpy, I have no doubt I would have lost the entire rig and perhaps even *Freethinker*.

Yet again, another tow and more torment. What would I do tomorrow? Come back to this spot before restarting the next leg? And it's not as though being towed was the preferable option anyway. No matter how long the tow rope and how slow and steady the speed of *Everest One*, *Freethinker* would snatch and jerk every time the tow line became taught, which would force my head, made heavier by wearing a helmet, to yank backwards, causing a nasty stabbing pain in my neck, at exactly the point where I had broken it. At the same time, if the rudder was not dead-centre, the tiller would be violently ripped from my hand with enough force to break a finger if I wasn't quick enough to react. Travelling in *Everest One*'s wake was also smelly from the diesel fumes and noisy from her knackered old engine. And as if that was not unpleasant enough, witnessing a member of the crew visiting the solicitors was enough to make even the most sea-fearing individual prefer to be sailing rather than under tow. Thankfully none of them ever had to visit the High Court.

Ian had radioed through to Spike, who was shore crew that day with Elaine and Mike, and by the time we were making our way past the Hoe and into Plymouth Yacht Haven, Spike had already identified a selection of tools for the job. Between him and Ian, the rivets were drilled and the offending mast collar repaired within a few hours, clearing the way for a 1000 hours start the following day.

It was yet another nine-hour sail, arriving Falmouth at 1900 on the night of Sunday 3 June. Fears over my backside were becoming a distant memory, although I still had the indignity of daily checks. Apart from the hiccup with the mast, the equipment was holding up and the crew were settling into their routines and responsibilities well. Yet again the road crew had done us proud and, despite turning up unexpected, had secured us an absolutely prize location for the vehicles, right on the edge of Mylor Harbour, a matter of feet away from the river and the beautiful view.

That night the Met Office forecast was borderline, but not in our favour. Both their shipping forecast and their inshore waters forecast warned of a southwesterly force 5, which was above the limits we had set in our risk assessments. Whatever the wind speed, with our next destination being Newlyn, the southwest wind would have been right on the nose anyway, and that alone may have decided whether we sailed into it or not. But the reason I made a note of this in my diary was because it was the first time I had bothered to check other weather websites, and it seemed it was only the Met Office who were forecasting force 5. All of the others were forecasting force 4, which, although at the upper limit, was within my capabilities. Based on the forecast, both speed and direction, Ian declared the following day a 'no-sail' day, and I was able to take the opportunity to venture into Falmouth and buy Elaine a birthday present for the following day. But I kept a quiet and private eye on the weather. That evening I once again reviewed the wind data for the previous twelve hours on several weather websites and, sure enough, at no point during the day had the wind exceeded force 4. Had the wind been in a favourable direction, we could have potentially lost a valuable day's sailing because of an overly pessimistic weather forecast by the Met Office. Perhaps I was just clutching at straws, trying to find any reason to press on, and I knew that these borderline decisions would be few and far between – but they could also be critical. I resigned myself to the fact that the Met Office had simply got it wrong, but I made a mental note to monitor the situation.

Celebrating her birthday in a motorhome – not the most salubrious of surroundings – was not necessarily what Elaine would have chosen, had she been given the choice. But the morning of

Tuesday 5 June 2007 was at least bright and sunny, and the whole crew gathered in Mylor car park by the side of the river to watch her open her presents. And it was a welcome distraction, at least for an hour early that morning, from the business of sailing.

At 0900, with the brief celebrations curtailed for the time being at least, Elaine put aside her new shoes and T-shirts and got back to the business of getting me dressed in my sailing gear and preparing me for another forty-five miles, nine hours, at sea. At 0945, and with a few passers-by looking on curiously from the quayside, I was launched and weaved my way sailing through the many yachts at anchor, out towards the main channel. For the first time in a long while, I had remembered to wear my helmet-cam, identical to my normal helmet but with a built-in camera. It was just as well, because leaving Falmouth I had a terrific sail, very fast but with a flat sea, very comfortable too. It was a bit of a fumble turning the camera on, and I had no idea if it was working, but if it did, it would be capturing some great footage from my perspective.

Unfortunately, the Chartplotter that was fixed to the port side of my cockpit had started to mist up due to water getting inside. Although supposedly waterproof, it's no great surprise that a sophisticated electronic item, when subjected to such a continuous drenching of sea water, does eventually leak. Spike had dismantled the housing, dried the unit out and re-sealed it as best he could, but the salt, having found its way in, just sucked up moisture, it was never going to get better. It meant that the unit was not only becoming temperamental in its operation, but it was also very difficult to see through the moisture on the inside of the screen.

It was more a nuisance than a major worry at this stage, but I would be needing a fully functioning unit for those passages where I would be out of sight of the coast. Besides which, it was good to have data from the Chartplotter on speed, course and position relative to the land. In the circumstances, effectively sailing blind, Ian gave me a course to steer using the Chartplotter on *Everest One* and, using my compass, I followed that course. Meanwhile, Ian phoned Raymarine from his mobile and a new unit was dispatched the same day.

We were just settling in for another long day at sea when, out the corner of my eye, a speedboat suddenly appeared. Bizarrely I could see my son Timothy, Mike and Andy, all of whom were on road crew that day, sitting in the bow of the boat as they raced towards us, and I saw them go alongside *Everest One*. It transpired that it was nothing more serious than having forgotten to pack our Thermos flasks of hot drinks, and they had commandeered a passing speedboat to bring them out. I'm sure we could have just about survived without them, but I wonder if it was partly an exercise to add some excitement to their day.

Having rounded the Lizard, the most southerly point on mainland Britain, I turned and made a course directly across the bay towards Newlyn. It was a stonking sail, exceeding 10 knots on several occasions as I surfed down the waves, the wind blowing 15 knots from astern. Sailing at such great speed, although exhilarating, is not without danger, not least from gybing or pitchpoling – in other words, flipping the boat head over heels. I could actually feel the adrenalin pumping as I fought to keep the boat in a straight line as she accelerated down the waves, and I had to continually monitor even the slightest wind shift to prevent the sail from slamming across to the other side and unbalancing me and throwing me into the sea. It really was edge-of-the-seat stuff, and I felt completely alert, a similar feeling to that of being petrified, but excited at the same time. It was a fantastic buzz.

Slowly, the unmistakable outline of St Michael's Mount detached itself from the coastline of Penzance behind and I could make out the picturesque fishing port of Newlyn on my bow. I had visited the town only a couple of years earlier, having studied the Newlyn copper industry as part of an Arts & Crafts metalwork assignment for my antiques degree. It was interesting to see the massively reduced fishing fleet that now operates from Newlyn, and to compare it to the huge fleets that used to operate there. And the late Victorian colony of metal workers and artists who settled there – it's a much changed place now.

We arrived too early and were forced to wait outside the harbour, just off the town beach, until the tide had come in enough to give access to the slipway. *Everest One* dropped anchor and I sailed alongside and was made fast.

Day 17, Tuesday 5 June 2007:

Sitting at anchor off Newlyn, waiting the for tide, looking at the old Penlee lifeboat slip brought back memories of that tragedy back in 1981, such brave guys.

Meanwhile, on shore, the road crew had been faced with a dilemma. There were two options available for establishing camp that day, either next to a funfair that was in town for the week, complete with big wheel, dodgems and on-demand candy floss, or Newlyn fish market car park, complete with the adjacent round-the-clock loading and unloading of fishing trawlers, fuel deliveries, the biggest ice-machine I had ever seen and, perhaps it's *pièce de résistance*, its smell. As it was Elaine's birthday, she was given the choice and opted for the latter. I was surprised at first, thinking she would prefer all the fun of the fair, but she had wisely put safety and security of our equipment as a priority over the inconvenience of noise and smell. And, to be honest, after an hour or so, we had gotten used to both. As a birthday treat, we even had a Chinese takeaway and watched some of the helmet-cam footage that I had taken that day, which came out much better than expected.

Having discarded the empty takeaway cartons and sprayed the motorhome liberally with a sickly sweet air freshener to disguise the smell of fish that had now permeated every crevice, birthday girl Elaine turned to me as I settled down to sleep that night and, shouting to make herself heard above the din of fishing trawlers unloading their catch, said, 'Don't you ever let anyone tell you that you don't know how to spoil the ladies.'

'The RIB's on fire, the RIB's on fire!'

The urgency in crew member Joel's VHF radio transmission was enough to fill me with horror, and quickly halted the TV interview I was doing with BBC South West, early that Wednesday morning.

No one else had heard Joel's transmission, only me, because I had been wearing my helmet with the VHF radio switched on.

'Shit. Spike. Quickly! Get down to the pontoon as fast as you can. Joel has just radioed to say the RIB is on fire!' I shouted.

Without needing to be told twice, Spike left at some speed, running down towards the pontoon where *Everest One* was moored, and where Joel had ventured down some minutes earlier to start the engine.

The lady interviewer and the cameraman looked uncertain whether to stay with me, still sitting in *Freethinker*, minutes from being launched from Newlyn, or whether to follow Spike and capture footage of the possible disaster that was about to unfold.

I had an anxious few minutes whilst I waited to hear the outcome. Elaine, Mike, Ian and Andy were blissfully unaware of the drama as they were back at the motorhomes in the fish market car park, getting changed into their sailing kit.

'It's OK,' came the calm voice of Spike over the radio, 'it's only the batteries shorting out and causing a bit of smoke, nothing I can't fix.'

I breathed a huge sigh of relief.

'Is everything OK?' asked the interviewer. I guess she was worried that we might not be going after all, and being dragged out of bed to interview and film me in the fish market car park at some ungodly hour would turn out to have been a complete waste of her time.

Worrying about the RIB only added to the anxiety I was already feeling about the prospect of sailing to St Ives that day, a voyage of some forty-five miles that would take me around Land's End.

Day 18, Wednesday 6 June 2007:

> Once at Land's End, the wind died, the currents and sea became very confused, it was quite eerie. The tide slowly carried us past Land's End, leaving Longships rocks and lighthouse to port. About an hour later the wind picked up from the northeast which meant a long, slow, cold and arduous beat up the north Cornish coast. The old tin mines clearly visible, clinging precariously to the sheer and rugged black cliffs.

Maybe it had been a subconscious psychological barrier that I had been unaware of, but rounding Land's End was strangely emotional. I didn't really know what or how I would think, finally turning the corner and heading north. But when it happened, rising and falling on the vast north Atlantic swell, craning my head backwards to look up at the iconic Land's End hotel above, it felt as though I was now entering unknown territory and the adventure was well and truly about to begin.

Thanks to the interview filmed earlier that morning, and broadcast at 1830 hours that evening on the local BBC channel, when we arrived at St Ives at 1930 everyone in the town knew of my imminent arrival. And so it was no surprise that we were met in St Ives Bay by a flotilla of dinghies from the St Ives Sailing Club, who provided an escort for me into the inner harbour, and that the harbour wall itself was lined with sightseers and well-wishers. Unfortunately, we arrived at dead low water and, with the harbour completely dried out, I had the indignity of being sat in *Freethinker* whilst the crew pulled her across the sandy harbour in front of scores of people, all applauding and cheering – now that was a classic goldfish-bowl situation.

Some months ago, when we had compiled the 'bible', we had noted that this particular leg, for the road crew at least, would be the shortest journey at only thirteen miles. So they had arrived early on in the day and, having spoken to the local lifeboat station master, had secured us, without doubt, the best view in town. Parked in line along the RNLI-owned harbour wall, the three vehicles looked very striking and imposing to all who passed.

For the first time in twenty-three years I met the consultant spinal surgeon, John Russell, who had treated me at Odstock Hospital when I had first broken my neck. John had long since retired and moved to St Ives so, seeing news of my voyage on TV, couldn't resist popping down to the harbour with his wife Sally, who was herself head of physiotherapy on the spinal unit at the same time. It was great to see them again – and with John immediately putting a hand on my forehead to check my temperature and Sally concerned about my seating posture in the boat, it was good to know that they still cared.

Later that night, having been told by Ian that the Met Office forecast was again just above our limits, so we would have to endure yet another lay-day, I went to bed, tired and exhausted, but feeling happy with our day's work. As I lay there in the privacy of the motorhome, listening to the evening strollers walking by, I could clearly hear them talking. 'Oh look, Dave, what's all this then?' – 'Blake Lapthorn summat, love, I dunno' – 'Some disabled thing, I think.' I would hear this all the time, wherever we went, and it always made me smile. Obviously I hadn't designed the vehicle branding clearly enough to inform passers-by. Must try better next time.

Day 19, Thursday 7 June 2007:

> I was feeling quite physically and mentally exhausted last night but so relieved to be finally heading in the right direction. Feeling much better this morning after a good sleep, I didn't even notice the seagulls, although Timothy has pointed out that they've been carrying out some overnight bombing raids and using our vehicles as target practice with some success – forgive me if I don't upload these particular pictures. What is it about little boys and poo that creates such hilarity?

Early on the morning of 8 June we set sail for Padstow. The previous day had been another frustrating day, delayed because of a Met Office forecast of force 5 that never materialised. In the event, with the wind in a favourable direction, we could have sailed, which only added to the frustration. But far from sitting around doing nothing, the crew took every opportunity they could to catch up on small jobs such as routine maintenance of the engine on *Everest One*, servicing the Land Rover and, with the new Chartplotter arriving from Raymarine, Spike installed it onto *Freethinker* – so when we did leave I could at least now see where I was going.

Day 20, Friday 8 June 2007:

> A mixed day. Left St Ives 0730 hours and towed out to sea. Completely windless for an hour. Made steady progress up NE Cornish Coast sailing into light northeasterly breeze. Spotted first basking shark of the trip about 0900 – they are easy to spot with large floppy rounded dorsal fins, unlike other sharks and dolphins. They are also more docile and tend to just roll along beneath the surface. You could certainly hit them if you did not take avoiding action and they don't exactly rush to get out of the way. We saw three in total, with the biggest about 15 foot long, small apparently by normal standards.
>
> Continued to beat up the Cornish coast against wind and tide to Padstow, arriving relatively early about 1700 hours, making our way up the narrow and very shallow River Camel.

Although sighting the basking sharks had broken the monotony, with long, windless periods and time rushing by, I elected on a couple of occasions to take a short tow from *Everest One* until the offshore breezes kicked in. They weren't necessarily long tows, maybe twenty minutes here, ten minutes there, but they were tows nonetheless, and the guilt that I felt for not sailing every inch of the way continued to eat away at me.

Unknown to us, behind the scenes, Susan Preston-Davis had worked her magic – and it was a great surprise when Elaine told us that Susan had spoken to Rick Stein's management in Padstow, or 'Padstein' as we learned the locals now call it, and all of us were treated to a fish and chip supper in his restaurant. I'm not sure I would normally have paid £9.50 for fish and chips, so had they not been free I would never have tried them. But they really were first class, and only highlighted the awfulness of those fish and chips we had consumed a fortnight earlier in West Bay. We never got to meet Mr Stein himself but his staff were a credit to him, and we all left the restaurant with full stomachs and high spirits.

One of the difficulties of the north Cornwall and Devon coastline was water, or rather the lack of it, particularly when leaving or arriving at a destination. And this was never so clearly illustrated as on the run of passages which included St Ives, Padstow, Bude and Ilfracombe. Our daily passage plan was always calculated to take advantage of the tide, for quick as *Freethinker* was with the wind in certain directions, in others, most notably anything forward of 100 degrees to port or starboard of the bow, she was incredibly slow. With tides running at anything up to 2 knots for six hours one way, and then up to 2 knots for six hours the other, it always made sense to pick a six-hour period to sail when the tide was in my favour.

But with the tides ebbing and flowing every six hours, it goes without saying that if we left on a high tide for a six-hour voyage and had the ebb tide flowing with us for six hours, we would arrive at our destination at low water. On this stretch of coastline in particular, the problem with this was that, because the sea bed was so shallow, arriving at low water could make it impossible to get within half a mile of our destination, simply because the harbours completely dry out. So, if we wanted to arrive at a destination at a time when there was enough water to get in, then typically we would be trying to leave when the tide was out.

It may seem straightforward, but the calculations needed to determine optimum tidal flow in my favour, to coincide with a time of departure when there would be sufficient water to leave and an estimated time of arrival when there was also enough water to enter the harbour, were extremely complex and were left to Ian – and boy was this where he excelled! Sometimes it meant unusual start times, sometimes even mid-afternoon or, worse, before dawn – but at least it meant we could continue to make progress.

Day 21, Saturday 9 June 2007:

> Thanks very much to the harbour master here in Bude, Kevin Benson, for making us so welcome and sorting out parking for the PE circus and spaces for the boats, not easy for such a busy holiday resort on a sunny weekend.
>
> We left Padstow at 0900 this morning for another relatively uninteresting slog in the light NE breeze; at least the tide was with me. Only saw one basking shark but he was a biggie, and countless gannets, guillemots and fulmars. Still no dolphins. It was a bit hazy so not easy to see the coastline but the silhouette of Tintagel castle is quite evocative and the neighbouring harbour of Boscastle a reminder of the floods a few years ago.
>
> On arrival here, Jeff Sacree, the owner of Gecko Headgear who provided me with my specialist helmet, was just coming ashore in his boat. It was a complete coincidence but good to see him and tell him in person how pleased I am with the helmet.
>
> Forecast still for light northerly winds, exactly the direction we need to go to Tenby, so we have decided to add an extra stop and head for Ilfracombe. It's about 30 miles and if the wind remains the same, it will make the trip to Wales a better angle for sailing. At least we are making steady progress now.

Our parking space for the night was behind Bude fire station. Having negotiated the busy river inlet, full of holidaymakers on the sandy beach either side and with only inches to spare under the hull of *Everest One*, we weaved our way as far as we could go upstream. *Everest One* was secured in a tidal lock, but there was nowhere secure to keep *Freethinker* overnight, and it was some distance from our encampment, so we took her on her launching trolley on a road trip of nearly half a mile and parked her alongside the motorhomes in the fire station car park.

That afternoon, for some reason, Spike had forgotten to switch off the Marinetrack device and, unknown to any of us, it was happily broadcasting *Freethinker*'s location coordinates via satellite to my website. Having just finished supper and with us all sitting around chatting, a young lady appeared in an electric wheelchair from behind the Land Rover.

'I'm glad I've found you,' she said. 'My name is Juliet and I've been following your progress since you left Southampton. I knew you were here because we tapped the coordinates into our sat nav.'

Blimey, our first groupie! We only spent an hour or so chatting, but I was really touched that someone I had never met before, someone I didn't even know existed, had been inspired enough by my story not only to have followed my voyage on the website, but to have taken the trouble to get in her car and drive some considerable distance to find us. It was my first ever encounter with 'fame' – I suppose you could call it. I felt unworthy and uncomfortable, the same as when people I knew well, like friends and family, praised me for attempting the expedition. But to know that complete strangers were in some way being inspired by what I was doing sat very uncomfortably on my shoulders. Every day I would read messages left on my blog, every single one supportive and encouraging, and many from people I did not know, but Juliet suddenly put a face to those people and, in an instant, they and their praise became real. It felt odd, but it felt strangely comforting too.

We managed to leave Bude the following morning and put in the extra leg to Ilfracombe, our final stop in England before heading north across the Bristol Channel to Wales. The following morning, whilst waiting in Ilfracombe to depart for Tenby, I wrote the following in my blog:

> I think it's fair to say that if there ever was a honeymoon period, it's long since over. Sailing daily, the guys crewing the RIB and the daily road crew trips have taken on an air of work rather than pleasure, and each day feels like 'business as usual'. I know there are many who would

love the opportunity to sail around GB and be supported by such a great team but the aches and pains are slowly creeping up on us all – certainly I'm noticing them. At times I think I'm the luckiest person alive to be sailing every day but there are some days, yesterday included, when being hunched up in such a tight space for nine hours is quite uncomfortable and boring. With my headgear setup with VHF radio and, with the Challenger being quite a wet boat, it's not practical to have a radio or even a phone, so nine hours can seem like a week.

At times I look at how far we've come and feel we've accomplished so much, other times I look at how far we've come and feel disheartened at the distance still to go, but at least making daily inroads means we are slowly but surely eating into the miles. One thing is for certain – the arbitrary figure of 60 days that I plucked out the air a year ago will not be met, not by a long way. Of course we intend to carry on until we finish, but it could well exceed 100 days. I would hate for anyone to have the impression of this being a walk in the park. Every day is very much a Personal Everest for every member of the team.

14

I watched the green, emerald-like Isles of Scilly slowly appear on the horizon and then grow in size as the helicopter neared. Set against the clear sapphire-blue waters of the Atlantic ocean, each fringed with golden sand, the islands appeared to sparkle like diamonds as the morning summer sun reflected off the greenhouses below. Against the deafening whining noise of the helicopter engine, it was impossible to hear a word anybody said on board. Elaine tapped me on the shoulder to get my attention. Looking through the small aircraft window, she pointed downward to the airport, where we could just about identify my mother and Andy waiting for us in the small car park. We waved but they didn't see us. This was it. This was my new home and, for the time being at least, I could think of a great many worse places to be.

My mother's home was a rented nineteenth-century stone-built semi-detached farm labourer's cottage owned by the Duchy of Cornwall Estate. In every sense it was a perfectly normal home – three up, three down – but this house had something extra-special: the view. Set back only a few yards from the beautiful isolated sandy beach at Porthloo, it had views across the bay to the capital, Hugh Town. And out to the west I could see many of the off-islands and, further still, right out to the north Atlantic Ocean beyond. It was the perfect vantage point from which to see all the comings and goings of ships and boats in the busy harbour.

In preparation for my arrival, one of the downstairs reception rooms had been converted into a bedroom for me, and the downstairs bathroom had a shower specially fitted. Being an older house, there was a step to the front door, the internal doors were very narrow and I still needed help to be wheeled from room to room in my heavy NHS wheelchair – but it was warm, comfortable and liveable.

It was July 1985, and there were five of us living in the house, including my young sister Lucy. This was the first time I had lived with my mother since I had left home aged sixteen, and the first time I had ever slept under the same roof as my new stepfather Andy. To complicate matters, I was now cohabiting with my fiancée. With so many issues, not least the fact that I was a quadriplegic and needed so much personal care from Elaine simply to live my life, the only surprise was that cracks in the family dynamic did not start sooner.

Elaine had introduced me to her parents in the spring of that year. It was a perfectly pleasant meeting and we had an enjoyable lunch at their house in Bristol. Although our relationship had been developing for some weeks, Elaine had thought it best not to tell them about us at that time. Even when she handed in her notice at Salisbury, her parents were under the impression that it was to work for me privately as my carer. Her instincts were proved right – when Elaine did break the news that we were to be married, perhaps more from shock than anything else, they made no secret of their disapproval. Whilst it is understandable that they wanted what was best for their daughter, they openly voiced concerns about my disability, and the discussions were always about how Elaine's life would be ruined because of it. It was a difficult time for Elaine, who was torn between not wanting to upset her parents, whom she loved dearly, and feeling embarrassed that their old-fashioned and uninformed views were so hurtful to me. She did what she thought was right and, in an effort to keep the peace, adopted a policy of only telling them what she wanted them to hear. What she really needed at that time was their unconditional support, but without it, and living with me and my family so remotely on Scilly, it was a lonely time for her.

If I was to have a honeymoon period as a quadriplegic in the outside world, then living on Scilly was to be it. Just about everyone in the small island community had heard about my accident, and some, like the local Round Table group, had even played a part in getting me repatriated by raising money. I was made most welcome wherever I went – whether to the shops or to the pub, the reception was always warm and the thought that I was disadvantaged in any way because of my disability never even crossed my mind. There was a 'can do' attitude, and it made for a non-threatening existence whilst I considered what my future held. Of course some places remained inaccessible, but there was always a pair of willing hands to help bump me up the steps into the pub, drag me over the sand or help Elaine push me up a hill. I'm very grateful for that immediate acceptance by the islanders because I didn't feel I was a burden on them, nor did I feel any injustice because of the way I was treated as a disabled person – there would be plenty of time for that later in my life.

Of all things, it was my weight which continued to pose a threat to my wellbeing. I was discharged from Odstock weighing less than eight stones and the doctors put me on a high-risk register for the likelihood of getting pressure sores. In an attempt to fatten me up, I was prescribed a liquid carbohydrate drink and was made to drink pints of the stuff every day. Unfortunately, it filled me up so much I simply could not eat normal food. The obsession with my weight continued, and Cornish Social Services even threatened to section me under the Mental Health Act if I did not put on weight, which really troubled me. Apart from Elaine, who actually witnessed everything I ate, it seemed that no one believed me, and that really upset me and gave me many sleepless nights. It was like being accused of a crime I had not committed. Each week, Elaine would push my wheelchair a mile or so to the island medical centre, where she would lift me onto the weighing scales. Since I was unable to lift my paralysed legs off the floor myself, the nurses would use bandages to truss my legs up under my chin, like a turkey before it goes into the oven. I suffered this indignity week in, week out for months until I refused to go any more. I wasn't ill, I didn't feel ill, it was the worry and pressure that I was being put under because of my weight that was causing the problem.

Elaine and I quickly got into a good daily routine, and as time moved on I began to lose the feeling of dependency I had subconsciously developed at the Spinal Unit. Once washed, dressed and into my wheelchair, I would be pushed through to the living room, where I sat at the dining room table, looking out to sea. Usually, at my mother's instigation, I would receive, Queen-like, a succession of well-meaning visitors to the house, all telling me how difficult everything had been for my mother since learning her son had become paralysed, all saying how lucky I was to be on Scilly, and all expressing their delight at seeing me looking so cheerful. I'm not quite sure what they expected from me but, no matter how I actually felt, I was certainly not going to let anyone see anything but a cheerful face. At least once a day Elaine and I would just go for a walk around the lanes and footpaths nearby. It not only gave me an opportunity to take in some fresh sea air, but it was important to get out of the house and experience a bit of space away from everything. Having spent so much time in the Caribbean in recent years, I had become used to the islands' exotic splendour so I did not immediately consider the beauty of Scilly to be anything out of the ordinary. But I did take great pleasure, as I had always done on beaches all over the world, simply sitting, slowly inhaling the salt-rich air through my nose, tasting it on the back of my throat, just looking out to sea and thinking. Whether it be a still, warm day or blowing a gale, the many moods of the sea provide a great medium for thoughts, some nostalgic, some forward-looking, but always private and always calming. It was not uncommon for Elaine to push me over the road and leave me to sit there on my own on Porthloo beach, wrapped up in my quilted jacket and woolly hat, just looking out to sea. I knew that my mother was watching me from the living-room window behind me, I could sense her concerned attention and, in some ways, that violated my privacy, but it was a small price to pay for having a bit of time alone.

The loneliness and isolation that Elaine had been feeling since announcing our relationship to her parents was made worse by my mother, who grew increasingly maternal and protective in her attitude towards me. As the days turned into weeks, it was clear that my mother began to consider Elaine a threat. At first, she would try and pre-empt Elaine in her care for me, for example ensuring it was she who emptied my leg bag of urine before Elaine noticed it was full, or rushing to fill up my glass of water before Elaine. Then the vacuuming started at 7.00 in the morning, a routine she started to perform daily, purposefully banging against the bedroom door with the vacuum nozzle – partly my mother's way of suggesting laziness on Elaine's part and partly to prevent us spending private time together. Later my mother would speak to me secretly, trying to undermine Elaine's competence: she would complain that Elaine had not done the washing-up or that Elaine had not helped with the ironing, or that I was in danger of catching a cold because Elaine wasn't putting enough warm clothes on me. She was bringing into question my choice of future wife – and that was a battle she could not win. It was a tough time for Elaine, though, unable to confide her feelings to anyone, not even me for fear that I might side with my mother. Perhaps because of my immaturity I let it go on too long, but there did come a point when my patience was finally broken and I would tolerate the conflict no longer.

Despite some talk of voluntary work with the island's tourist board, which came to nothing, I had not earned a penny since leaving hospital and had little prospects of a proper job. The same applied to Elaine, but with looking after me taking up much of her time and the physical effort needed to lift me and push me everywhere, finding a job to suit her circumstances was not easy. As autumn arrived on Scilly and the tourist season came to an end, many of the locals turned their attentions to potato picking to supplement their income. One afternoon, my mother entered the front room where Elaine and I were drinking a cup of coffee.

'It's a beautiful day out there,' my mother said. 'Robin up at the farm said that if you want to earn a few pounds, Elaine, he could do with some extra help picking potatoes in the fields.'

This was not the first time my mother had suggested this, and I had already clearly explained the situation to her – as had Elaine.

'Thanks Patti, but I lift Geoff at least a dozen times a day and you've said yourself that potato picking is back-breaking work. What would happen if I hurt my back?'

My mother quietly left the room, and we heard her climbing the stairs to her bedroom above where Andy was taking an afternoon nap. We heard mumbled talking, followed by Andy's heavy boot-steps stomping down the stairs.

He burst into the front room, rushed up to Elaine and, sticking his finger right in her face, shouted, 'So, potato picking is too fucking good for you is it, Mrs Lardy Dah? It's OK for us to do it and to put food on your table but you're too precious to pick a few potatoes!'

Both Elaine and I were stunned. I'd never seen anyone so possessed. He was like a mad man, shaking and trembling as he threatened her.

'That's enough,' I shouted. 'How dare you? How dare you speak to Elaine like that!'

I knew what my mother had done. She had gone upstairs with the intention of firing him up, knowing that by twisting the conversation it would infuriate him. She succeeded, but her motives backfired.

The following day, and still dumbstruck by his tirade, Elaine pushed me out of the house and up the hill to a neighbour. As we went, I could see my mother peeking out from behind her bedroom curtain. We left my mother's house in exchange for a wooden holiday chalet that we were kindly loaned, rent-free, by a neighbouring farmer. The chalet was very small but it was all we had and we were very grateful. Normally only used in the summer, the thin-walled wooden chalet had a small bedroom with twin beds, a kitchenette/dining area and a bathroom which I could not get into because the door was too narrow for my wheelchair. It had a two-bar electric heater to keep it warm, powered by an up-rated electrical meter. What we saved in rent, we more than made up for in electrical costs, often more than £30 a week in heating just to stop the net curtains freezing to the condensation on the inside of the windows. There was a step into the chalet at the end of a muddy path. Once again, I was effectively housebound.

We started getting visits from Andy at the chalet demanding that we pay back-dated rent for our time living with them. Even before I left hospital, I had offered to pay rent and had the relevant paperwork sent to me by social services so I could claim it on my mother's behalf. But, on the basis that it would constitute subletting a Duchy property – and because my mother said she would not take money from her son – the suggestion was dismissed and the matter forgotten. Andy's visits became quite menacing, so one day I got Elaine to push me into town to Barclays Bank to withdraw some money so I could pay them the money and bring an end to the situation. As was not uncommon, I couldn't get into the bank because of the steps so I sat outside and sent Elaine in on my behalf with my completed withdrawal slip.

She returned moments later, in shock and pale-faced. 'It's all gone,' she said, 'It's all gone. Your mother came in yesterday and withdrew all of your savings.'

My mother had withdrawn almost £500, money I had saved from my disability benefits, all the money I had in the world. Because the bank teller knew my mother, she considered it OK to give her my entire savings when she requested it, allegedly, on my behalf.

We now had no money whatsoever and my mother knew this. I can only speculate her motives, but she knew I had been thinking about leaving the islands and maybe it was her way of trying to stop me.

If she had been concerned that we were planning to leave, then she was right to be. As beautiful and as friendly as Scilly is, it is no place for a nineteen-year-old quadriplegic. There were no job prospects, indeed no life prospects, for us as a couple. Leaving was not a difficult decision to make. All I had to look forward to was a lifetime of gossip, being mothered and being housebound. My one regret is that, leaving in such haste, we did not give ourselves enough time to say our goodbyes and thank-yous, nor did we have the opportunity to explain the reasons for our departure to everyone. We took out a bank loan, booked our tickets on the ferry and, with Elaine's faithful Austin Allegro packed to the roof with all of our worldly belongings, we left in January 1986.

I can't say or remember exactly why I considered Southampton to be destination of choice for our return. To be honest, most of my friends and family lived nearer Portsmouth and just about all of Elaine's friends and family lived in Bristol, but Southampton it was.

We found out very quickly that we no longer had the Scilly security blanket wrapped around us. Here we quickly found that we would have to fight every inch of the way for everything we were going to need, and first on that list was housing. With no fixed abode and staying in a B&B, it was not possible to get paid my disability benefits, not even to have a bank account. And with no address Elaine couldn't start to earn money as an agency nurse, so we could not even afford to pay a deposit on a rented flat. It was a catch-22. Thankfully, after much negotiation, Elaine's father agreed to act as a guarantor on a ground-floor two-bedded flat that we found in the Freemantle area of the city. There were two steps up to the front door so I knew from the outset that I would once again be housebound. I could only access the bathroom by being dragged through the door on a narrow kitchen chair, but the flat was warm and clean, it provided us with an address so I could start to apply for disability benefits and, most important of all, it was our first home.

Determined that her father would never have to be called upon as guarantor for our rent, Elaine's first priority was to get some work as an agency nurse. At first she began taking eight-hour day shifts, but it quickly became apparent that they were not as lucrative as the night shifts, which paid almost double the hourly rate. It was one thing for me to be left in the house during the daytime, on my own – at least I could watch TV or speak to people on the telephone. But when Elaine worked nights it was extremely hard on both of us. With Elaine needing to be at work by 8.00 p.m., I would have an early dinner and then go to bed by 7.30 p.m., the TV remote control resting on my chest, the telephone placed to my left and a glass of water on a table next to me with a long rubber tube taped to the headboard so I could drink if I was thirsty. And there I would stay, alone and fearful of anything that could happen, until 8.00 the following morning. Tired from her long night shift, on her return Elaine would then wash and dress me and lift me into my chair. I would spend the day sitting quietly in the front room typing on my new Amstrad word-processing machine or watching TV whilst Elaine slept. It was not ideal, but we knew nothing else and we needed the money.

When we did go out socially, the community support that we had enjoyed in the Isles of Scilly was conspicuous by its absence wherever we went in Southampton. I lost count of the occasions that I was refused entry to restaurants, pubs or night clubs on the grounds that I was a 'fire-hazard', each occasion as hurtful as the last. People didn't seem to consider that I was a human being. They only saw the wheelchair. Having been able-bodied to the age of eighteen, it was the realisation that I was being discriminated against because of my disability that I found hardest to stomach. For the first time since my earliest days out as a disabled person in Salisbury, I found myself wanting to shout out 'I wasn't always disabled', as though it would make them change their attitude towards me.

One Sunday, on a rare day off from his lucrative estate-agency job in London, my friend Sean was visiting and a group of us decided to go to the Odeon cinema in Southampton to watch a film. I knew the cinema had a flight of steps up to the entrance, but we assumed that the management would not mind me being carried up them – after all, everything was on the level once inside. Upon enquiring, Sean was told that I was not allowed in because of the risk I posed to other cinema-goers, should they have to evacuate the building in the event of an emergency. Sean bought me a ticket anyway. When the cinema staff were out of sight, three of my friends lifted my chair up the steps and pushed me swiftly into the cinema just as the film was beginning. A matter of minutes later, an usher appeared and asked me to get out of my wheelchair and into one of the cinema seats. Aware of the danger of getting a pressure sore on a cinema seat, and certain that such a move would surely increase the risk in the event of fire, not reduce it, I declined. When he asked me to leave the cinema, I refused. Minutes later, the manager appeared and repeated the request to leave and I repeated my refusal, at which point he grabbed my wheelchair and tried to push me out of the cinema. Outraged and feeling that I was being assaulted, I elbowed his arms off of my chair and it was at that point that he called the police. When they arrived, I was cautioned and evicted from the premises.

Still shaking and feeling sick at the indignity and prejudice I had just been subjected to, we returned home. The others had picked up a pizza on the way home and were busily chatting away about the afternoon's events but I could not eat – my blood was boiling. It was the first and most stark display of prejudice I had ever been subjected to, and for no reason other than that I was in a wheelchair. Is this what other disabled people were being subjected to? I learned that day that becoming disabled had also removed my physical ability to stand up for myself.

Being 6 feet 3 inches tall meant nothing when I was sitting in a wheelchair, and could not retaliate against even the smallest of officious cinema ushers.

For the first time in my life I decided to use the media to get publicity. I picked up the telephone to the local BBC radio station, where I was given a couple of minutes, live on air, to vent my grievance. Buoyed up by the support from the presenter and the outrage of subsequent contributors to the programme, I wrote a letter the following day to Odeon Cinemas detailing the event and explaining how upset I had been. To be fair to Odeon, they did have the courtesy to reply – but the letter informed me that I was banned forthwith from every Odeon cinema in the country.

I realised that being subjected to this kind of discrimination was turning me into a different person, a person I neither recognised nor liked. By nature I was a happy-go-lucky chap, all my life I had avoided conflict, and I preferred the company of positive, outward-thinking people. I don't recall ever getting 'angry' at anything before this. As an able-bodied person I might have complained about the odd plate of cold food in a restaurant but now, as a disabled person, I realised that, in order to make my voice heard, I was changing. The succession of injustices that I felt made me cross inside, and extremely stressed – and all of this because I was disabled. I wasn't angry at my disability – I have never had an issue with my disability. What made me angry was the prejudice and injustice I faced because of it. I didn't like the 'angry' me, but this was one of the cruel side effects of disability that I had not bargained for. Maybe it was my genetic make-up that gave me the determination to fight injustices when they arose, maybe it was because I had experienced life as an able-bodied person and felt I continued to deserve the same respect – but I was feeling this anger and hurt because of my disability, and I resented that.

Preparing for my circumnavigation

◄ Testing the crane fitted to the Land Rover

▶ Branding one of the motorhomes

▲ Elaine and Spike with the Land Rover

▲ Concentrating, during a final trial run

▲ All systems go

▲ With Sir Robin Knox-Johnston and Tracy Edwards before the start

▶ The team ready for the start (clockwise from the left): Joel Whalley, Ian Clover, Andy Cockayne, Sarah Outen, Mike 'Spike' Spencer, Mike Golden, Elaine, me and Timothy

◄ 10 minutes to go

▶ The Southern Union Chorus

▲ Off to a lively start – seconds before the near-disaster

Face down in the water ▶

▼ Rescued

▲ Testing a new lifejacket after the accident

▲ Out into the Channel – the view from the RIB

▲ How it should be – between the sea and the sky

◄ Off Dorset's chalk coast

▼ Ian keeping in contact

▲ We have lift-off

▲ Arrival at Portland

Passing Portland Bill the next day ►

▲ The entourage on the quay at West Bay

▲ Entering Brixham

▲ My lunch is conveyed to me in a shrimping net

► Into the waves off Salcombe

▼ The slipway at Plymouth

► Eddie

► Ian and Spike

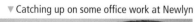
◄ Timothy with his mackerel at Plymouth

▼ Catching up on some office work at Newlyn

▲ Rounding Land's End

▲ Across Ilfracombe harbour at low tide

▲ Off Skomer

◄ Honoured by the Fishguard Rotarians

► This is the life – scudding before the breeze, after leaving Fishguard

▲ Synchronising watches –

and launching at Aberystwyth ►

▲ Unwinding at Oban

◄ Not every port of call had a slipway

◄ Mike and Spike

On the Crinan Canal ▼

▲ A tense moment, as the sea lock at Ardrishaig threatens to stir us into a cappucino

 The Caledonian Canal

Dolphins in the Moray Firth

Bass Rock, screaming with gannets

▲ A seal breakfasts at Dunbar

◄ Speeding southwards

▲ Sometimes there was no access for our crane

◄ Andy with Timothy

Forty winks at Wells-next-the-Sea

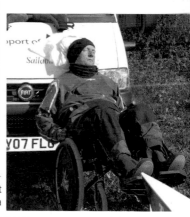

◄ Passing a wind farm off the Norfolk coast

'This way up' say the flags

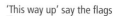

Done it!

In the autumn of 1986 I took a call from Barry Rice, my old employer on *Endless Summer*. I had not spoken to him since my accident, and his call took me by surprise. He had got my phone number from my mother and, explaining that he was back from the Caribbean for a short while, asked if he could come over to see me. Not having given Barry much thought since my injury, I agreed, and a couple of hours later he was sitting in my front room drinking a cup of coffee.

He had come to see how I was feeling and how I was coping, which I thought a noble gesture. Our conversation was perfectly convivial, and he explained that he was back in the UK because, ironically, he was unprepared to risk letting his wife Rosalind have their first baby in Tortola. They wanted the safety and protection of an NHS maternity hospital in England. We talked about various things but he never referred to my accident or his decision not to fund my repatriation, and I didn't ask. Nor did he mention the reason behind the company's refusal to acknowledge that I was in the Caribbean to work for them, but he did tell me about the lovely new villa he and his wife had recently bought in Tortola. The more he spoke, the more I looked at him and found myself beginning to feel a dislike for somebody that I never felt before. I looked into his eyes and realised that in a matter of minutes I had come to detest this man so very much. The accident was not his fault, but I believed that his actions immediately thereafter were causing the difficulties I now faced and he had, albeit inadvertently, just rubbed my nose in it. I thanked him for his visit and, when he had finished his cup of coffee, I bid him farewell.

I was incensed. He had stood in my home, a flat that he could clearly see was unsuitable for me, and had told me all about his lovely new villa. He then had the nerve to tell me that rather than entrust the birth of his newborn child to the Caribbean health service – the same health service that he knew I had endured with a broken neck – he had flown his wife back to the UK to give birth. To that point I'd not even entertained the thought of litigation against my former employer, but his visit changed all that.

I asked Elaine to pass me the phone.

'Hello? International Directory Enquiries, please. I'd like the name of a lawyer on the island of Tortola in the British Virgin Islands. Just give me the name of the first one on the list.'

Before Barry Rice had even left our drive, I was speaking to Mr Archibald QC at his chambers in Tortola – and so began a twelve-year law suit against Barry Rice and Endless Summer Charters.

15

My first ever sail across the Bristol Channel was a damp, wet and misty affair. Somewhere en route we had passed the island of Lundy – I could see it on my Chartplotter – but with visibility at times less than 500 yards, all I could do was rely on my instruments to steer a course for Tenby, and rely on the radar on *Everest One* to warn me of any potential shipping dangers. We passed close to a couple of small fishing vessels, but ever since rounding Land's End it had been noticeable how few sailing boats we had seen. Perhaps it was the lack of easily accessible marinas, but we had probably seen no more than two or three yachts in the past week.

Tenby was a pleasant surprise. In fact I didn't know what to expect, with many people telling me it was a little piece of England in Wales. Certainly the orderly and colourful Georgian houses that lined the parade along the cliff top would not have looked out of place on Brighton seafront.

The road crew had driven their longest leg to date, in excess of 300 miles, up the M5 from north Devon to Bristol before crossing into Wales and following the coast road around to Tenby, arriving only minutes before us. The Tenby Sailing Club had allowed all three vehicles and trailers to park in their tiny car park on the harbour front, and within minutes of arriving the road crew had hooked up mains electricity, topped up the freshwater tanks and even secured a key for the club showers.

It was another tricky harbour entrance for me. In these little harbours that dry out, with no marina or pontoons, local pleasure boats and fishing boats are often tethered fore and aft, with a line from the harbour wall securing the bow of the boat and a stern anchor set some yards behind to prevent the boat swinging around. It's all well and good, but not so easy when trying to negotiate your way through the moored boats to the slipway in a twelve-foot-wide trimaran with no brakes.

It was 1800 hours by the time we finally came ashore, where we were met by a small group from the local Rotary group and the sailing club. But there was another visitor waiting for me, a chap in a wheelchair who introduced himself as Alan Thomas. I'd seen some comments left on my website from Alan wishing me well but I had never thought he would go to the trouble of coming to see me. Whilst chatting in the evening sunshine I learned about his disability, cerebellar ataxia, which is degenerative, and how it was slowly affecting his body, but he was so cheerful and positive in his outlook. I felt lucky in many ways by comparison, not least because, as brutal as my accident was, and even there is no cure for spinal injury, at least it is not going to get any worse, nor do I suffer any pain. Meeting someone like Alan, who was so positive yet was living in the knowledge that his condition was only ever going to get worse, really made me stop and think. I found it difficult to fathom how Alan, and for that matter Juliet, whom I had met only a few days earlier, could heap praise upon me and say that I was inspiring them. Certainly anyone who does not understand the intricacies of different disabilities could be forgiven for believing that my sailing expedition was in some way 'special', but I think that for disabled people like Alan and Juliet, and for the many others who wrote to me, what made the difference was the positive high profile being given to someone with a disability who was not letting his disability be a barrier to ambition – and that I guess is a very powerful message. It's not a message I consciously set out to promote, but finding myself as some kind of 'unofficial ambassador' for those disabled people who believe in getting on with their lives, it was a responsibility that I was proud to bear. But as a disabled person who has lived and breathed disability for many years, and seen thousands of people doing the same, I knew that people like Alan and Juliet were living their own Personal Everests every day – only their story, like those of thousands of others like them, never makes the papers.

That night, after Alan left, we ate a takeaway pizza and I retired to the motorhome to catch up on emails, to write my blog, and to get an early night. One message left on my website by an employee of my sponsor didn't register as too important at first, but it was to prove prophetic:

> Message from J White – The sail to Tenby sounds better than the drive! My condolences to the motorhome massive. Keep an eye out for the tank ranges at Castlemartin, one of my old stomping grounds. Thinking of you all in a stunning part of the world. To fair winds and empty roads. We are all following you closely here in the office. Good luck!

Having read my messages, I finished my blog for day 24, Tuesday 12 June 2007:

> It appears we may have a motorhome problem on the horizon. The crew motorhome we have is on a three-month hire, May, June and July. With the event almost certainly over-running by another month, I called the motorhome company to extend the hire only to discover there are other bookings on the van. So unless we can find another vehicle to rent for all of August capable of sleeping four individuals separately, then we are going to have to invest in some tents!
>
> Going to try and make Dale tomorrow, only a short hop but in the right direction. Another issue regarding lack of water in the harbour tomorrow morning so it looks like an 0700 start to catch tide and wind, yippee!

And finally, at nearly 2330 hours, having been up since 0500 and having spent eight hours at sea, I fell asleep.

Blog entry, Day 25, Wednesday 13 June 2007:

> Left Tenby 0700 this morning for Dale. Had an absolutely cracking sail, perhaps the fastest and most exhilarating in its entirety so far this trip. We beam-reached out through the passage with a following tide, often in excess of 8 knots. Both wind and tide in my favour meant we sailed fast but the shallow water caused a lot of confused sea, and by 0730

hours I was completely soaked with very cold Irish Sea from head to toe. It's one way to wake up and, to be honest, not my favourite.

We continued to sail well until we were diverted around a local gunnery range by an officious gunnery protection vessel, which meant sailing three miles out into extremely confused seas. The following three hours were like riding a roller coaster, and at times the wind blowing over the now flooding tide caused the biggest and most confused seas yet. I had to let the mainsail forward of the beam to try and de-power the rig and prevent her from nose-diving. Even so, I continued to make in excess of 6 knots. We arrived Dale at 1300 tired but completely exhilarated.

At first I didn't let on just how cross I was about the gunnery range incident, but I was really upset by it. When I first encountered the problem off Lulworth some weeks earlier, it had been a slightly different situation. There was a potential danger and, with calm seas and light warm breezes, it caused me as skipper of my boat no hardship to move out of the area. However, on this occasion, as forewarned by the message on my website the night before, the Castlemartin gunnery range did indeed cause me difficulties. The gunnery range vessel was quick to pounce when it saw us and, having spoken to Ian on the VHF, he instructed me to move nearly three miles further out to sea. I had been sailing with the wind behind me and a following tide so I was moving quickly and the sea state was calm. Being forced out to sea took me further from my direct course and wasted more than an hour, in which time the tide turned, and now, with wind over tide, I was forced to sail in potentially dangerous conditions, *Freethinker* being tossed all over the place. I was very angry and had only acquiesced because directed by Ian, even though it was against my better judgement. It didn't help that I was by now extremely wet, cold and, to be honest, frightened. I don't like sailing *Freethinker* in those conditions at the best of times but in doing so then I was putting my own safety in jeopardy. I later learned that if a skipper of a vessel believes he has a strong navigational case for retaining his course, then he should do so and gunnery operations would be suspended. I should have had the courage of my convictions and done just that. There is no doubt in my mind that I had a valid a case, and I made it clear to Ian that should a similar situation arise in the future I would, depending on the circumstances, make up my own mind whether to change course or not. It was the first and only time I ever challenged Ian over a matter of navigation. To be fair, he didn't disagree with me, but I think he was more surprised at how upset I had been over the incident. Sat in the relative comfort and stability of *Everest One*, and unable to see the agony on my face behind my visor, I think he simply did not realise.

Day 25, Wednesday 13 June 2007:

Dale is a small harbour tucked just inside the northwest entrance to Milford Haven. From our camp in the car park, courtesy of Dale Sailing, I can look up river to the refinery and see huge tankers at anchor.

For the second day on the trot, I was met by Alan Thomas, a local chap who has been following my travels, and I really appreciate him taking the effort to come and see me arrive.

We had hoped to be sailing to Fishguard tomorrow and all was set, including the passage plan requiring an 0335 start (no, that is not a typo) to get through the notorious Jack Sound in time before the tides turned. However the 1800 shipping forecast has just issued a weather warning claiming potential force 6 in the west of our region. I'm not a great lover of Met Office forecasts, ever since the Michael Fish incident – on balance they always seem to forecast worse than the weather that actually arrives. I find the other websites to be far more accurate but, with the boat difficult to sail in winds exceeding 15 knots in seas bigger than moderate, what do you do when the Met Office says potential force 6? No doubt we'll be sat here tomorrow frustrated at not going and another day wasted, but without crystal balls it's a difficult decision to make. The boat is certainly up to big winds but it's the seas that can cause the problem, especially with big following waves. The last thing we need is another lay-day due to weather – it just increases the pressure on us all as time will become a major factor.

Sure enough, the Met Office forecast of force 6 never materialised, although the force 5 that did arrive would have been beyond our limits. With yet another enforced lay-day, the team headed into Milford Haven, where we spent a somewhat surreal afternoon playing ten-pin bowling and eating pizza, but at least it took our minds off sailing for a while.

Day 27, Friday 15 June 2007:

> Left Dale 0415 this morning in complete darkness, Ian finally deciding on going outside Jack Sound which proved good decision with strong tides in our favour and few overfalls. The number and variety of seabirds between Skomer and Skokholm islands was simply amazing, most particularly thousands of puffins, so many the sea and sky was black with the little clown-like birds. Hurriedly flying single-file in strings of twos, threes, fours or more, only a metre above the water, backwards and forwards to their nest sites on the islands. Those that we passed on the water you could see had bills full of sand eels – it was a privilege to see them at dawn in the early morning sun.

Less than an hour later we arrived at Ramsey Sound, where I was quite literally tossed around in extremely violent overfalls for almost forty minutes. Even with no wind I was being pushed through at 9 knots. I try not to over-dramatise situations, but this was worthy of an adrenalin rush. The waves were appearing from nowhere and coming at me from all directions, their white foaming crests breaking all around. They towered over me, and with zero wind *Freethinker* was just spinning out of control as I was carried through what felt like a washing machine. It was the longest forty minutes I have ever spent at sea, and being sat so low down in a tiny, fragile dinghy, I was unashamedly petrified.

We arrived in Fishguard relatively early at 1300, some nine hours after leaving Dale. With a mile or so still to go, the Fishguard RNLI fast inshore RIB raced its way out to escort me in. I smiled when I saw Timothy riding up front in the bow.

'Hello Daddy, I'm a lifeboat man,' he shouted as they passed by.

I was pleasantly surprised on rounding the enormous breakwater to see such a large, empty harbour – it was vast. The Stena ferries which sail across to Ireland were only in harbour a couple of times a day, and when these monsters weren't there it was a remarkably peaceful place. My welcoming committee consisted of just about every member of the Fishguard RNLI, including the station manager and, for the third consecutive location, my new friend Alan Thomas. Tucked away in a far corner of the harbour, right at the beginning of the breakwater and difficult to see at first, is a tiny little inner harbour which is the domain of Fishguard RNLI. Entering it, I couldn't believe that it hid an enormous, top of the range, Trent class lifeboat. And at the end of the inner harbour was the slipway leading up to the RNLI station, without doubt the steepest slipway I have seen in my life. So I was somewhat nervous when told it was my only option for getting out. With the Land Rover parked at the top, and its steel wire cable winch extended, ever so slowly I was pulled in *Freethinker* up the 45-degree slope, the only thing stopping me flipping over backwards being the winch-wire made fast to my bow.

But the ride was worth it when ex-RNLI coxswain Roger gave me a mug full of whisky. 'This'll warm you up,' he said, and sure enough it did.

The RNLI in Fishguard made us very welcome, and once again provided us with all facilities whilst allowing us to park in the best spot in town.

Day 27, Friday 15 June 2007:

The RNLI guys here have been so kind. I can also recommend their child-minding services; Timothy has so far had a tour of the main Trent class lifeboat, a trip around the lifeboat station with Coxswain Paul Butler, a trip out on the inshore RIB, and one of the crew, Roger, has taken Timothy out to check the lobster pots with a 3 out of 3 success rate. All three lobsters have been donated to the crew and Mrs H has already cooked them – I can't wait for my sandwiches tomorrow! A special thanks to Rev Brian Barnes, lifeboat operations manager, for organising our stay.

We are off to the Bay Hotel in 30 minutes courtesy of Fishguard Rotary for dinner, so we are much obliged for that. It will not be a late night as we are supposed to be heading for Aberystwyth at 0545 tomorrow morning.

Sure enough, it was indeed an early start – but by now, with everyone so attuned to their responsibilities, it was like watching a well-oiled machine at work. For an 0545 start, Ian would arise first at 0345, checking the weather, charts and tidal data. The guys in the crew bus would be up at 0400 and after a light breakfast Spike, Andy and Joel would start to rig *Freethinker*: hoist the mainsail, replace the battery that had been charging overnight in the battery box, check the rigging and electronics. Meanwhile Ian would have been to the RIB to get her ready for a day at sea and Mike, in the crew motorhome, would start his daily chore of sandwich making, using up to two loaves a day for the three RIB crew and boiling water for their Thermos flasks. Only when the RIB and *Freethinker* were ready would those on RIB duty get dressed into their sailing gear.

In my motorhome, on the other hand, Elaine would rise first at 0400 to make her coffee and give me a twenty-minute warning, after which time she would struggle to lift me and dress me in my salopettes and special drysuit top, all in a cramped confined space, trying not to wake Timothy. Getting straight out of a warm bed to have a damp, cold, salty neoprene neck seal pulled over your head and to feel that clammy wet sensation on your neck every morning was a daily torture. And then I would appear like some prima donna as the electric lift on my motorhome swung me out of the van and lowered me to the floor, dressed and ready to go – the only thing missing was a puff of dry ice and a fanfare of trumpets.

I would then be lifted into *Freethinker*, and a series of checks would be carried out on me and the boat before Ian would give the OK. In no particular order these included that my helmet was on and secured, that the VHF was set to channel 77 and a radio check was successfully completed, that my lifejacket was securely fastened, that my Spare Air, a James-Bond-like underwater breathing apparatus, was tied to my helmet in case I fell in, that my drinking water tube, which was fed from a two-litre bladder behind my seat, was fixed to my left shoulder and I had checked to see that it flowed correctly, and finally that my leg-bag tube was attached and positioned in the centreboard slot so I could pee. Only then could the anti-tip bars be fitted around me and the backboard positioned behind my seat. But it was the fact that everyone knew their roles and, without a word being spoken, all the preparation could be achieved with time to spare which was so admirable. We had become a very slick and highly professional team.

Two days later, on Sunday 17 June, we arrived in Abersoch:

> We left Fishguard yesterday morning at 0600 for the longest, most boring slog into misty drizzle for nine hours, the boredom alleviated only by arrival of the trip's first pod of dolphins. One even jumped about five foot off my starboard hull, quite moving. I've seen hundreds in the wild but they never cease to surprise and please.
>
> Arrived Aberystwyth 1500 into tiny harbour at low tide; interesting disembarkation up precarious slipway over large rocks and boulders. Once again met by my new Welsh friends, Alan Thomas and his partner Dawn.
>
> Left there at 0900 this morning but hardly any wind, arrived here in Abersoch at 1530 to a very busy holiday beach. North Cardigan Bay scenery quite spectacular.
>
> Overnighting here in car park, ready for 0600 start tomorrow, hopefully for Holyhead but may not get that far. Spike's last day tomorrow – he'll be missed by us all.

It was a shame that Spike's last full day with us was spent drifting across Cardigan Bay from Aberystwyth to Abersoch in *Everest One*. It was a hot, sultry day, and once again I had to be towed for an hour or so until we found just enough wind to push me along at a couple of knots.

Arriving on that Sunday afternoon was like a busy day on Bournemouth beach. It was heaving with people of all ages, surprising for what I thought would be a remote part of north Wales. And having got permission from the resident beach patrol to take the Land Rover on the beach to pull me out, we created quite a spectacle, attracting the attention of scores of children, all running along beside *Freethinker* wanting to know what was happening.

Before even arriving in Abersoch, we knew that it would be a complicated stop. The distance from Abersoch to Holyhead is about sixty miles, but it is not direct. First you have to round the Llŷn peninsula, which is tipped by an island called Bardsey. Between Bardsey and the mainland is a notoriously difficult and dangerous stretch of water called Bardsey Sound, which could only be navigated in a boat my size at slack water and with minimum wind from the right direction. It was therefore highly unlikely that I could make Holyhead in one hit. The only solution was to split the journey into two legs by stopping overnight at a place called Morfa Nefyn. As the crow flies, Morfa Nefyn is no more than five miles from Abersoch, but by sea around the Llŷn peninsula it was about thirty. To really complicate matters, Morfa Nefyn is not a safe anchorage: it is southwest-facing and is little more than a beach with a slipway. So to make the trip to Holyhead, we would need a 48-hour weather window to sail both legs back to back. It would be no good sailing to Morfa Nefyn and then finding ourselves weather-bound, especially as there was no shelter for either *Freethinker* or *Everest One*.

In many ways, with it being Spike's last day, I wasn't unduly worried when Ian knocked on the motorhome door at 0500 hours to say that it was too windy to sail. In fact I didn't need him to tell me, as I had been kept awake most of the night listening to it whistling through the trees and feeling the motorhome being rocked from side to side. So everyone went back to sleep and re-emerged at 0800 hours. We had now been away thirty days, a whole month, and it was amazing how quickly time had passed. Although we all knew Spike would be leaving, I for one had shut it out of my mind, I hate goodbyes at the best of times. And with Spike being such an integral part of the team, we had all grown to respect and care for him very much indeed. One of life's 'good men', his absence was going to leave a big hole in our group and he was going to be missed, not least by Timothy, who had come to idolise him. He would follow Spike everywhere and bombard him with questions, wanting to know how things worked and why. So it was no surprise when Timothy, still dressed in his pyjamas, asked Elaine for some tin foil and some string early that morning.

'What for?' she asked.

'I want to make Spike a medal for being such a good crew member,' he replied.

It was indeed sad when Andy drove him off to catch his train, and I consoled Timothy, who cried 'I miss Spike.'

The Met Office forecast that morning took a turn for the worse, and even the other weather websites were predicting up to five days of unsettled weather, certainly of sufficient unpleasantness to prevent a two-day sail to Holyhead. And with Abersoch Beach Patrol telling us that we could not continue to park in the beach car park, it made sense to find something a bit more suitable where there were at least showers and toilets.

Ian volunteered himself as scout, and returned no more than thirty minutes later to tell us he had told our story to the owners of a nearby campsite and they had said we could spend a couple of nights with them. As it was not yet high season, they had some space and kindly agreed to waive the charge. So with wagons rolling – the two motorhomes, the Land Rover and the two boat trailers – we made our way only a mile or so to the Deucoch Caravan Park in Sarn Bach, and were directed with military precision into our allotted space by a tall, slim, elderly gentleman, wearing a flat cap and a long brown coat. It may have been our first campsite, but it was a cracking view, looking out across Cardigan Bay with the Snowdonia mountains in the distance. And Timothy liked it too – real grass, something we had not seen for a month, perfect for riding his bike and playing football.

Freethinker was taken around by sea to the little harbour in Abersoch and was left secure in the boat pound of Abersoch

Boatyard Services. *Everest One* meanwhile was moored at sea, just off the South Caernarvonshire Yacht Club.

Being told that the weather would be bad for five days at least got the shock over and done with. It was inconvenient, but there was no ambiguity. We could do nothing to change the situation, and once it had sunk in and I'd finished swearing there was no choice but to get on with it and make the best of the situation.

On the morning of Wednesday 20 June Ian took an urgent call from the bosun of yacht club to say that the RIB was looking dangerously low in the water. Joel and Andy were quickly dispatched and made their way by small inflatable dinghy out to *Everest One*, which was tethered to a swing mooring a few hundred yards from the shore. It was far worse than expected. Overnight, with a strong tide pushing the boat one way and the wind blowing the opposite direction, the waves had been lapping over the back of the boat. Sea water was now filling the boat and had virtually submerged the diesel engine. It was a major problem: without a RIB there would be no more sailing. Taking a tow from a neighbouring boat, they managed to get *Everest One* into the inner harbour at high water, so that when the tide went out all of the water would drain out, and they could at least see the extent of the problem.

Luckily we were weather-bound at the time, or the prospect of being prevented from sailing because of a mechanical failure would have been too much to bear. Ian was optimistic, and twenty-four hours later she was at least drained of sea water, at which point Andy, Ian and Joel effectively stripped down the whole engine and drained all the fuel and oil – not an easy job, but they did so whilst she was either afloat at high tide or lying on her side on the sand at low water.

Day 33, Thursday 21 June 2007:

Longest day of the year.

As if the weather was not enough to cause despondency, we had a major mechanical problem with the RIB yesterday. How bad? Bad enough for Ian to be working on it till gone 2230 last night, back again at dawn and he's still there now. We won't know whether it's fatal till later today, at which point we'll have to find another solution.

Last evening it really felt as though everything that could be going wrong was going wrong. Don't get me mistaken, I'm not a quitter, on the contrary, 'the higher the barrier, the taller I become', to quote a good song – but wallowing in frustration I had neglected one thing, and that was how lucky I was.

When reading my blog, I strongly encourage you to read the comments people leave. I'm embarrassed to think that I had become so obsessed with our own set of trivial problems like 'bad weather' that I failed to see two important things: (1) just how lucky I am to have been given the opportunity to do this amazing project, to have actually conceived it, planned it and brought it to fruition. And (2) that this whole event is much bigger than me. Without consciously setting out to do so, it has touched the lives of many people and I apologise to anyone who has been inspired by this project if I gave the impression of not appreciating it.

To read those comments on my blog last night was very emotional for me and made me realise how lucky I am, and it put everything into perspective.

If just one person is inspired by what I'm doing to the point that it encourages them to sail, then this whole experience will be worth it and I'm humbled to think that so many people are emotionally involved with what our team is achieving.

There were many messages left on the website that night, but the ones which hit me most were as follows:

D McClellan – Despite the frustration of not being able to sail today remember that it's nothing compared to the many 'normal' days that all we disabled people endure. Please keep at it. Your Everest has already encouraged me to sail again. I had my first sail in a Challenger last Monday. It was fantastic. Thank you so much.

Class 5SM, Manorside School, Poole, Dorset – Hi Geoff, we have been watching your progress as we used your trip as part of our class assembly (all about perseverance). We are all rooting for you and hope the weather improves so you can continue your exciting journey. Keep smiling and keep happy.

J Prentice – Geoff, I think you, your team and all you've set up and stand for are touching the lives of more than you can imagine in a deep 'ripple effect' way. I read your blog every eve because it positively inspires me and puts me in a good frame of mind about life and all its richness before I go to bed. Thank you.

S O'Callaghan – Keep at it Geoff, eyes are on you from around the world, good luck to you and best wishes to Tim, Elaine and all the crew.

Maybe it was tiredness, or maybe a feeling of letting people down, but with the delays, and now the problem with the RIB, I felt emotionally fragile – and just reading those messages of support was very moving.

I couldn't understand what was happening, and being so isolated I had no way of benchmarking any interest that was being generated by Personal Everest. For the first time on the trip I went to the site which monitored back-end visitor statistics for my website, and I had to refresh the screen and look again because I couldn't believe what I was seeing. Since departing on 20 May, my website was averaging nearly 30,000 hits a day. Perhaps this explained why I was getting so much support and encouragement from complete strangers.

Despite being fed up and totally pissed off, I genuinely felt a wave of inner strength just knowing that Personal Everest was touching people's lives, and with that came a feeling of responsibility and a renewed determination. And I was certainly going to need all the determination I could get.

It was now Friday 22 June. We had been away for thirty-four days and, despite the doom and gloom of being stuck in Abersoch, the mood lifted enormously when we were joined by new crew member Sarah Outen. I had only met Sarah a couple of times beforehand, both times before we left and, despite reassurances from her and the guys in the crew motorhome, I could not help being concerned about her having to share the campervan with three strange men, Mike, Andy and Joel. Perhaps I was being old-fashioned, but I was obviously worrying unnecessarily. Sarah had just graduated from Oxford University and was supremely funny, outgoing – and a damn good choice for Spike's replacement. Timothy fell in love with her immediately, and within a day she had fitted in to crew life as though she had been with us from day one.

Day 35, Saturday 23 June 2007:

> I've not seen TV for over a month now nor even heard a radio or seen a newspaper, but I do see the BBC homepage when I log on. I gather most of the UK is experiencing floods and this lousy weather, which somehow seems to justify our inability to move on.
>
> It seems so strange stuck in this beautiful campsite on the Llŷn peninsula in bright sunshine looking across to Snowdonia but knowing the wind is so strong and there's so much rain out there.
>
> There is a glimmer of hope on the weather horizon. Mid next week could bring a significant change in our favour – fingers crossed.

The glimmer of hope quickly faded that evening when the long-term forecast indicated another sequence of low-pressure systems that would take us well into the second week. Elaine drew the short straw and was elected to break the news to Norman and Audrey, owners of the caravan park, and thankfully, although I'm certain they must have been getting worried, they allowed us to stay longer.

In many ways, perhaps the poor weather forecast was just as well. Once the RIB engine had been put back together it was started for the first time – with catastrophic results. Somehow sea water had remained in the system, and the head gasket blew, buckling one of the pistons and the crank shaft. When Ian told me, I said nothing. I couldn't speak. I just retired to my bunk and went to bed to try and sleep away the mental torment.

Each night, from the seclusion of my bunk, I would hear the crew outside on their mobile phones to loved ones, family, friends or employers, apologising that there would be yet another delay. I had sold the whole concept to them on the basis that we would be back home within 60 days. We had now been away for 35 days and we were not even a quarter of the way around. There was no suitable weather on the horizon and now, to cap it all, we had a completely buggered RIB. Two big problems, one total disaster. In short, a bloody mess. I was utterly devastated. Desperate. I could sense that this might actually be the point where it would be better to give up than to prolong the agony.

To nip it in the bud, over dinner one evening in the mess tent (which we had bought and erected so we could at least eat together, further adding to our already sprawling presence on the campsite) I put the situation to the crew –

'The bottom line is that we have a buggered RIB, no prospect of getting out of here until the weather improves and the RIB is fixed, and even when we do, there's every possibility we may not get back until mid August at least. I want you to have a think about it. No need to let me know now, but talk amongst yourselves and, over the next few days, let me know your thoughts. I won't think bad of anyone who wants to call it a day.'

It wasn't easy pretending that I wouldn't mind. Of course I would mind, but it wasn't fair on these good people if they felt obliged to stay and help me when they had their own lives to get back to. Ian had already pledged his support to the very end and I was immensely grateful for that. And it was only a matter of seconds before everyone else did likewise.

'Look, the RIB is fixable, but it's going to take about a week,' reassured Ian. 'She'll need to be lifted out and taken to a proper marine engineer to re-skim the cylinder head and rebuild the engine. It's not going to be cheap either. If the weather is keeping us pinned in anyway, let's just accept that and get on with fixing the RIB.'

It was incredibly generous of them all to pledge their support so quickly and willingly, though I knew they must be harbouring some reservations. And Ian was right. If we were weather-bound anyway, what difference did it make to get the RIB fixed?

After sending the RIB off first thing Monday morning to a local marine engineer, at Elaine's suggestion I proposed that the crew might like to go home for a few days' R&R. Over the next day or so, Mike, Joel and Ian took me up on the offer, leaving Sarah, Andy, Elaine, Timothy and myself on site.

On our eleventh day in Abersoch, with a lot of time on my hands, I started to monitor the weather forecasts more closely and, in particular the actual winds compared to the Met Office forecasts. Time and time again, most notably on the borderline force 4 and force 5 forecasts, the Met Office would go with force 5, the other sources would go with force 4. And time and time again, when reviewing the forecast, the Met Office had been overly pessimistic and it was the other web sites, most notably Weather Online, who were getting it right. It may seem an insignificant matter, but these pessimistic Met Office forecasts were enough to convince Ian not to sail.

Whilst Ian was away for a couple of days, I emailed Weather Online and asked if they would be prepared to sponsor me – I could offer publicity on my website in return for a personalised telephone forecast from one of their specialists. Literally within thirty minutes of sending the email I took a call from one of their directors in Germany. I explained my problem and she kindly agreed to give me direct access to a forecaster until the project was concluded. I learned that all weather forecasts are in fact interpretations of a single set of synoptic data charts produced by the Met Office; it all came down to how the data were interpreted. Even though we were well and truly weather-bound with storms and gales, Weather Online still gave me daily forecasts and were able to tell me, hour by hour, what the weather would be doing in Abersoch. Time and time again, it was spot on. I was very excited, and couldn't wait to tell Ian when he got back.

'And what do I tell the coroner?' was his response when I did speak with him.

'I don't understand,' I said.

'If the Met Office forecast a force 5, Weather Online forecast a force 4, we go out, it blows force 5, your boat flips over and you drown, what do I tell the coroner when our risk assessments clearly state that we won't sail in anything above a force 4?'

It seemed to me that this was more about Ian protecting his reputation than about accepting the facts, and it told me that the Met Office's pronouncements were gospel in the world of sailing instructors, to the exclusion of all other sources. I was actually extremely annoyed too, as his comments implied a recklessness on my part which is not true. As a husband and father, I would do nothing to endanger my own life.

'Ian, the stark reality is that if we only listen to the Met Office and their overly pessimistic forecasts, we are losing sailing days. I have found a personalised one-to-one service that seems to be giving some consistently accurate data. We've got to get real an start taking a few risks if we are ever to get out of here.'

I'd made my point. To be fair to Ian, he took on board my comments – but I remain convinced that his attitude had more to do with preserving his impeccable safety record, and that is no bad thing.

Later that week I inadvertently stirred up a bit of a hornets' nest with Rotary, but it brought to a head an ongoing niggle of mine and resolved it, for the better, once and for all. An innocuous comment on one of my blogs read simply:

> Haven't seen any Rotarians at this stop; not sure if there are any in these parts. That said, we have almost every facility we could wish for at the caravan park and they are charming hosts.

Clearly I had touched a nerve. Within hours of the message being posted, my friend Mike Gallon was on the phone to see what was going on.

'The bottom line, Mike, is that this relationship just isn't working. We are meeting the odd Rotarian at some ports, and they are all very amicable, but in practical terms we are achieving nothing.'

In my view the relationship needed coordinating. It was simply unthinkable that a member of my crew could find the time to speak with every Rotarian at the next destination and then ask for help – maybe it's not human nature, maybe it's not British, but none of us could bring ourselves to ask for help. And what we really wanted was people able to smooth the way for the arrival of the Personal Everest circus when we were on the move. Someone, ideally a Rotarian, needed to notify the local Rotary group at each destination and ask them, on our behalf, for names of harbour masters, marina managers and so on. And then I had my brainwave – David Cheatham. The guy from my local Hamble Valley Rotary whom I had met at the Rotary conference in Bournemouth in April. I plucked up the courage and called him and explained what I had in mind. Thankfully he agreed. We had no idea if it would work, but it was a last-chance effort to get the relationship back on track. All we needed now was some fine weather, and for the RIB to be fixed.

But still the weather kept us firmly trapped in Abersoch. Every day I would check the weather forecasts, all of them, even the Met Office, for any hint of fair weather. I can only describe it as mental torture. We had now been here for three weeks. The crew were all back on site and taking their minds off the torment by getting away from the campsite as often as possible – not easy when your only transport is the home you are living in. Andy, Joel and Mike were quick to discover the various watering holes in Abersoch, whilst Ian made himself busy with odd jobs on the RIB now it had at last been repaired. Sarah chose to take advantage of the countryside, and she and Timothy would often disappear for the day with a picnic and walk some nearby coastal path. On one occasion, Andy, Joel and Sarah even left for a couple of days to climb Snowdon.

It was a bright, albeit breezy, day on Saturday 7 July – pleasant, but too windy to sail. I was sitting outside, sheltering from the wind behind our motorhome whilst soaking up some warmth from the sun, reading one of the latest yachting mags, looking for any press updates on my challenge, when a small classified advert caught my eye. It read simply, 'Have you sailed around

Great Britain? Would you be interested in completing a short questionnaire for a forthcoming book?' Well, I hadn't yet completed the trip but I felt confident enough to phone the number and have a chat. But I was to get much more than a questionnaire, for that brief conversation was to relieve me from a secret agony that had been haunting me since my first stop in Lymington. The lady conducting the research, Samantha Steele, was keen to ask me questions about the trip and, to my surprise, had been following my progress in the yachting press. Knowing that I was using only a fifteen-foot dinghy, she asked me how I managed for power when the wind died or the tide turned, or when coming into harbour. Unintentionally, she had found my Achilles heel.

'Can I share something private with you?' I asked. 'I'm rather embarrassed about this and it has been troubling me, but in those situations I take a tow from my support boat'.

'So, what's your problem?'

'Well, just that, that I am sometimes being towed. It feels like I'm cheating.'

I could hear her laughing on the other end of the phone.

'I'm sorry,' she said, 'but did you seriously think you could sail around the country without power? Certainly some boats do it, mostly when racing, but when cruising, of the dozens of boats I've surveyed for this book, just about every single boat has used power at some stage. What else are they supposed to do when they are not moving? On average, skippers used power for more than 50% of their time at sea. Stop worrying. If you had a motor, no doubt you would have needed to use it, so taking a tow is completely understandable.'

Suddenly I felt rather stupid, especially as I had only been towed for a small percentage of the time and only when it was essential. And now, knowing that most other boats cruising around the UK used power, a weight had been lifted from my shoulders and I found that I could talk about it without fear of embarrassment.

Day 50, Sunday 8 July 2007:

Another day, another false hope ... once again the weather conspires against us at the twelfth hour – it's so demoralising for every one of the crew.

We had quietly been keeping our fingers crossed that there would be a window of opportunity today to break the grip of the Welsh dragon that has kept us here but not so. It's 50 days today that we left Southampton and exactly 21 days since we landed in Abersoch, if that is a milestone, then it's not one I wish to celebrate.

We now need to regroup and start assessing the next fragile opportunity that may present itself.

I was having recurring nightmares and had convinced myself that this would be where the project ended. I recalled the smooth, slick, operation of moving on each day that we had enjoyed, for the most part, up until Abersoch. Try as I might, I could not envisage regrouping and operating in that way ever again. Each day I looked at myself in the mirror and thought that I was beginning to look ill – not poorly, but a deep sadness in my eyes. In my heart I wasn't happy. I was on the verge of being beaten by the weather. I recorded a daily diary-cam, confiding my innermost fears to my pocket video camera. The anger and frustration had long gone, and it was now the voice of a beaten man that I heard when I replayed the recording. We had now been sat in a wet and windy field in north Wales for more than three weeks, nearly half the total time we had been away, and we still had more than a thousand miles to sail.

Ian asked to have a private word in my motorhome. 'Shit,' I thought, 'this is it. He is about to throw his towel in the ring, and who can blame him?' But it was not the conversation I was expecting.

'Geoff, I know we've been here before, but I think we are going to get the two-day window we need. We could be off tomorrow.'

The funny thing was, I had heard the Met Office forecast: it had clearly stated a possible force 5. And I had spoken to Weather

Online, who had clearly stated no more than a force 4 – I had given that same information to Ian. Bloody hell, was Ian going to take a risk? Not that he would ever admit it, of course.

'The tides will be in our favour too. I've got a feeling we may get stuck in Holyhead, but we will at least be able to leave here,' he continued.

As kind as the owners had been to us at the caravan park, it was important to move on, a psychological step if nothing else. I could feel a wave of happiness and excitement, even butterflies in my stomach. We called a crew briefing to break the news and you could sense the renewed spirit and joy amongst the team. But having been in a similar position several times already, their excitement was tempered.

Ian issued a job-list to everyone to make ready for a departure the following day. Ian, Andy, Sarah and Joel disappeared into town to prepare the RIB and *Freethinker*, whilst Mike and Elaine started to re-stow the motorhomes, which had become completely disorganised and unprepared for any lengthy road trip. Another of Elaine's duties was to inform the owners that we would, finally, be vacating our pitch the following morning and to ask for the invoice.

I could see Elaine returning from their house at the top of the field accompanied by park owners Audrey and Norman, daughter Ruth and her young daughter Rebecca. 'Oh heck, it's worse than I thought.'

I opened the motorhome door and was surprised to see Norman quite emotional. In his thick Yorkshire accident he said, 'There'll be no charge, son, no charge. It's been our absolute pleasure having you here. What you are doing is wonderful and we wish you every success.'

I was deeply touched. Once again, I realised this wasn't about the money, although it was a huge relief to be let off £2,000 of fees, it was about touching someone's life – and that was priceless. I kept remembering Mike Gallon's phrase, 'synchronicity'. It was indeed strange how my life, and the life of the project, kept crossing paths with wonderful people who, by becoming emotional stakeholders, were enabling the project to succeed – I was a lucky man indeed.

Day 54, Thursday 12 July 2007:

Go ... Go ... Go ...

We're off at last. After 23 days weather-bound in Abersoch we finally managed to restart our epic journey, and the feeling of elation amongst all the crew is almost tangible. Bardsey Sound was fast becoming my nemesis, so it was with some trepidation we finally set sail from the beach at Abersoch Boatyard Services and headed out past St Tudwall's towards the Devil's Ridge and the aptly named Devil's Mouth bay (I told you this was a notorious stretch of coast). Within half an hour we had a visit from dolphins, which proved to be a good omen. We arrived Bardsey Sound bang on slack water and, just as stated in the Almanac (slack water Bardsey HW Dover + 3 hours), it was like a sleeping monster. The wind had come around to SW in my favour blowing a good 15 knots plus which meant I powered through the Sound and past the overfalls called 'the Tripods' at speeds occasionally hitting 10 knots. Arriving Morfa Nefyn at 1800 was a great feeling. Although only a few miles as the crow flies, the 30-mile sea journey around the peninsula had been giving me nightmares for weeks. Now it is over and we can think about moving on. Setting off 1200 hours today for Holyhead, ETA about 1900. It feels wonderful.

16

After we'd been living in the flat in Freemantle for a year, Southampton City Council recognised the unacceptable housing situation we were enduring, and Elaine and I were placed in a one-bedded, purpose-built 'wheelchair-friendly' maisonette in the Polygon area of the city.

What we lost in space we more than made up for in ease of access. For the first time I could not only enter my own front door without the need to be bumped up a step, but the bathroom was huge and had a wheel-in shower. I could get under the bathroom sink to clean my teeth instead of cleaning them over a washing-up bowl. I could reach the light switches, I could reach cupboards to help myself to food in the kitchen, and I could even open the front door if someone called. It was fabulous, and with our modest income from benefits and Elaine's agency nursing we furnished it ourselves and were very proud of it.

Despite some difficult meetings with Elaine's parents since moving back to Southampton, their opinions were never going to change either Elaine's mind or mine about our future together. I accepted their right to be concerned for their daughter and, for Elaine's sake, I bit my tongue when confronted with what I regarded as distasteful and hurtful questioning. 'How are you going to provide for Elaine?' 'How are you going to be able to work and pay a mortgage?' 'What sort of life will Elaine have, spending it looking after you?' And, perhaps the cruellest of all, 'Did you know that Elaine always wanted children?'

I didn't know the answers to many of those questions apart from the fact that, at that time, there was almost no chance of us having children. But Elaine and I had discussed all of these things in great detail, and it was her decision to continue. It had to be her decision, I could not make it for her. But the one thing I did know was that the pair of us loved each other very much, and we were so determined to prove ourselves right that we were not going to allow the concerns of her parents to get in our way. Thankfully those concerns were to mellow as we demonstrated, time and time again, our ability to get on with our lives. Over the years they have often commented on how proud they are of our achievements, and we have since become very close. But in those early days their misgivings only made our resolve stronger.

Conceding that we were serious about our future together, Elaine's parents thankfully gave their blessing, and we were married in Bristol on 19 September 1987. It was a magnificent affair with over a hundred guests, and Elaine looked resplendent in her long white dress. Sean was my best man and a convoy of friends and family made their way up from Southampton for the big day. I had not spoken to my mother since leaving Scilly so neither she nor Andy were invited to the wedding, but the guests included the Pennells, all twenty of them, my brother Richard, sister Lucy – who was one of Elaine's bridesmaids – plus my old school friend Simon Lawton and Si O'Callaghan, who was just back from the Caribbean.

My mind now turned to the thought of work. Not only to earn much-needed money (we had taken out several loans to try and keep our heads above water), but also to give myself back some dignity. Just because I was now using a wheelchair did not mean that I did not have the same aspirations to get a job and to earn a salary, but I had to accept that I certainly had no sailing career any more. I scoured the job adverts in the local paper, but in truth, apart from a lot of sailing experience, I was unskilled, I had only two O levels and I was quadriplegic. My job prospects didn't look rosy. By chance one day I saw a scheme being promoted by Southampton City Council to get housebound people back into work. What made this particular scheme unique was that it was an IT-based training scheme which was going to provide ten applicants with their very own desktop computers and a dedicated tutor for the eight-month duration of the course. This was 1987, and still very early days in the development of computers. I applied for one of the places and was fortunate to be selected. Over the next eight months I studied hard. Working closely with my tutor, whom I saw weekly, I specialised in database management, spreadsheets and word processing. In those pre-email days, I would save my work to large-format floppy discs and send them off to be marked each week. I succeeded in gaining my certification of competence in all three subjects.

For the project to be considered a success, the final phase was to get the students into employment. An evening reception at the Guildhall was arranged, where we would meet prospective employers. I was struck by the fact that only six of the ten students bothered to turn up, and I was the only one of those six wearing a suit – albeit one of Sean's cast-offs, a Savile Row pin-stripe!

The reception was a casual affair: a glass of wine, a few canapés and an opportunity to chat with people from various agencies and firms in the city. I returned home not particularly optimistic but tired from having spoken to every prospective employer I could. At 9.00 the following morning a very excited lady who worked for the Council phoned to say that the senior partner of accountancy firm Deloitte Haskins & Sells had been impressed with our conversation and would like me to attend an interview for the position of database manager within the firm's Southampton-based marketing department. Of course I was delighted, but it presented me with an unexpected dilemma. I knew that to accept a job would mean automatically losing entitlement to most of my disability benefits, plus I would lose my entitlement to financial help with my rent and other local authority taxes – a net loss of £7,500 a year, which was a lot of money to me. But in terms of self-esteem, I knew that a job would be priceless.

The following week Elaine drove me down to the interview, and I sat in their plush boardroom awaiting the arrival of Paul Oakley-White, the partner who had spoken with me the week before. His secretary came in to offer me a drink whilst I waited.

'I don't need to wish you good luck,' she said. 'Paul has already told me that the job is yours, so you can relax now. But shhhhh! Don't let on that I told you.'

With that she gave me a thumbs-up and left the room. Her comments were confirmed minutes later when Paul went through the formal interview process, though he made me sweat over salary. I later learned that he had been prepared to pay twice the agreed sum of £7,500, but the money was only secondary as far as I was concerned. I always knew that it was the job itself which was the vehicle to future opportunities. Once on the employment ladder there was only one way I intended to go, and that was upwards.

I was so incredibly proud to have a job. I had never heard of the firm Deloitte Haskins & Sells before, but I quickly learned that they were a major player in the accountancy world and they were highly respected. It was my first job as a disabled person so I didn't know what to expect. I needn't have worried. I was given my own office, my own telephone with a direct extension, a computer and even my own secretary. But most importantly I was accepted as just another member of staff. There was not one occasion when my disability caused a problem for my employers, and that gave me a huge sense of comfort and security within the firm. Every single member of staff was so positive in their attitude towards me that even I forgot about my disability when I was at work – and that's the highest compliment I could pay anyone.

My job consisted of one main task, to establish and maintain a database, from scratch, of clients and potential clients. Up until this point most companies had been using data-cards, brown pieces of card with holes punched in them, to analyse client data.

My new computerised database was revolutionary, and slowly, over the months, I created a system that was then loaded with detailed data on more than 10,000 contacts. For the first time, the firm could use its data to underpin its marketing efforts, and the results greatly improved the firm's market position in the local area. I loved my job, not least because I could see a direct link between the success of the firm and the work I was doing, but also because of the sense of pride that it gave me. The more complex I made the system and the more data I loaded, the more sophisticated the data reports I produced, and so my role became more respected by the staff. Within a year I had received two pay rises, and after a merger with another major accountancy firm and a round of redundancies, I found myself managing an entire marketing department for Coopers & Lybrand Deloitte.

For me, my new-found employment status was nothing more than I would have wanted for myself, and I failed to see anything unusual. But inadvertently I found myself becoming a bit of a local celebrity. The local newspaper and the local TV station were quick to pick up on the story of me finding such a good job and, knowing that the publicity would also be good for the firm (after all, I was in marketing), I agreed to a series of interviews which generated a lot of positive news coverage. I was asked to join various business-related organisations and committees in the city and I was also asked to speak at conferences as an example of someone with a disability who had re-trained and found work. Even local politicians jumped on the bandwagon, and my name was put forward by my local MP for the national Total Ability Award:

> in recognition of his outstanding determination to discover, develop and apply his many talents, thereby encouraging others to reach out beyond their handicap and have access to education and employment in the same ways as the rest of the community ... [!]

I was flattered to win the award, and it brought about another flourish of publicity for the firm and myself, but it all seemed slightly odd to me. Couldn't anyone see that I was merely a paralysed body with a working brain? Did no one stop to think about how I actually got to work in the morning, or how I got to London to collect my award? It was partly my fault – I wasn't going to start volunteering that sort of personal information, nor was Elaine going to start asking, 'Hey, what about my role in all this?' – but Elaine's support was an invisible aspect to my life which no one seemed to consider. Luckily for me, Elaine was now working in telesales and had the flexibility to spend a considerable amount of her time running around after me.

In fact, I chose not to discuss any aspects of my disability. It was a charade. So long as I looked smart and clean I would do whatever I could not to draw attention to my disability. If my leg went into spasm and started jumping, I would retreat to my office until it calmed down. If my leg bag was full, I would phone Elaine and ask her to leave her work to come and empty it. It wasn't that I was embarrassed by my disability. I just felt that if my work colleagues had seen any aspect of my care it would have highlighted the disability, and they might have subconsciously started making allowances for me. I did not want sympathy or special allowances, conscious or subconscious; I wanted to be like them. If I did something wrong, I didn't want them attributing it to weakness or failure because I was disabled.

At a conference in 1989 I had been asked by Hampshire County Council to speak about my experiences to an audience of prospective employers. It was a big conference with nearly 200 delegates. Whilst I sat waiting for my turn to speak, smartly dressed in my suit and tie, I got talking to a chap next to me. He had cerebral palsy, and apart from my mates with spinal injuries at Odstock he was probably the first disabled person I had ever spoken to. His body was extremely twisted and contorted, he writhed about in his wheelchair with involuntary movements, and his personal carer next to him periodically wiped the dribble from his chin. His head and body were strapped to the wheelchair so he didn't fall out. I don't recall his name but I do recall our conversation. At first it was a bit difficult to understand him, with his arms flailing as he fought to speak. But slowly it transpired that he had two degrees, one in advanced mathematics, the other in psychology. He was in his mid thirties, single, and had never had a job in his life.

When it came my turn to speak, I chose to discard my notes and speak from the heart. How could I have the nerve to sit on a stage and tell everyone that employing a disabled person was to be applauded when it was clear that I was being used for exactly the reason which I had been so at pains to hide? It did not take a genius to see that I had been asked to speak because I represented the 'nice' face of disability, the safe, non-threatening face, and that was partly because I chose to hide the reality.

I began by telling the audience about my sailing career, my accident, retraining and getting a job with only two O levels and a few months' IT training. I then posed a question, pointing to the man in the front row –

'Why then, with two degrees, has this chap not got a job? I'll tell you why. Maybe no one in this room is brave enough to say it, but it's because employers are frightened of his disability. He's far better qualified than me and could do my job with ease, but you would feel more comfortable employing me than you would him, wouldn't you? Until employers can overcome their fear of disabled people, then conferences like this are a waste of time.'

I acknowledge that it was a slightly anarchic thing for me to do, most definitely presumptive and possibly even patronising. I had no idea what his reaction or that of the delegates would be, but I felt so strongly that I had to say something. I felt that I was being used because I was 'safe', and to have kept quiet would have been betraying other disabled people.

As I came down off the stage and took my place in the front row, there was a deafening lack of applause from the audience and I thought I had completely blown it. I turned towards my new-found friend to apologise but he cut me short. 'Thank you,' he said, 'you are the only person in this room who could say that and you were right to do so.' I thought about what he said, and knew he was right. I was uniquely placed to make that point.

By this time, Elaine had taken a job in medical insurance, and with both of us now gainfully employed we settled into a regime that was incredibly tough. At the time we were both younger and more resilient than we are today, but it was punishing for both of us. The most striking fact was that Elaine was acting as my full-time carer without any help from social services or any financial benefit. Of course she would argue that she has never cared for me for monetary gain, but it is so desperately unfair that if a disabled person has a partner, that partner is expected to provide whatever care is needed without financial help. Had she not been there I would have qualified for nursing care provided by the local authority, and I would have received financial benefits to help cover the costs. But because we lived together, and because she supplied all of my care, I did not even appear on any social services register. And because she worked in another job in addition to her care for me, she did not even qualify for a carer's allowance.

The only reason I was able to work at all was because each weekday morning Elaine would get up at 5.00 a.m. to get herself ready and to make our sandwiches for lunch before getting me washed, dressed and into my wheelchair an hour later. After she had dropped me off at work at 8.30 a.m., she would then drive ten miles to her place of work for 9.00 a.m. She would drive back to me at lunchtime to empty my leg bag and then drive back to her office, all within her lunch hour. At the end of the day she would return to pick me up at 5.30 p.m. and we would go home, arriving about 6.30 p.m., at which point she would start preparing our dinner and doing housework. This is a routine we adhered to, day in, day out, for more than a decade.

Had Elaine not provided that level of care, it would have been impossible to get any home-delivered nursing care to start that early in the morning. But even if we could find nursing care to start that early, with no accessible public transport I would not have been able to get to work anyway. It's little wonder that so few disabled people can access employment, and it's no wonder so many people were so surprised at the ability of a quadriplegic like me to hold down such a job.

Another ongoing stress was the legal case I had begun following Barry Rice's earlier visit. I had engaged the services of J S Archibald QC on a no win, no fee basis. He agreed to take my case, and the grounds of my claim against Endless Summer Charters Ltd were on a breach of contract: specifically that I was not insured against any personal or medical injury, as Barry had assured me I would be that day at our meeting at Moody's on 1 September 1984. Ignorant of the legal system, I was encouraged by Archibald's optimism for my chances of success and I did everything that he asked of me. At first we spoke weekly and I spent many hours typing statements, copying paperwork and working with my medical team at Salisbury and the Spinal Injuries Association to obtain detailed medical reports on my condition. As time progressed, I became aware of just how slowly the legal system worked in Tortola. Weeks turned into months, which turned into years. Every so often I would speak to Archibald, there would be another flurry of activity, and then it would go quiet again. Having started the process, and with Archibald's infectious positive attitude, I reluctantly accepted the slow progress. But my legal case sat, monkey-like, on my shoulder. Every minute of every day. The worry and concern it gave me, though slight, was omnipresent and would last another twelve years before resolution.

In late 1988, after much hard work, we were finally in a financial position to make the biggest decision of our married life so far – to buy our first house. It meant a tremendous strain on our finances and, at a time when interest rates were at a record high of 15 per cent, it left us no extra money at all for emergencies. We discussed it at length, weighing up all the benefits of remaining in a rented council flat against the costs of buying privately. In a decision made more with our hearts than with our heads, we found a two-bedroom bungalow in the Bitterne area of the city which became our very own home.

17

Holyhead marina was a brand new facility, tucked away behind the longest breakwater in Europe. It had been quite a drive for the road crew up to this remote top-left-hand corner of Anglesey but, after their enforced break in Abersoch, they had quickly settled back into the routine of life on the road.

It felt so good to be sailing again, and the trip up to Holyhead had reinvigorated me with a new sense of 'getting on with the job'.

Blog entry, Day 55, Friday 13 July 2007:

Well, after a cracking five-hour sail from Morfa Nefyn, we arrived Holyhead at about 1930 hours yesterday. We had a steady 15 knots of breeze from the southwest, which gave great sailing conditions. However, when we reached the spectacular South Stack lighthouse, the skies darkened, the cloud level lowered, the wind disappeared and we rounded the headland with minimal visibility, the only hint of its presence being a ghostly grey silhouette through the cloud, and the deep boom of the fog horn – even the beam of light from the lighthouse was obscured by the low cloud.

With the euphoria of having resumed our journey still in evidence, Ian and I set aside time to discuss our passage plan. It was no use pretending that our twenty-three-day delay in Abersoch hadn't affected our plan – in truth, it had decimated it. And in so doing it had forced us to re-examine our route in detail.

Most immediately pressing was our next leg, to Scotland. The direct route was due north, via the Isle of Man. Once again it would be a two-day, back-to-back sail, with each leg being about sixty miles. But this time it would be across the full might of the

Irish Sea. There would be no safe havens in an emergency: this was an ocean passage. And there would be no road-crew support either. The RIB would be loaded with essential supplies, and Elaine and Timothy would have to fly into the Isle of Man for the night so Elaine could help me with my medical needs, then fly back off the island the following day; being a chronic seasickness sufferer, there was no way she could travel on the RIB. Meanwhile, the road crew would have to drive in excess of 330 miles to our next stop, Portpatrick in Galloway, our first port of call in Scotland. The only alternative open to us was to sail a succession of legs, each of about forty miles, along the north coast of Wales, up past Liverpool, Blackpool, Barrow-in-Furness and back out again to Portpatrick, a minimum of six stops and at least a week to complete.

Optimistically, we agreed to go via the Isle of Man, accepting that we might have to wait for the right weather window. It was a gamble and we knew it. There might come a time when the extended route past Liverpool would have been the quicker option, but we had to take that risk. It was a tough call, and we understood that a delay of more than seven days in Holyhead would mean the end of the project, regardless of route. That was the stark truth.

Perhaps the most important decision I have ever taken as a yachtsman was taken that day whilst discussing our route around Scotland, assuming of course we ever got there. From the outset, the intention had been to sail up through the Western Isles, up to Cape Wrath on the northwestern tip of Scotland, then to turn right and sail through the Pentland Firth before turning south at John o' Groats. With the weather as bad as it had been, it was almost certain that, by sticking with the original plan, we might never round Cape Wrath – at least, not in 2007 – and the overall objective would never be achieved. The only alternative was to sail through the Caledonian Canal, which would effectively cut off the top part of Scotland. I knew that sooner or later the decision had to be made, and I had wrestled with it privately since leaving Abersoch. But the time had come to make that decision, and to plan for it. On the positive side, it would not only shave off about 300 miles, but a trip through the Caledonian was unlikely to be affected by the weather, no matter how bad it became. Conversely, I was worried about how it would be received by the press and the critics. Was it a false circumnavigation of Great Britain? Or was it a prudent route that would still achieve the overall goal? Ian could see it was troubling me.

'It's the route Ellen MacArthur took,' he said with a reassuring smile.

That was good enough for me. 'OK then, let's do it.'

Twenty-four hours into our stay in Holyhead, we had an unexpected stroke of luck with the weather. A low-pressure system had fizzled out and my new personal forecaster at Weather Online was predicting forty-eight hours of decent weather, after which it would again deteriorate if we remained in Holyhead. However, if we could at least reach Scotland, we would be well north of the next weather system and could potentially have a succession of better weather. It was too good an opportunity to miss.

At 0300 hours on Sunday 15 July Ian awoke to confirm the weather forecast. By 0430 we were prepared, rigged and had put to sea. *Everest One* was laden with essential supplies for the journey including tool kits, engine spares, food, even my special low-pressure mattress and my wheelchair, all strapped to the steel framework above the RIB. With no access to land crew or vehicles for at least the next two days, we had to be self-sufficient. The weather proved even better than we could have hoped for, and we made good time in a calm sea. It was a marathon journey, over thirteen hours at sea, sailing 68 nautical miles – the longest I have ever sailed single-handed in one hit and, I would guess, further than any other quadriplegic had ever sailed single-handed. I was shattered beyond words when we arrived, as were the RIB crew, but it felt great to sail into Peel harbour and to see Elaine and Timothy, who had flown out earlier from Liverpool, waiting there on the beach.

After overnighting in the only wheelchair-accessible hotel we could find during peak holiday season, some fifteen miles away in the south of the island, Sarah, Andy, Elaine, Timothy and I made our way back up to Peel to rejoin Ian, who had stayed in a B&B to keep an eye on *Everest One* and *Freethinker* as they rode at anchor in the bay nearby. On our taxi ride into Peel, from the cliff tops above in the early morning light we could see far out to sea – and my attention was drawn to the white horses, signalling strong winds, strong tides, or both. I began to get butterflies in my stomach.

On paper, it was a straightforward sixty-mile sail, due north to Portpatrick. The wind was blowing a steady 15 knots from the south, so it would be directly behind me, as would the moderate sea state. The forecast was unambiguous – in twenty-four hours the weather in the Isle of Man would deteriorate and, when it did, there was every chance we would be trapped on the island without the road crew – indefinitely. The forecast also confirmed that only sixty miles to the north we could expect a prolonged settled period of finer weather. There was no alternative, we had to press on. I kissed Elaine goodbye as she rushed to catch the morning plane back to Liverpool, whilst Timothy decided that he wanted to go on the RIB with Ian, Sarah and Andy.

From the moment I poked *Freethinker*'s bows outside the harbour wall, I was in no doubt as to what lay ahead of me. Within minutes I was surfing down two-metre-high waves, forced to let the mainsail go forward of the beam to try and spill the wind and de-power the boat. Every single wave that passed under me had a breaking crest, which, for the most part, I managed to avoid. But occasionally one would creep up from behind and break across my back with a lot of force, swamping me and flooding my tiny cockpit with sea water, which seemed to drain out only just in time before the next wave hit.

I had to remain mentally alert for every inch of the trip. At the base of each wave I had to steer *Freethinker* to one side or another just enough to prevent her burying her nose into the wave in front. With immense power in the sail and with the following wave lifting her stern high in the air, it would not take much to flip her over, head over heels. I was using every sailing skill I had learned in my life to keep her upright.

After only two hours, I was running out of strength and, unable to bear it any longer, I allowed my boat to come around into the wind so I could relax my tired arms. We had already come a good fifteen miles and the Isle of Man was now some way off in the distance. Even if I wanted to take a tow, with the waves so high there was no way the RIB could safely come alongside without risking damage to both vessels. I also knew that the prospect of sailing back towards the Isle of Man was futile: there was no way I could beat into those seas and that wind. I had no alternative. I had to press on to Scotland.

So turbulent were the waters that I could barely push the transmit button on my VHF to talk to the crew, and with the RIB completely disappearing in the trough of each wave that passed, I had a feeling of vulnerability and isolation. I'd not felt like that since those days as a teenager when sailing across the Atlantic Ocean, but there was a big difference between sailing a large yacht and sitting huddled in my tiny dinghy.

Day 58, Monday 16 July 2007:

Timothy came on the RIB and although he enjoyed it the rough conditions meant most of his breakfast ended up in Andy's lap. The sail across to Scotland was without doubt the most physically and mentally exhausting of my life. For almost the entire eight hours I had a stiff force 4 blowing from behind with a large rough following sea. To prevent the boat broaching or pitch-poling as it accelerated down the waves, I spent eight hours looking over my shoulder anticipating, then steering the boat down every wave. It was not pleasurable in any way, just downright scary – and with hindsight not a trip I would do again. Being only 2 feet above the water, the following seas were actually breaking over my stern and flooding my cockpit. It required so much concentration that I could neither eat nor drink the entire journey. If there was one consolation, I saw a 5-metre shark jump vertically and clear of the water. I was not entirely sure what I had seen, it happened so quickly. I lifted my visor, stared across the waves, and it did it again – it was one of the most spectacular things I've ever seen at sea. Sarah, our resident marine biologist, informs me it was probably a basking shark and, although a rare occurrence, they are known to do this. It was incredible.

When the voyage was just about over, and suffering the first signs of dehydration, exposure and severe exhaustion, I mustered up every last ounce of energy to line *Freethinker* up to negotiate the twenty-foot-wide entrance into Portpatrick harbour. As I looked down, I was surprised to see that my white mainsheet was stained red with blood. At first I thought it was from my hands, which had been chafing on the rope the entire journey as I sheeted in, then let the rope out to control the speed of *Freethinker* down every wave. My hands were indeed bleeding, but the majority of the blood was coming from my mouth. Having now slowed the boat down, and with the constant sea spray abated, I could feel the warm, iodine taste of blood coming from my gums. Unable to control the rope with my clawed hands alone, I had been lifting the rope to my mouth with my wrist so that I could clench it between my teeth and use my neck muscles to pull it in, unknowingly ripping my gums in the process. It didn't hurt, but seeing the blood was pretty shocking. Having threaded *Freethinker* through the narrow harbour entrance, I was so physically and emotionally drained that I collapsed and momentarily lost consciousness. Only for a few seconds, but I don't recall anything about sailing across the harbour and coming ashore on the beach until Elaine lifted my visor, handed me a large mug of whisky and announced –

'Welcome to Scotland!'

Still dazed from the previous day's exertions, and with every muscle in my neck and arms throbbing and aching, I awoke to the news that we had indeed got ahead of the bad weather system and we would be pressing on. Luckily it would be a midday start, but as Elaine helped me get dressed in my still-damp sailing gear, I felt numb and looked at my hands, which were trembling uncontrollably. I didn't feel ill, I just realised that I was now pushing my paralysed body to the absolute extreme in terms of exertion. Possibly further than any quadriplegic had ever pushed themselves before. I had got used to the constant salt in my eyes, and the skin on my face was now toughening up from the never-ending wind and salt spray. But no matter how battered and bruised I felt, when I logged onto the internet that morning to file my blog, I looked at the Marinetrack reading and was over the moon to see the progress we had made since leaving Abersoch, a string of bright orange arrows heading due north and now placing us firmly in Scotland. We absolutely had to be back home in time for Timothy to start school – but that was not until 3 September, seven weeks away. There was now every chance we could succeed.

The road crew left before us that day, a massive 230-mile journey ahead of them to Campbeltown on the Kintyre peninsula via Glasgow. For us it was still a forty-mile trip by sea, but it would take us significantly less time, especially as the favourable southerly wind would be pushing us up, past the imposing granite island of Ailsa Craig, which rises steeply from the sea, to Campbeltown, a pretty harbour on the eastern side of Kintyre.

Day 60, Wednesday 18 July 2007:

Sat here in the motorhome overlooking Campbeltown harbour, it's a lovely calm morning and we are all feeling so much happier. We've now got all the vehicles and crew back together. Having made so much progress in the past week, we are on a real high at the moment.

Yesterday's sail was another long one, taking almost seven hours, but we covered another 40 miles, arriving here about 1930 at exactly the same time as all three vehicles rolled in from their mammoth road trip. We were met by members of the Campbeltown Rotary and the Campbeltown Sailing Club who, appropriately, were mostly the same people. They had even laid on a lovely spread of food for us, so much in fact that I think some of it will find its way onto the RIB for today's lunch. We are setting off about 1100 for Ardrishaig at the top of the Kintyre peninsula with the intention of crossing the Crinan Canal tomorrow. This is a significant change to our route but has been made to ensure we maintain momentum and do not get caught by potentially bad weather and strong currents going up the west coast of Kintyre.

With David Cheatham having taken over responsibility for pre-notifying Rotarians of our arrival, the relationship with Rotary had been transformed for the better in an instant. Elaine would call David first thing in the morning with our anticipated destination and estimated time of arrival, at which point David would swing into action telephoning the local Rotary group and not resting until he had found, or persuaded, a volunteer to identify suitable parking and facilities, thereby making life easier for the road crew when they rolled into town. And Campbeltown was one example of that system working at its best. Of course, it helped having a Rotarian who was also a member of the Campbeltown Sailing Club, Frank McHardy. Not only had Frank mobilised the local troops to provide parking and help drag *Freethinker* up the slipway, but he had also talked to his sailing club, who had laid on food for our arrival. But Frank had another string to his bow, for he was also production director at the Campbeltown whisky distillery, Springbank, and he was kind enough to leave us with a bottle of his finest. It should have only been a bottle, but early the following morning Joel and Mike slipped into town with Frank for a private viewing of the distillery and returned laden with bottles – so many that the crew motorhome developed a 'chinking' sound whenever it moved.

The weather had improved, but we would be faced with some quite fierce overfalls if we chose to go up the west coast of the Kintyre peninsula, and there was barely any port of refuge there, should things take a turn for the worse. The alternative was to go up the eastern side, to a port called Ardrishaig, and cut across the top using the Crinan Canal. It was a short canal, only nine miles long, and the trip across could be achieved in a day. And sailing to Ardrishaig, some forty miles away, we would be in protected waters. Having already accepted the benefits of traversing the Caledonian Canal, I was happy that we use the Crinan Canal for the same reasons, and it would also be good practice for the Caledonian too.

With the decision made, we said our farewells and made our way out to sea. Campbeltown harbour is very beautiful but I couldn't help thinking the grass-covered mountain to the south of the harbour looked somewhat unusual. I later discovered that the mountain itself was man-made, and was a NATO fuel storage site.

The sail up the east side of Kintyre was one of those rare days at sea when you would give everything you owned just to stay exactly where you were, it was so perfect. To my left the Kintyre peninsula, to my right the Isle of Arran. The sun was out and I could feel its warmth on my back, all around gannets were diving into the sea, and we saw several pods of dolphins, some heading north and some south. At one point, after a couple of hours, we were about a mile off the coast and sailing north, just offshore from what must be the most perfectly situated house in the British Isles. A huge white Scottish manor house, sat right in the middle of its own horseshoe-shaped long golden beach, with a hillside covered in bright green pine forest rising steeply behind, it looked like something out of a fairy tale. For the first and only time on the trip whilst at sea, Ian turned off *Everest One*'s engines, and we made the two boats fast to each other and ate our sandwiches, our eyes trying to take it all in. It was so stunningly beautiful and peaceful. The realisation that today was the sixtieth day of our journey, the day I had told everyone we would be back in Southampton, was not lost on me – and it could have taken the edge off such an occasion – but, in a strange way, it didn't matter any more.

Day 61, Thursday 19 July 2007:

> We arrived Ardrishaig at 1930 yesterday evening and stayed in the motorhomes in the car park outside the Crinan Canal offices. British Waterways, who own the canal, waived all charges and at 0830, for the first time ever in a Challenger and accompanied by the RIB, I headed into Lock 1 of the Crinan Canal system. The first sea lock was the most turbulent but we had rigged a rubber dinghy between the central hull and each of the two outer floats of the trimaran, with Ian sat in one of them with an outboard motor to power us through the fifteen lock gates. All of the team were involved in crossing the nine-mile stretch of canal, either riding the RIB or operating locks. We arrived Crinan at 1700.

It seemed odd deciding to sit in *Freethinker* whilst crossing the canal, knowing that I could not sail her and that I would be motored through the canal by Ian in the little rubber dinghy lashed to my hull. And I presume all the sightseers at each of the lock gates were thinking the same thing. But if I was to complete this circumnavigation, by whatever route we chose, then I wanted to know that I had at least sat in my boat every inch of the way.

Sitting so low down in my boat, for the duration of the canal trip I had seen nothing but the RIB ahead of me, the banks of the canal either side of me, and the occasional lock gate in front of me. We descended the locks into Crinan, on the west coast, and eventually entered the final lock, the sea lock. Still I had no idea what lay beyond. As it opened, it was like revealing the most beautiful landscape painting I had ever seen. I only wish I had a more extensive vocabulary to find the superlatives to do justice to what lay in front of me.

Day 61, Thursday 19 July 2007 (continued):

As if the harbour itself were not spectacular enough, when the final sea lock opened, the view ahead of me was, without exaggeration, by far the most stunning I have seen in my life, looking out across to Duntroon castle and the Western Isles. I have never seen so many shades of green or such incredible light. I'm still in complete awe.

The only downside to Crinan was that there was no mobile phone coverage, meaning that Elaine could not make her daily calls to Susan and David. So it came as a bit of a shock, when we asked to use the telephone at a hotel, to be met by one of the rudest men I had encountered for a long time – though perhaps we had been spoiled by people's generosity to this point.

'You'll need to come back at 1.00 p.m., there will be a minimum charge of £5, and your call will be monitored,' he barked at Elaine.

Our next stop, Oban, was important to me. It was the destination where I had been privately arranging to rendezvous with Jonathan Lloyd-Jones, senior partner of my sponsor, Blake Lapthorn Tarlo Lyons. With such a changeable schedule, and needing to sail when the opportunity arose to make up for lost time, trying to find a date and destination to coincide with flights to a nearby airport for Jonathan's visit had been very difficult, but Oban it was to be. In truth, we could have sailed on the Saturday, the day we met with him, but there was something very empowering about saying, for the first time since Brixham, 'today, even though we could sail, we are going to take a lay-day.' It felt as though it was us in control again, not the weather.

Day 62, Friday 20 July 2007:

We set sail from Crinan at 1330 today headed Oban. With offshore breezes of 15 knots and no sea state and the tide in my favour, I made the twenty-five-mile journey in little over four hours. Once again the scenery is simply breathtaking. I would say that today's run was the most dramatic and scenic I have ever seen. We arrived all too soon at the slipway of the Puffin Dive Centre in Oban at about 1800 and are settled at a nearby campsite enjoying, for the first time since Deucoch in Abersoch, the luxury of showers, electricity and laundry facilities. It does however miss the friendliness and wonderful view of our friends' campsite in Sarn Bach, Abersoch.

We spent the morning of Saturday 21 July shopping in Oban, doing laundry, stocking up on supplies, and I even managed a haircut – my hairdresser telling me a hilarious story that he had been told by a US naval rating whose hair he had cut earlier that morning. This guy was a sailor on a US naval ship moored in Oban harbour, and he had been out night-clubbing in Oban the night before. On his way back to the ship, at 0300 hours, he decided to join a queue for another night club. In a drunken state, he waited three hours for the queue to move, and when it did start moving at 0600, he got to the front only to realise he had been queuing outside Waterstone's for the latest Harry Potter book to be launched. Unfortunately my hairdresser found the story so funny, I came out looking like a skinhead because he'd used the wrong grade clippers.

It was really good to see Jonathan and his wife Sarah again, even though we were worried that, after living in such confined accommodation and with so little opportunity to shower or wash our clothes, we had started to smell. If we did, they were too polite to mention it. Being so far north, and having been away for such a long time, we were reminded by meeting them that we hadn't been forgotten – and he reassured us of the firm's support for the project, something I needed to hear. It was a joyous few hours, and having dinner that night, recounting our stories from the past nine weeks, enabled us momentarily to forget the enormity of the journey that still lay ahead.

Day 64, Sunday 22 July 2007:

We left Oban at 0700, sailed past Jonathan and Sarah's hotel and saw them waving from their bedroom window. Sailed 35 miles up Loch Linnhe and arrived Fort William 1430. We are now just inside the sea lock at the very start of the Caledonian Canal, ready for an early start tomorrow up through the locks. Despite passing the 700-mile barrier since leaving Southampton, it was a tough voyage today, with northerly winds meaning I had to be towed some of the way. Being towed is horrible, not least because of the constant drenching, which makes me feel very cold. I tend to suffer from the cold, hunching my shoulders, which ends up giving me bad neck and back pain. Today was the coldest I have been on this trip and I don't feel particularly well. I'll have a Lemsip and an early night to try and sleep off the aches and pains from today.

It seems strange to think that once through the Canal we'll be on the east coast and we will start heading south on the long run home – my goodness, home. I can't even recall what home looks like.

I was glad of a good night's rest, and pleased that most of the day would be spent moored alongside *Everest One* as we made our way slowly through the unnavigable sections of the canal. The cold of yesterday had caused a chill in my bones and I felt shivery, and it was bad enough sitting huddled up in the cockpit for eight hours without feeling poorly.

There was some confusion as to the exact time we could start our ascent up the lock system from Fort William. There are apparently only two occasions each day when you can start, and – with an average crossing taking three days to cover the sixty miles – we did not want to miss the first opportunity. So we had risen early and ate our breakfast on the edge of the dock, the imposing Ben Nevis rising in front of us, its top third obscured by cloud.

Ian returned from the canal office at some speed, announcing that they had brought the time forward by an hour. Our only opportunity to go, if we wanted to get in a full day, would be in twenty minutes.

Inside the sea lock of the Caledonian Canal was the first stop on the journey where there was no slipway or marina, just steep sloping grass banks to the water's edge. On arrival the day before, I had been lifted out of my boat from a pontoon outside the sea lock, and *Freethinker* had then been brought inside the lock ready for our ascent. We had already decided that the only way to lift me into *Freethinker* that morning was to use the extending crane that we had fitted to the roof of the Land Rover, and to lower me in from above. We had never used it in a real-life situation before, and now we had less than twenty minutes to do so. The crew sprang into action, and after Elaine had lifted me into my special seat and connected me to the overhead hoisting and safety wires, the Land Rover was positioned with a chock under each wheel to prevent it rolling into the canal, and I was winched up about four feet, then the crane was extended six feet out over the water with me dangling below. Once lined up over *Freethinker*, afloat in the lock, I was gently lowered some ten feet until my seat slotted into the narrow cockpit. I think we were all as surprised as each other at how painless it was, and at how well, in practice, the system had lived up to the theory.

With progress up the first flight of eight locks, known as Neptune's Staircase, taking a couple of hours, Mike and Elaine had so much time to pack and stow the vehicles that Elaine was also able to provide a waitress toast delivery service to myself and the RIB crew. She would arrive with our various orders piled high on a faux silver platter, wait for the water to rise enough in each lock for the boats to be level with the footpath, and simply pass them over – very civilised.

Day 66, Tuesday 24 July 2007:

> After a fascinating two days travelling through the Caledonian Canal, we find ourselves this evening at Dochgarroch, only a short run and five locks from the end of the canal, Inverness and the east coast.

The following day, after three full days of travelling, having negotiated twenty-nine locks, been pulled through twenty miles of unnavigable sections of the canal and having sailed through nearly forty miles of navigable lochs, including Loch Ness, on day 67, Wednesday 25 July, we finally reached the end of the Caledonian Canal.

Having a three-day break from sailing at sea was a welcome break, although there were some hairy moments in Loch Ness when the wind funnelled down the loch with tremendous speed. I was struck by several things in the Caledonian, not least how black the water was, but how cold it was too – bitterly cold water – and when it splashed on my face it seemed particularly odd that it was fresh water and it no longer stung my eyes like the salt water of the sea. But perhaps what I found strangest when sailing through Loch Ness was the depth. Having sailed the Irish Sea with depths of forty or fifty metres, it beggared belief that this long, narrow inland stretch of water was up to 230 metres deep in parts.

Day 68, Thursday 26 July 2007:

It took an agonising five hours of waiting for swing bridges, locks and the final rail bridge to eventually exit the Caledonian Canal at the Inverness sea lock. Once out, we were officially on the east coast and the North Sea. We rounded Fort George and were welcomed by many dolphins, well in excess of twenty, and a huge colony of seals. With an offshore breeze gusting to 15 knots at times and with dead calm seas, I broad-reached the twenty miles to Nairn at a fantastic speed, at times touching 10 knots. In fact, we arrived so early, there was barely enough water to get *Freethinker* over the sand bar, and the RIB had to wait another hour to get in. Considering it was an unexpected stop, the Nairn Sailing Club and Alex the harbour master made us extremely welcome, providing overnight facilities for the boats and vehicles. It was a lovely spot. This morning, just before we left Nairn, we were provided with a bag of home-grown veggies from a local well-wisher which will go perfectly with our haggis tonight (well, you've got to try it, haven't you?).

With light winds forecast, we headed off at 1000 for Buckie, but with such excellent sea conditions and a following tide we made good time and once again changed our plans, this time going an extra fifteen miles to Whitehills, another previously unconsidered port of call but an extremely pleasant surprise. It's a tiny harbour, perfectly protected from all wind directions, and we've got good parking facilities with electricity, laundry and showers – what more could you ask for?

Popping out of the Caledonian Canal into the Moray Firth on the east coast was a good feeling. From now on we wouldn't be sailing north – we were as far north as we were going to go, which was just as well, with the air and sea temperatures considerably lower than further south. I was also struck by the colour of water, a light brown, tea-like colour, so different from the crystal-clear waters of the west coast. The weather was bright but blustery, and our morning call to Weather Online had not filled us with confidence. As I made my way into the tiny harbour of Whitehills, I could see the ominous black clouds already brewing out to the southeast.

Back in 1983, as a young lad, I had worked for several months in Beth's Restaurant in Hamble. One of the trainee chefs there was a girl called Annie Hammond, and we had been good friends but had lost touch when I departed for the Caribbean. Unknown to me, her mother had been charting my sailing exploits via our local TV station and had been keeping Annie updated on my progress. Some weeks earlier, Annie Crabtree, as she was now, had contacted me through my website to say 'hello' and to say that she was now married with three kids and living in northeast Scotland. And, like many others who emailed and sent messages, she said she would like to meet if we were passing. Unable to commit to a schedule, I had long since lost count of all the missed opportunities to meet up with people on the way. Arranging to meet people on this trip had the same falseness about it that one feels when writing 'we mustn't leave it so long next time, I promise to be in touch' on a Christmas card. And part of me believed the same would be true with Annie. But what I hadn't bargained for was being weather-bound in Whitehills.

When we arrived, and not really knowing where she lived in relation to Whitehills, I sent Annie a quick email to say where we were, and that we were likely to be stuck for a couple of days, so would it be OK to meet up? As luck would have it, we were only a matter of miles away – and less than an hour later Annie turned up with all three daughters, Mollie, Louisa and Pippa, and a basket full of local cheeses and home-made bread. It was so good to see her again, especially after all this time, although it was bizarre that circumstances meant it should be in a motorhome in a remote fishing harbour in northeast Scotland. I had been telling the crew about Annie's cooking, so there was much merriment when she invited us all over for roast dinner at their house, assuming we were still weather-bound, on the Sunday lunchtime.

Day 68, Thursday 26 July 2007 (continued):

> We have several changes over the next few days which could affect our progress. Joel leaves us on Saturday, having been with us from day one. We'll be really sorry to see him go. We then have an issue over camper-vans, or the lack of them, for a week to 7 August, plus new crew arriving etc. It's going to further complicate an already complicated set of logistics. With any luck, we may even get some decent weather for the run south, but in the short term things are not looking very promising. Whether we sail or not tomorrow will very much depend on tonight's forecast – but it's not looking good.

It was sad to see Joel leave that Saturday, especially because, had we finished the voyage in sixty days as I said we would, we would have been back by now and he would have completed the whole trip. As it was, he was having to leave us at the halfway mark. Ian and I had looked at options for replacing Joel, with one idea being to operate with one less crew – not an ideal situation but it would be manageable, just. I had also shared my concerns with Susan Preston-Davis, and she reminded me that Eddie Edrich, husband of her friend Pam, had offered his services. I exchanged emails with Eddie and, on the basis that he could help out for a couple of weeks, he was going to make his way up from Southampton to Scotland and would join us, wherever we might be at that time, on Tuesday 31 July. We had met briefly before but I certainly didn't know him well and, as far I was concerned, Eddie was very much an unknown quantity.

That same Saturday was Mike's birthday, but he chose not to join Andy, Sarah, Elaine, Timothy and myself at the Dufftown Highland Games, preferring instead to stay behind and catch up on some letter writing. It was the first time I'd ever been to a Highland Games, and it was everything I had imagined it would be: caber tossing, hammer throwing, pipes, drums, and even a private audience with the local Chieftain. It pelted down with rain all day but it seemed not to bother Annie's kids, who spent the whole afternoon running around with Timothy in the rain-soaked fields. Not wishing to neglect Mike on his big day, that evening the whole crew visited a hotel in Cullen Bay for dinner, where we tried their local speciality, Cullen Skink, a creamy smoked fish soup which met with mixed approval from the crew. It was nearly midnight by the time we got back.

The following day, and still (thankfully) weather-bound, we all took extra trouble getting showered and putting on our cleanest, smartest clothes. After all, it wasn't every day that we were invited to someone's house for lunch and, secretly, we had all been dreaming about the prospect of succulent roast lamb and roast potatoes, all cooked in a real oven, a treat not enjoyed for more than two months. Nor were we disappointed – it was simply delicious – and nor were any of us embarrassed when asking for seconds and thirds. And afterwards, with stomachs full to bursting, whilst Timothy and the girls ran riot outside in the garden with their black Labrador and new litter of adorable puppies, we sat in Annie's huge front room, drinking port, some of the crew sprawling across her deep, plump sofas, just reading the Sunday papers. It was fantastic, and for a few hours at least we felt human again. But I did feel sorry for Annie's husband Tim, who must have wondered what the hell his wife had let into their beautiful home.

Without doubt the single largest concern to me at this time

was the issue of the motorhome. I first flagged my concern on my blog back in Tenby about the project over-running and the crew motorhome having to be returned on Monday 30 July. For the past month, whenever I found spare time between sailing, I scoured the internet on my laptop computer and made countless telephone calls trying to find a replacement motorhome to arrive the day the original one had to be returned. The crew were aware that the time was fast approaching, but I'm convinced they thought I wasn't giving it the attention it deserved. On the contrary. Not only was I trying to locate a seven-berth vehicle for an eight-week hire, but even the *Portsmouth Evening News* had run the story to try and help me locate a suitable vehicle, all to no avail. After a lot of effort, I finally had a breakthrough and found a company who could provide what we needed, except they were based in Luton, which was 570 miles away, rental would be a £1,000 a week, and we could not take possession until Tuesday 7 August, a week after the original vehicle had to be returned.

With no alternative, during the interim period the crew would have to stay in local B&Bs, which would not be too much of a hardship whilst we were weather-bound and stuck in one place, but if the weather improved it would prove very complicated to continue on the journey with the crew living out of different accommodation and in different destinations each night. And with no motorhome for a week, there was nowhere to stow all of their personal belongings and pieces of equipment – a substantial amount of kit.

So electric light bulbs were flicking themselves on in my head when I saw Annie's horsebox sat on her drive that afternoon. It wouldn't exactly be secure, but it would enable us to stow all the non-essential items and keep mobile if the weather improved. I'm not sure that Annie entirely approved, but thankfully she agreed, and for the next seven days we added a horsebox to our inventory of vehicles.

With the original crew motorhome now gone, its contents emptied into the horsebox and the crew booked into a B&B a few hundred yards from the harbour in Whitehills, once again we started the waiting game for the weather.

Day 72, Monday 30 July 2007:

> We are now on day four into our unplanned stay at Whitehills. The force 4 on Friday has slowly built into a steady force 7 today, the sea state has also increased to rough, and the view from our motorhomes out across the Moray Firth is of nothing but white horses breaking on huge waves.

The following day, Tuesday 31 July, new crewman Eddie arrived. With none of us knowing his background, and with time to spare, we explained the daily routine of life at sea on the RIB and on the road with the road crew, and tried to illicit from Eddie his experience, so we knew what responsibilities to give him. It was a 'granny sucking eggs' moment to discover Eddie had been chief marine engineer and mechanic for a Formula One power-boat racing team. He had also owned and run his own sailing school, so we were in safe hands. But Eddie's biggest asset was himself. He was an affable and immediately likeable bloke, an instant favourite with the entire crew. Within minutes of Eddie's arrival, Ian was capitalising on his expertise and had him changing the injectors on the Land Rover.

With Eddie came improved weather, and we made ready to sail on Wednesday 1 August. What should have been a normal departure routine was thrown into chaos when I logged into my blog that morning to leave a quick message.

I noticed that crew member Andy had left a message on my blog at midnight the night before from his B&B which read:

> Meeting Annie and her family has been a huge positive in an otherwise grim time. The folk in Whitehills have been fantastic in their generosity and if you are ever sailing this region, stop here, you are sure of a welcome. Otherwise morale is being tested to its limits, onwards and upwards!

My heart sank. A seemingly innocuous comment, I knew that it was enough to spark controversy. And I wasn't wrong. As I was actually reading the message and deciding what to do, another message was left by a well-intentioned, but ill-informed, supporter which read:

Dear Geoff, From now on you will be gravity-assisted heading south. Regrettably, I have kicked your main sponsor for not giving you adequate support. If morale is low, rest assured you have some supporters who think you, your family and team are not too bad. Good luck.

And no sooner had I read that than my phone rang. Elaine answered it.

'Geoff, it's the *Portsmouth Evening News*, they've read your blog. Can you give a comment on morale and what's going wrong?'

'Tell them I'm busy, I'll call them back,' I hissed.

I was still considering my options when, less than a minute later, the phone rang again – it was still only 0830 hours. Once again Elaine took the call. 'Geoff, it's Adam, they've had an email they need to speak with you about.' Adam was marketing manager for my sponsor, Blake Lapthorn Tarlo Lyons.

'Hi Adam,' I said, taking the phone from Elaine.

'Geoff, we've had an email from someone, addressed to Jonathan Lloyd-Jones, critical that we've apparently not given you enough sponsorship so you can't afford a motorhome for the crew. I'm going to have to show him it. Can you explain?'

What was frustrating was that the motorhome issue was never about money, it was about availability, and it was certainly nothing to do with my sponsor.

'It's OK,' I reassured him, 'it's a misunderstanding. I'll take the blog message down and email the chap and put him right.'

'For fuck's sake,' I shouted, passing the phone back to Elaine, 'that's all I need, someone having a go at my sponsor over something that is not their fault, and all because Andy left that comment.'

Having worked with the press for years, I was highly sensitised to the media, and in particular I was very careful about what I said on my blog – why else did it take me more than an hour to complete it each day? It certainly wasn't because of my typing. It was because I would read, re-read, and read my words again, at least three times, checking for the slightest hint of ambiguity that could be misconstrued by the press. And now Andy's unchecked comment, coming from a member of my crew stating morale was low, was picked up by the press, and by someone who then used it to have a go at my sponsor. I was seething with fury.

I immediately took the offending blog entry down and sent an email to the person concerned, who did in fact retract his accusations straight away and wrote an apology on the blog and to my sponsors. But it would be another two days before I could raise it with Andy, who I knew was going through a tough time himself.

This was the last thing I needed, just before heading out into the North Sea on another gruelling eight-hour sail.

18

'Were your ears burning this morning?' asked Elaine as she came through the front door one Saturday lunchtime.

'No, why?' I replied.

'Does the name Diana Campbell mean anything to you?'

I thought for a moment before replying, 'No. Should it?'

'Well, she remembers you,' Elaine explained. 'She was the job I was sent to this morning by the nursing agency. She's a disabled lady, lives in Hamble, says that you used to help her when you worked at Beth's Restaurant. Apparently you used to help bump her wheelchair up the restaurant steps and made sure she was comfortable. She obviously took quite a shine to you.'

I did vaguely recall helping a lady in a wheelchair, but working in a restaurant you get to meet a great many people – and besides, much had happened in my life since then.

'Well, she's asked us around for drinks next week,' said Elaine.

Being self-conscious of my disability at this time, I never particularly liked going to meet strangers in a social setting. I normally enjoyed it once I got there, but never knew what to expect, so I wasn't especially looking forward to meeting up again with this lady who remembered me more than I did her.

To my surprise, I recognised Diana straight away. As soon as I saw her, I remembered thinking all those years ago how frail she looked in her small wheelchair, and she still looked the same. In her mid sixties, Diana, or Tid, as she was generally known, her body cruelly twisted by a mixture of chronic rheumatoid arthritis and a rare arthritic condition known as Still's disease, was a charming host. I didn't realise it at the time, but she was also fighting cancer, and the combination of the three left her in acute pain, which she hid well.

Despite her crippling disability, she was an imposing character with a wicked glint in her eye. Within minutes of arriving at her flat, I had a rum and soda in my hand which Elaine had been gruffly ordered to make by Tid. She then showed me around her home, paying particular attention to a magnificent oil painting of a cavalry scene in north Africa hanging on the wall of the dining area. She told me that it depicted her father, Major Jock Campbell, an accomplished horseman who had won the Victoria Cross for outstanding valour. She opened a drawer in the mahogany bureau which stood beneath the painting and produced a smart burgundy box, slowly opening it to proudly show me her father's VC medal; it was a magnificent thing. She fell silent, and I could see that she was becoming emotional.

After a moment's awkward silence, she barked, 'Right, so you were a yachtsman were you?' changing both subject and mood entirely, which took me by surprise. Putting the medal back in the drawer, she ushered me through to her small but immaculate living room. 'So, tell me all about it, where you worked, who for and what it was like.'

I spent the next hour or so recounting my nautical stories as though I were talking to a complete novice, blissfully unaware of Tid's own experiences. Once I had finished, she started to tell me snippets of her life story. I began to cringe with embarrassment as she told me of her experiences at sea – sailing across the Atlantic, the many and varied boats that she had owned and had built for her, and the great lengths she had gone to in helping to design a new class of boat for disabled sailors called a Challenger trimaran dinghy. I began to realise that this frail little old disabled lady was not quite what she seemed. She certainly knew a lot of influential people, and she was clearly wealthy, but there was much more to this truly enigmatic woman than that. The key to Tid Campbell lay in her strength of character, her confidence and her sheer bloody-mindedness. Unwittingly, my previous acts of thoughtfulness at the restaurant some years earlier had earned me the right to call myself one of her friends, and I was very lucky in that respect. It was a friendship that was to grow and that I was to cherish very much indeed. Without doubt, the synchronicity that brought the two of us together that day was to change my life as much as my accident had done a few years earlier.

Over the following weeks and months we met several times. On each occasion she would drill me for my views on the sailing opportunities that existed for disabled people in the UK, and my thoughts on which boats were most suitable for disabled people to sail. I had very few views on disabled sailing, simply because I had no experience in that respect. Since my accident in 1984 I had not once been on a sailing boat – it was now 1991, seven years later – but I did not have the nerve to tell her that. In fact, I had not told anyone. Of course Elaine knew, but as far as anyone else was aware I was still sailing. I had managed to bluff for seven years, but the moment came in August 1991 when that would all change.

'Geoffrey,' Tid bellowed down the phone – previously, only my mother, my Nana, Elaine or Joyce could ever get away with calling me Geoffrey, and it normally meant that I had done something wrong –

'I've been listening to what you've been saying and I have spoken with the boat designer Reg White about a modified version of the Challenger trimaran. We've called it the Mark 2 Challenger, and the first of the new boats arrives in Southampton next week. I've phoned the BBC and they are sending a film crew to record you taking her out for her first sail. I've also phoned Bugs Hughes and he'll be there too.'

Brigadier Bugs Hughes was the Director of the Seamanship Foundation, a charity run by the Royal Yachting Association, and he was a leading light in the development of sailing for the disabled. To that point, I'd only ever heard of him and the charity from what Tid had told me, and she was not over-complimentary about either – but, then again, she wasn't about most things.

Putting the phone down, I felt a mix of emotions. I was obviously excited at the prospect of sailing again, but I was somewhat frightened too. I was worried that I might have forgotten how to sail or, worse still, that I might crash the boat into something, and then what would people think? I had several sleepless nights that week.

When the big day arrived, nerves were getting the better of me. Wearing only jeans, a T-shirt and a lifejacket, I felt dizzy and faint. As Elaine lifted me down into the tiny boat she whispered in my ear, 'I hope to God you know what you're doing.' Her words didn't exactly fill me with confidence, but I shared her sentiments.

Luckily for me the weather was kind and my sail, the first in seven years and my first ever as a disabled person, went off without incident. Just being back on the water again felt wonderful, but despite spending so much of my life at sea this time was special. For the past seven years I had got used to the fact that I was pushed everywhere in my wheelchair. But just because I'd got use to it didn't mean that I liked it. Sometimes I made the decisions where I went, sometimes the person pushing me made those decisions, but it was always someone pushing me. The moment I sailed away from the pontoon and steered the boat out into Southampton Water, I had an overwhelming feeling of freedom and independence that I'd not experienced before. It was like a rebirth, and I found myself yelping out loud with excitement. I pulled the mainsheet in and, with the wind rushing through my hair, my boat accelerated across the river. It felt magical. It felt as though I was completely free again. When I turned to come back, there in the distance, on the pontoon alongside Elaine, Tid, Bugs and the film crew, was my wheelchair, a distant silhouette, empty. It felt strange looking at it from afar. Normally I only ever get to see my wheelchair when I'm lying in bed, so to see it so far away but still to be mobile and free felt very odd.

'Just five more minutes,' I shouted as Bugs bellowed an

instruction to return. It was such a great feeling. I struggled a bit pulling the ropes with my clawed hands, and the hard plastic seating was in danger of giving me a pressure sore on my bum, but I knew these were only minor issues and would be easily rectified.

Back ashore, with a grin stretching from ear to ear, I gave my interview to the BBC.

When it was broadcast that evening, both Tid and I were to receive unexpected benefits from the coverage. Less than ten minutes after it was shown, Tid took a call from her estranged sister, Dill Fortescue, who lived on the Isle of Wight. Dill had not seen or spoken to Tid for many years, but seeing her on television that evening prompted her to phone and to call a truce to a family disagreement that had lasted too long. Despite their happy reconciliation, Dill had some sad news for Tid. Since they had last spoken, Dill's son and Tid's nephew, Billy, a thirty-year-old father of two, had recently died after a brief fight with cancer. Having seen the broadcast on TV that night, Dill was so moved she offered the money to buy a new Challenger trimaran dinghy, to be given to someone nominated by Tid, so long as the boat was called *Billy* in memory of her son.

Without a second thought Tid requested that I be the recipient of the new boat, and I was both surprised and grateful when Tid phoned with the news.

Bugs Hughes was not as I had expected. A typical ex-brigadier, he had a voice that could knock you backwards if he chose to use it. A no-nonsense man, he was also a true gentleman and was driven by the motivation of seeing the joy and pleasure sailing gave to disabled people. We quickly became friends, and I respected everything he said and stood for.

When my new boat *Billy*, sail number 121, arrived a few weeks later, Bugs put me in touch with other like-minded disabled sailors, and it was not long before I was dragging poor Elaine to reservoirs and gravel pits around the country most weekends racing my new boat, getting to know the other sailors and beginning to understand the political structure of disabled sailing, which was still very much in its infancy.

To show my appreciation to Dill, and as a means of raising awareness of the Challenger – which I knew would please Tid – in 1992 I decided that I would try and sail around the Isle of Wight in *Billy*. I also hoped that it would help to raise funds for the RYA Seamanship Foundation. Quite how or why I came up with the idea I don't know, but it was a challenge that I felt was just about achievable.

Juggling work with my renewed interest in sailing was not easy, but poor Elaine was kind enough not to complain. My employers too were most accommodating, and with a few hundred pounds in sponsorship Coopers & Lybrand Deloitte not only provided me with much-needed money to fund the record attempt – I would become the first disabled sailor ever to achieve it single-handed – but also allowed me several hours a week of work time off work to spend preparing for my project, which I rather unimaginatively entitled Challenge '92.

I had frequently spent six or more hours in my boat when racing at regattas without any particular difficulty, so I reckoned that spending a few extra hours in the boat, assuming I resolved matters like seating, eating and drinking, would not be too much of a problem for a trip around the Isle of Wight. With a distance of some sixty miles, I knew it would be a genuine test of my stamina and my sailing skills. Bugs kindly offered to help me train for the voyage, but I hadn't quite realised what I'd let myself in for.

Several evenings, after we finished work and when tide and weather permitted, Elaine and I would meet Bugs at Weston Sailing Club on the banks of Southampton Water. Elaine would help me into my waterproof sailing clothes and lifejacket before launching me, and Bugs would follow me out to Southampton Water in a fast rescue boat. On one occasion it was blowing a strong force 4, gusting force 5. Arriving at Calshot Spit in the Solent in *Billy*, Bugs ordered me to sail across to Osborne Bay on the Isle of Wight. It was only about a four-mile trip but it took me across the notorious Brambles Bank in the middle of the Solent, where the water shallowed and became increasingly choppy. Half an hour later I arrived at Osborne Bay where, without pausing to rest, Bugs ordered me to sail back across to Calshot. Sailing back into the wind and against the waves was tough, and I took a lot of water on board, but forty minutes later I arrived, feeling rather pleased with myself. Bugs immediately ordered me back across to Osborne for a second time. I arrived about thirty minutes later, feeling much more tired and exhausted, so it was through a false grin that I agreed to sail back to Calshot again, my fourth crossing of the Brambles Bank. By the time I arrived at Calshot for the second time I was close to tears. I was extremely cold and wet, and my shoulders were so hunched up because of the cold I could hardly move my arms to steer. The salt water was stinging my eyes so much I could barely see, and I could tell that we were fast running out of daylight. So when Bugs shouted at me to commence my third crossing back to Osborne Bay, I found myself losing control –

'No Bugs, I can't do any more!' I didn't want him to see that I was within an inch of crying. 'Why are you deliberately trying to do hurt me?' I bellowed at him, partly hoping he wouldn't hear, partly hoping he would. To this day I don't know if he did.

'Good. I've found your breaking point,' he shouted through his loud-hailer. 'Now, get back to the sailing club and into the warm.'

As we headed back up Southampton Water to the sailing club I was really cross with Bugs. Didn't he know that I was a quadriplegic, and didn't he realise that his instructions had caused me so much pain and discomfort? The truth is that of course he knew, and it was his way of determining the extent of my stamina and how much punishment I could take, which would be essential for the sail around the island – but at the time I felt rather sorry for myself.

Challenge '92 was a great success in almost every way. Although it took me a gruelling fourteen hours to circumnavigate the Isle of Wight, with Bugs alongside me in a support boat every inch of the way, in so doing I became the first disabled person to make the trip single-handed. Most importantly, apart from severe fatigue, my body had held out. I suffered with minor dehydration, which was my fault for not drinking enough fluids, but my biggest fear, that of a pressure sore on my backside, did not materialise, and that was entirely due to the special seat that had been custom-made for me by the Department of Medical Engineering at Salisbury Hospital. I suffered a few cuts on my hands and had a rather sunburned face, but crossing that finishing line off the Royal Yacht Squadron made me feel ten feet tall. My achievement was reported on local television and published in the mainstream yachting press, raising awareness for disabled sailing and the Challenger trimaran, all the more satisfying considering it was at a time before email and the internet. My efforts also raised £10,000 for the Seamanship Foundation – but it was seeing the pleasure it gave Tid that was my greatest reward. The Challenger dinghy had not only given me back sailing, but out on the water it provided me with a means for my mind to escape the difficulties of everyday life as a disabled person. Were it not for Tid and her ambition to develop a boat for exactly that purpose, my life would have been much the poorer.

A few years later I took a phone call at work.

'Geoffrey, what are you and Elaine doing next week?' asked Tid. It was unusual for her to call me at work, so I presumed there was a problem.

'Nothing,' I replied, still rather concerned.

'Good,' she said. 'I've spoken to your boss and he's given you the week off. You and Elaine fly out from Heathrow first class on Saturday to Antigua, all expenses paid. You are staying at a hotel in English Harbour.'

I didn't know what to say. My 'thank you' seemed a rather inadequate response to such a generous gesture.

'There is one condition,' she continued. 'I want you to take photos, as many photos as you can of the islands – and when you get back, you and Elaine will come to dinner and I want to hear all about it.'

Tid had spent many years in the Caribbean when she was younger, and since becoming friends we had spent many an evening reminiscing about the islands, especially our favourite, Antigua. Apart from periodic trips to the British Virgin Islands for my ongoing court case against Endless Summer Charters, Elaine had never had a holiday in the Caribbean, and a week in Antigua was a timely break that we both enjoyed very much.

The Tuesday immediately following our return was spent eating a Chinese takeaway and poring over hundreds of photographs of Antigua with Tid in the front room of her flat in Hamble. For the first time in my life I saw her drink, only a small rum cocktail, and she looked happy. I watched her as she laughed and recounted raucous stories of her times in the Caribbean, and for the first time she looked at peace, she showed no signs of pain, she looked beautiful. As we left that evening, she asked if I was sailing that coming Friday. It was the Easter Bank Holiday weekend.

'Yes, I'm taking *Billy* out for the Good Friday race at the club. High tide is at midday.'

'No it's not,' she corrected me, 'it's at 1.00 p.m.'

It wasn't the first time I had been corrected by Tid over one thing or another, but the reason why an elderly disabled lady would know tide times for three days hence didn't register with me at the time. With hindsight it was obvious.

Good Friday was a beautiful sunny spring day with a light breeze blowing from the west. I had been sailing *Billy* in a race at the Weston Sailing Club when I started to feel a bit cold, so I headed back at about 1.30 p.m. I could see Elaine, up to her waist in the water, wearing her wetsuit, waiting to catch *Billy* as

I returned to shore. This was our normal routine so I wasn't concerned – but as I got closer I could see she was crying.

'What's wrong?' I asked, as she grabbed the front of the boat.

'It's Tid,' she said. 'They found her body in the River Hamble this morning.'

My heart sank, and for a moment the world stood still. I just sat there, in *Billy*, a boat which owed its existence to her and which was named in memory of her nephew. If I had to hear of her death, then you could say this was perfect timing. Still floating on the water, I buried my head in my hands and wept. I felt empty, helpless and so desperately sad. Poor Tid. Suddenly it all made sense: the holiday, the photos, the dinner, knowing the time of high tide. She had it all planned, and that's why she had been so happy and contented on Tuesday. The previous evening, at about midnight, when it was high tide on the river, Tid wheeled herself around to the quayside at Hamble in her electric wheelchair and, in an act that must have taken huge courage, propelled herself over the edge and into the bitterly cold, black waters below. She could not swim. At least she was now at peace where she could feel no pain, but she left a huge hole in my life.

Having a wicked sense of humour, Tid had saved her best surprise until last. She named me specifically in her will to dispose of her ashes on the River Hamble whilst sailing *Billy*. She also stipulated that nobody attend her funeral and that *My Way* by Frank Sinatra was to be played whilst she was cremated, so typically Tid. When the urn containing her ashes arrived at the Hamble Point Boatyard, where twenty or so mourners had gathered that blustery and solemn day, I suddenly realised the physical difficulties I was about to face.

Needless to say it was blowing over 20 knots of wind, which was only going to add to the comedy about to unfold as a quadriplegic sailor tried to control a boat whilst at the same time struggling to pour his friend's ashes on the sea. Upon seeing the enormous urn of ashes, which was the size of an old fashioned sweetie-jar and far too cumbersome and heavy for me to hold, I asked a friend to slip discreetly down to the waterside and find something more practical. In the distance, I could see clouds of ash blowing around as he tried to decant Tid into a smaller container at the water's edge without drawing attention to his actions. As I was launched from the slipway with a small bouquet of orchids on my lap, my friend presented me with a white plastic scoop containing only a fraction of her ashes, the rest long since blown out to sea. It was an old dinghy bailer that had been fashioned by cutting a chemical carton in half, and the warning *Danger Highly Toxic Contents*, written in red with a skull and crossbones emblem, was still clearly visible. Hardly the most appropriate – but Tid would have seen the funny side. With *Billy* heaved-to in the middle of the river, I respectfully removed my woolly hat and proceeded to pour Tid's ashes, what was left of them, downwind into the River Hamble. Unfortunately, the blustery wind ended up blowing her all over the place, including over *Billy* and me, and I had to wipe a cement-like mix of sea spray and cremated Tid out of my eyes before I could see well enough to lay the orchids on the water.

'Good bye Tid, look after me,' I whispered as I set the flowers adrift.

Life felt empty without Tid. I understood Tid and she understood me. She had given me back the means and the confidence to sail again, but she had also set me on the road to becoming involved with the rapidly developing world of sailing for disabled people in the UK. And to help that development, she had left more than £250,000 in her will to the RYA Seamanship Foundation. The legacy was to be spent entirely on purchasing new and maintaining old Challenger trimarans, which she had dedicated so much of her life to developing so that people like me could experience the same freedom and enjoyment of sailing that she had. If she needed a missionary for her dream, she had one in me.

I first met Princess Anne in 1992. A combination of factors, most notably my sail around the Isle of Wight and my interest in the Seamanship Foundation, had brought me to the attention of the UK's governing body for sailing, the Royal Yachting Association. At that time, a forward-thinking chairman of the RYA, Peter Cotgrove, had persuaded the RYA Council that it would be beneficial to have someone representing disabled sailors on their national council. My name was put forward, and less than a month later I found myself wheeling into the Royal Thames Yacht Club in Knightsbridge, smartly dressed in a blazer and my new RYA tie. Everyone in the room stood as the Princess entered the room directly behind me, and I felt myself getting quite nervous. She walked around the group of standing, mostly elderly men, and took her seat directly opposite me. She gave me a warm smile, and after the meeting had begun she personally welcomed me to Council.

At home later that night I was phoning all of my friends. 'Guess who I was with today?' I asked each of them. It all seemed slightly odd, little old me, sat in a room with the Queen's daughter.

A year later I was asked to sit on a working party that was to bring together the two disabled sailing charities of the UK, the RYA's Seamanship Foundation, which predominantly looked after the interests of blind sailors, and Sailability, which primarily looked after the racing, both at home and abroad, for physically disabled sailors. Both charities served an important role, and many of the sailors and helpers were well known within both organisations. At the time there were probably a hundred or so disabled sailors who sailed regularly on 'the circuit' at a handful of clubs, which had evolved, on their own and without help, to offer sailing for disabled people. It made sense to bring the two charities together and to consolidate efforts to find more sailors and volunteers. And becoming one organisation would bring the added benefit of helping to raise money to fund the development of new clubs and provide the necessary specialist training.

Thankfully, all parties agreed to the idea of a new charity, to be called RYA Sailability. The road to the merger was anything but straightforward, however, and after more than two years' hard work brokering deals between the parties, finally, in the autumn of 1995, and with Princess Anne agreeing to be patron of the new charity, it was approved by the members and the Charity Commission, and RYA Sailability was born.

Along with nine other people selected for their business acumen and understanding of disabled sailing, I was elected as one of the ten trustees. The first item on the agenda of that very first meeting in November 1995 was the election of a chairman, and there was only one candidate, my friend Ian Harrison, a very experienced disabled sailor with a sharp political mind. With only one candidate, I was asked privately by another trustee to allow my name to go forward so that it would be a true election rather than a coronation – and much to my surprise I was duly elected by a majority vote. It came as quite a shock to me, as well as to Ian. I was just 29 years old and I found myself chairman of a national charity with a monumental task ahead of it. To be honest, at the time, I felt too immature and too naive for the role, but I was surrounded by nine much older, much wiser, much more politically motivated people, so I felt I was in safe hands.

The following six years that I spent as chairman, and a further two as vice-chairman, were very tough indeed. Effectively, the charity was starting again from scratch, albeit with a strong volunteer base. Disabled people had been sailing in various guises for years and had been helped by a dedicated group of volunteers at a few dozen clubs in the UK. But with the advent of RYA Sailability, every single sailor and volunteer now had a view about how the charity should be run – and they were not afraid to let those views be heard. With a publicly stated target to grow participation over a ten-year period to 20,000 disabled people a year, it was always going to be tough trying to please everyone. We not only had to raise the funds to implement the strategy, we also had to mediate and maintain good will with all the existing sailors and volunteers. The underlying problem with the charity in its early years was one of structure: too many trustees, many of them with entrenched views, micro-managing a staff who also had their own strong views. On top of this, there was a highly vocal group of sailors and volunteers who felt disenfranchised. And I was caught in the middle of what felt, at times, like full-scale warfare.

Inevitably, despite huge strides forward, the charity made some questionable decisions over the years, not least over staffing, and the decision to change the constitution and scrap public membership in favour of having only one member, the RYA. From that moment, the sense of ownership felt by the sailors themselves ceased to exist, and that was a key moment in the relationship between the charity and the sailors whom it was established to support. I was persuaded to vote in favour of the change. I was wrong to do so, I should have stuck to my conscience, but with a unanimous vote in favour by all the trustees it would have made no difference to the outcome.

Although I felt the membership issue may have been a mistake, it made no difference to policy. The overall objective of the charity, to develop and increase sailing opportunities for disabled people across the country, could not be challenged or ignored, even by the fiercest critic, and the rapid increase in numbers of sailors, volunteers and groups was a testament to that policy. Slowly, as the development plan was implemented, as more and more Sailability clubs were set up, as more and more specialist training was delivered, and as the charity gained a greater depth and breadth of expertise, to see the extent of its expansion was worth all of the hard work and heartache invested in those early years. As the national governing body for the sport, the RYA played its part in supporting the charity, and through dialogue and gentle persuasion disabled sailing was given equal footing with just about all of the other departments within the RYA such as racing and training. RYA Sailability even shared the same building as the RYA, setting a benchmark and sending out a very strong message to other sporting governing bodies throughout the country. And as awareness of the charity grew, so too did the number of disabled people participating. My involvement with Sailability taught me many lessons, and I was most surprised to discover that even in the charity sector there are people who play politically motivated games. In a business sense, I grew up fast.

The same year as RYA Sailability was born, I had been promoted by my new employer, Deloitte & Touche, to senior management in the marketing department. An otherwise un-noteworthy event, it turned out to be very significant indeed. With my promotion came the offer of a company car. When the memo arrived on my desk, I read down the list: Rover, Ford, Volvo, all the usual middle-management cars you might expect. My boss at the time was Ray Gibbs, a very easy-going partner in the firm whom I got on well with.

'Hi Ray, I've had this memo through,' I said as I wheeled into his office. 'I know this is a huge ask, but if the firm are prepared to give me a car, do you think they'd consider a company van, modified so I could drive it?'

I had played about with hand controls on a few cars since my accident. Once in a car I could just about manage to drive, but the habitual problem of 'normal' cars for me was that I needed to be lifted out of my wheelchair and into the car seat. It was tough enough asking Elaine to lift me in and out of my wheelchair, but in and out of the driver's seat of a car defeated the object of being independent, especially if I then needed help to be lifted out at the other end of my journey. For the previous ten years, Elaine had lifted me in and out of our family car at least twice a day when we went to work. Occasionally I would use a taxi, but finding a wheelchair-accessible taxi in the mid 1990s was not easy. I had seen on TV a specially adapted van that could be driven by someone in a wheelchair so I knew it was possible, but I was never going to be able to afford it myself.

'How much will it cost?' asked Ray.

'I've no idea,' I said, 'but I can find out.'

'Leave it with me and I'll speak to the other partners.'

Less than a week later, having provided them with all the estimates – some £30,000 – I was completely speechless when Ray told me that the partners had agreed to my suggestion. Regardless of the money, I don't think they realised just what it meant to me. The vehicle quite literally changed my life. I had already rediscovered my freedom and independence on water through sailing, and now I was to enjoy those same freedoms on land. My shiny new blue Transit van, completely modified so I could drive from my wheelchair, arrived some months later. It opened up a whole new world, not only for me but also for Elaine, who was relieved of some of the lifting and now had more time to herself without chasing around after me every five minutes. I later learned that the partners had kindly used their own office budget to cover the extra cost. I know it was a purely commercial decision on their part, because being more independent meant that I could do my job of regional marketing more productively, but it was a tremendously big step for them, and I was appreciative of the faith they had put in me.

With my new independence, I took on more committee roles in the world of disabled sailing. Chairmanship of RYA Sailability and sitting on RYA Council meant that I was already uniquely placed to have a sound understanding of the sport in the UK, but there was still a gap in what was happening on a global scale. The body which looks after international disabled sailing is called the International Foundation of Disabled Sailing (IFDS). If sailing for disabled people in the UK felt fragmented, then IFDS at the time was nothing more than a few highly influential countries who had banded together and organised international regattas. But at the Atlanta Paralympics, due to be held the very next year in 1996, disabled sailing was going to be a demonstration sport, the first stage towards a full medal-status event, so the stakes had suddenly got a lot higher.

Generally disabled sailors around the world were somewhat sceptical of IFDS and what they represented, so I didn't rush to accept the invitation of the Royal Yachting Association to become the UK delegate on the IFDS committee, but I did eventually agree. From the beginning it felt like a closed shop, and the intricacies of its committee structure were unlikely to be changed by the likes of me. To be fair, they were doing a difficult job trying to emulate the success of RYA Sailability on a global scale, but I found myself flying to meetings around the world to represent Great Britain on IFDS business, then when I got there it seemed all decisions had already been taken in private and were presented as a fait accompli. The whole process seemed undemocratic, a waste of time and a waste of money in expenses.

Being elected chairman of another new committee, the Paralympic Steering Group (PSG), in early 1996 squared the circle for me in terms of disabled sailing. The PSG was the committee appointed by the RYA to select our sailors for the Paralympic Games later that year. I was now chairman of the national disabled sailing charity, I sat on the RYA Council representing disabled sailors, I was the UK's delegate on the world disabled sailing group, and now I was chairing a committee which would be choosing our sailors for an Olympiad. Quite by accident, and perhaps good fortune, I was at the hub of knowledge and understanding of disabled sailing. Voluntary committee membership is not only a thankless job, it is also hugely boring to those not involved, including my wife and friends. But I was amazed at how many people were giving up so much of their time to try and advance the sport.

But it wasn't all committee work. The greatest pleasure, and the greatest reward for my commitment, came from seeing RYA

Sailability in action. I was still racing my Challenger trimaran *Billy*, so I got to see at first hand the development of disabled sailing around the UK, and I got to hear the views of the sailors and the volunteers. It would be wrong to pretend everything was rosy – far from it. Many sailors and volunteers were deeply unhappy about what they saw as the centralisation of services and funding. They were also upset that the RYA now owned the charity, not them. In many ways I agreed with them. But putting all the arguments to one side, it was happening – increasing numbers of disabled people were going sailing. At club after club, I would see ordinary folk giving up their time to volunteer, purely to help disabled people get out on the water.

I would often sit and watch, incredulous that someone whose only ability was to breathe could sail a boat using a sip-and-puff air system linked to the rudder and sail. From a distance you could see no difference in the performance of the boat, but to think it was being controlled purely by someone's breathing was spine-tingling. But the time when I was struck most by the power of sailing was during a visit to Rutland Sailing Club. I had been asked to attend an official disabled sailing event in my capacity as chairman of RYA Sailability. As I lowered myself down the ramp from my van in the car park, all I could hear was the squeals of children laughing on the water's edge. As I wheeled down to the pontoon I could see about half a dozen children, dressed in bright yellow oilskins and orange lifejackets, all under the age of twelve, sitting in a boat, splashing each other with water, laughing and screaming. Seeing their fun and enjoyment brought a smile to my face too, right to the point when one of the helpers told me that they were all deaf-blind children, and had been since birth. I tried to get my head around what I had just been told whilst seeing what I was seeing. If they were deaf-blind, how did they know there were other people in the boat? How would they know what another person looked like? How could they hear each other laughing? How did they know what water was? Why would they be splashing it at someone they didn't know was there? And above all, why were they laughing? My brain was doing somersaults. And then I realised that I was looking too deeply. This wasn't about psychoanalysing them, this was simply about the fact they were getting enjoyment from being on the water.

And such opportunities for disabled kids to have fun were not unique. I saw it happening time and time again, throughout the country. Most of the credit must go to the hard work and dedication of the clubs themselves. But it was also due in part to the awareness created by RYA Sailability, which helped promote these opportunities, and I was very proud of that.

We flew to Atlanta for the Paralympics in 1996; I was a member of the British technical delegation for the sailing event. It was a wonderful event and a spectacular regatta, made even more so when Great Britain took the gold medal after a thrilling final race. We all returned to the UK on a high, and that performance helped boost publicity for disabled sailing in the UK tremendously for several years to come.

Despite the highs, there were times, as I tried to juggle all of my sailing commitments whilst holding down a job, when I felt like packing it all in. Apart from basic expenses, there were certainly no financial rewards for giving up so much of my life for disabled sailing. Of course I did not do it for financial reward, but there were several occasions when I was pushed to my limit. Whether it was one of my more politically aggressive trustees bending my ear over a contentious agenda item, or an irate disabled sailor phoning late at night to complain about something, I always did my best to act as mediator. This went on relentlessly, day in, day out for more than six years. On more than one occasion Elaine came into my office close to midnight to tell me that if I didn't put the phone down and come to bed, she would do it for me.

However, my position as chairman of RYA Sailability opened up doors to people and businesses that I had only read about in newspapers or seen on TV. Whether I was hosting the then prime minister John Major at the launch of a new boat at a Sailability group in his Huntingdon constituency, or meeting King Harald of Norway at a reception at Holyrood Palace in Edinburgh, I never lost sight of who I was and my humble beginnings.

Princess Anne and I worked together quite closely. She was patron of Sailability, and I made it my job to keep her updated on the charity's progress. We would meet quite regularly in her private office in Buckingham Palace, often just the two of us poring over strategy documents for an hour or so. Of all the things I could have worried about, I was most conscious of my wheelchair leaving dirty tyre-prints on a beautiful polar-bear skin rug that lay in the middle of the room where I was parked, its head, mouth open, teeth bared, at my feet. On the mantle behind the Princess, photographs of her family and personal effects sat amongst the finest pieces of Meissen porcelain. This was her very private space and here was I, Geoff from Waterworks Road, Farlington, sat talking to a princess. It was all slightly surreal.

But the greatest treat for sitting on the RYA Council was always the annual August meeting, which was held in Cowes aboard the Royal Yacht *Britannia*. Tea for the entire RYA Council was taken on the lawn of the Royal Yacht Squadron before we were taken by boat to *Britannia* for the afternoon meeting. Unable to follow the others as they climbed the steps from the launch to the meeting room, one deck level above, I was always taken out to *Britannia* on my own in the Duke of Edinburgh's private flat-bottomed launch. Once alongside *Britannia*, and with the davits connected, the launch could be winched right up to the very top, the Royal Deck level. From here I would be wheeled through the aft deckhouse and taken down by an internal lift to the meeting room, one level below. Every year I looked forward to this day more than almost any other. I would love watching the boatmen on the beautiful blue launch, dressed in full uniform and plimsolls (so they don't disturb the Queen), do all of their fancy twiddling of boathooks – one at the bow, the other at the stern – as they came alongside at the Squadron steps; it was an impressive sight. The crowds of sightseers along Cowes seafront would be held back by police as they strained to see which, if any, famous face they could recognise. I would be accompanied by one of the naval commanders for the short trip out to *Britannia*, at which point I would have to don a bright yellow hard-hat whilst being hoisted vertically, boat and all, the fifty feet or so upwards.

Once at Royal Deck level, I would be piped aboard and met personally by Rear-Admiral Sir Robert Woodard, Commander of *Britannia*. He was a charming man who told me they had perfected the routine for his mother, herself a wheelchair user who lived in the Azores – where, he told me, one could get 'cheap NATO fuel'. I was never sure which of the two was his primary reason for visiting the Azores. Commander Woodard would then himself push me along the beautiful teak games-deck and through the Royal Quarters where, typically, there would be the Duke of Edinburgh, Princess Anne, Prince Andrew, Prince Edward, King Constantine of Greece, Prince Michael of Kent and no one else, not even a servant. They would all be sitting around on beautiful sofas drinking tea, reading papers and chatting. The first year I was taken aboard, as I entered their quarters, the Princess leapt to her feet, came over to me, shook me warmly by the hand and, gesturing towards the assembled group, without any hint of irony asked, 'Have you met the family?'

19

B log entry, Day 75, Thursday 2 August 2007, Peterhead:

Well, we had a great sail out of Whitehills heading east to Rattray Head before turning south to Peterhead. We saw plenty more porpoises and seabirds, especially around Troup Head, the UK's biggest mainland gannetry. It was one of those surreal moments when the sky was white with thousands of gannets, all flying high then diving like white arrows into the sea. At 1415 hours we officially changed course south, the first time since we left all those weeks ago, and it felt good to have the sun on my face again. Well, I say sun, it was a milky orb behind the high grey cloud, but at least I could see it. It ended up being quite a long day and quite a wet one too with both rain and fairly sloppy seas which broke over my small boat. The road crew have had to adjust to life in B&Bs since Monday, which isn't as glam as it may sound, especially with their belongings chucked in the back of Annie's horsebox.

There was something very satisfying about rounding Rattray Head and turning south. We had now well and truly passed the halfway mark and metaphorically, if not geographically, it felt like we were on the 'downhill' leg. The northeast Scottish scenery was still spectacular, huge cliffs rising vertically from the sea, but the lack of Atlantic swell was a welcome feature.

The thought of visiting Peterhead, our next stop, brought a smile to my face. In the summer of 1984 I had worked on a survey vessel in these parts, only for a few months, surveying the Cruden Bay pipeline which brings ashore much of the North Sea oil, and surveying the Pentland Firth for the Hydrographic Office. I had not long been back in the UK from working in the West Indies and, at that time, there had been a widely publicised case of suspected green monkey disease in the UK. Whilst at sea surveying one day, I started to feel quite ill, most notably a fever, rigors and the most awful sore throat. My skipper, Clive Ward, ordered me below to my bunk and decided to head back into Peterhead. Over the noise of the engine, I could just about hear him talking to someone on the VHF radio about me, and he was describing my symptoms. When we arrived at the main Peterhead fish quay we moored alongside the harbour wall and, through my cabin window, I noticed blue flashing lights. I rushed up on deck to see a police cordon had been set up with red and white striped tape, and there was an ambulance waiting. Everyone was wearing face masks. Not really knowing what was happening, I was taken by ambulance with a police escort, blue lights flashing and sirens blazing, to the nearest hospital, where a doctor climbed in the back of the ambulance, opened my mouth and made his diagnosis: tonsillitis.

As I rounded the breakwater, it looked much the same as it had twenty-four years earlier, although I was struck by how 'un-fishy' it smelt. Back in the eighties, I remember smelling Peterhead before I even saw it, and I recall dodging trawlers as they hurried to and fro across the inner harbour to unload their catch. I was surprised at just how few there were now – perhaps they were all away at sea.

Peterhead was a complicated stop, not least because we were a motorhome down, which meant Mike, Eddie, Andy and Sarah had to find a nearby B&B where they could stay the night – not an easy task at the end of a long day at sea and then de-rigging the boats, once we finally made it ashore at the Peterhead Sailing Club. The Personal Everest circus, for the time being at least, now consisted of Elaine's car, which Eddie had driven up from Southampton and which was towing Annie's horsebox, my motorhome and the Land Rover, where Ian slept.

Day 76, Friday 3 August 2007:

We departed Peterhead yesterday about 1100 and carried the 2-knot spring tides south, unfortunately straight into a southerly breeze. It became another mixed day, at times broad-reaching at 9 knots, at others just wallowing with no breeze. The highlight was certainly the sighting of a pair of whales, possibly minke, but we were not close enough to be certain. I got fairly close but when the RIB followed the engine noise scared them away. We also saw several dolphins and many puffins, which was surprising – I thought we had seen the last of them. They are such funny looking things, just like clowns with their rainbow-coloured bills.

We eventually arrived Stonehaven about 1800 and we were escorted into the harbour by members of the resident Maritime Rescue Institute, a charity offering training and advice on all aspects of waterborne emergencies, similar to the RNLI. They have been incredibly helpful in providing us with space for the vehicles and boats and also their facilities, as too has the Aberdeen and Stonehaven Sailing Club. It is another extremely pretty harbour, and when we arrived we not only had a reception from curious locals but, fortuitously, a reporter for BBC Radio Scotland was sitting having a quiet drink when we turned up. Curiosity got the better of her, and within twenty minutes of landing I was doing a radio interview, still sat in my boat.

Andy had been on edge and decidedly off-character for a few days now. I had still not mentioned the incident that occurred when Andy left his message on my blog just as we were leaving Whitehills, but I believed that he had said what he had because he was somehow cross with me. No longer was he encouraging and funny, he had become a grumpy bugger, and his miserable mood was noticed by everyone. He barely spoke with me, and when he did he wouldn't look me in the eye. It was crazy really, it was I who should have been angry with him, not the other way around. I most certainly did not want to lose Andy – more than just a valuable crew member, he'd become a friend – but I knew to challenge him about his attitude could risk him walking away. I really think that things had become that bad.

Ian took the initiative and told Andy what had happened in Whitehills, and how I was having to deal with a potential crisis with my sponsor, and how it was all sparked off by his comment on my blog.

'You should have told me,' Andy said to me, cross that I had kept it from him. I laughed – I might have guessed it was my fault!

'Andy, are you going to tell me what's going on. I'm not a mind reader, but something is clearly upsetting you – have I done something wrong?'

It transpired that Andy had taken a call some days earlier advising him that he had only a matter of weeks to move out of his rented home in Sussex and find somewhere else to live. Not that he had done anything wrong, it was just that the owner had decided to sell the property. And this had to be done well in advance of us getting back to Southampton. But our time with Annie and her family had also been causing Andy to miss home, not least his ten-year-old son James. He had not seen him for over seventy days now, and no amount of phone calls could make up for not being with him. Being turfed out of the motorhome, his personal belongings thrown in the back of a horsebox, and having to live out of a holdall in a different B&B each night was the final straw.

At least understanding how he felt meant I could find ways to help ease the problem.

'Look, you're free to go whenever you want, but if you want to continue with the project – and I hope you will – why don't you take a week off? I'll fly you back and you can sort out your house and see James at the same time.'

That seemed to do the trick. Andy worked out that he didn't need to be home for another few days, but just knowing that he was going back for a while seemed to lift his spirits. It was another crisis dealt with and, to be fair on Andy, it could not have been an easy time for him. Knowing how much he missed his son made me feel increasingly guilty about the time we had been away, especially as Elaine and I were fortunate to have our son with us. Being stuck in Stonehaven for two days because of more bad weather only added to my feeling of guilt.

Day 78, Sunday 5 August 2007:

It's a relatively calm Sunday morning here in Stonehaven after a fairly blustery couple of days. The weather can be so deceptive. Yesterday was blowing about 20 knots from the south so, with a wind over tide situation, there were fairly lumpy seas. We took advantage of having Elaine's car here to go into Aberdeen, only my second visit to a city since we left, but it was so hot, it seemed unthinkable that only a mile or so away out on the water it was very different.

It happened to be 'Tartan Day' in Aberdeen, so lots of pipe bands and people in kilts – well, it is Scotland. It seems extremely odd visiting a busy town or city and seeing so many people, so many shops and so much traffic. It was a relief to get back to the encampment at Stonehaven.

The weather forecast looks favourable for a departure today for Arbroath, but we must wait until 1300 hours to catch the favourable south-going tide. Fingers crossed for a prolonged period of more settled weather this week – we all want to be back by September.

The trip down to Arbroath was just like every other day-sail that I had completed thus far. Even though I had endured the exhausting trip across to Scotland from the Isle of Man, I had never felt anything other than safe and secure in my boat. And suffering no ill effects other than severe exhaustion, I was becoming increasingly complacent about the reality of what I was actually doing. Every so often, whilst sailing far out to sea off some new stretch of coast, I would remind myself that here was I, paralysed from the chest down, sailing a boat, on my own, around Great Britain. Then I would look over and see the RIB and the crew, and realise that all of them were there solely to help me. And to think what we had already achieved to get this far – it would be unbelievable were I not actually living through it. But no matter how much I tried to award myself a metaphorical pat on the back, and no matter how wonderful some of the experiences of the past ten weeks, it felt no different to getting up in the morning to do a day's work.

Freethinker and I were completely in tune with each other, but every day that we sailed it felt as though we were working together purely to get a job done. With the constant pressure to complete the challenge at the forefront of my mind, I could not honestly say that I had enjoyed one minute of the trip – not since that delay in Brixham when reality hit home. I wanted to enjoy it, I wanted to enjoy it so much, but there was no way I could relax, knowing that the next weather system could effectively write off my chances of finishing. That would be hugely disappointing, not just for me but also for all my crew, my sponsors, and my many supporters. With that pressure, there was no way I could enjoy myself. Occasionally I would find myself taking pleasure from a particular day's sailing, or from looking at a particular piece of scenery – then reality would kick in and I'd snap out of it.

Day 79, Monday 6 August 2007:

I was escorted out of Stonehaven by a fellow trimaran sailor – I think her name was Jenny – and it was great to have company, even if her boat had a jib and was better at sailing to windward than mine. Just after we parted company about two miles south, we had an encounter with a minke whale which would have been the highlight of most people's days, and it would have been mine had I not sailed straight through a pod of about twenty dolphins an hour later, all leaping and jumping as they headed north. I was so close, and one of them even knocked the centreboard of my dinghy up as they dived underneath. It was a terrific experience.

We arrived Arbroath to a wonderful welcome from a variety of folk, not least the Arbroath RNLI, who let us use their facilities, but in particular from Jim Ratcliffe, a Rotarian I had first met back in April at the Rotary conference in Bournemouth. Jim had promised to provide help on our arrival and he did just that, including organising berthing for the boats with the harbour master and overnighting our vehicles at Mackay Boatyard. Our sincere thanks to Harry and Duncan for laying on all facilities, which even included eating Harry's Arbroath Smokies for my breakfast – now there's fellowship in action ... I must also thank Ian (Micka) for bringing me a couple of packs of fresh smokies from the company he works for (M & M Spink). You won't get better, and they deliver too.

Any complacency that I had developed in recent weeks was soon to be violently undone by the North Sea, which was to live up to its ferocious reputation. It would be a stark reminder of just how quickly situations at sea can become life-threatening. If the trip from Peel to Portpatrick had been the most physically demanding on the trip, then the journey from Arbroath to Dunbar was, without doubt, the most frightening. We left Arbroath at 1100 for a routine forty-mile sail due south across the Firth of Forth, expected to take us about eight hours. It was damp and very misty when we left and I had to keep close to *Everest One*, which was using radar to locate nearby ships that might cause me a danger. By lunchtime the cloud had lifted and it was just like any other day's sailing, until, still with ten miles to go to Dunbar, the wind picked up. At first it wasn't too much of a problem, but it was heading me slightly so I could not make Dunbar on one tack and would have to beat my way to windward. Sailing into the wind always makes the wind feel stronger than it is anyway, simply because you must take into account your speed too. At first, the apparent wind speed was a steady 15 knots. I was getting wet with waves breaking over the bow, but this was nothing unusual and I was not unduly worried. The wind then started gusting, upwards of 20 knots, again nothing too much to worry about, although my arms were beginning to ache. But then, in only a matter of minutes, the tide turned, and the waves, which had been no more than a metre high, quickly changed to short, steep waves, at least three metres high, with breaking crests.

As I tried to sail into the waves, the breaking crests would simply overwhelm my boat and push her off course. Depending on my angle to the wind, the gusts would either pull the boat into the wind, ripping the tiller out of my hand so that I lost all power, or worse, if they caught side-on, with a wave breaking underneath me, they would lift my outer hull and try to flip me over sideways.

At first I tried to deal with it, and was certainly not scared. But when I began to weaken, and found I did not have the physical strength to control my boat in the fierce wind and confused seas, I began to worry.

To make matters worse, with Mike having caught the train south that day to collect the replacement motorhome, we were a crew member down, which meant that for the first time on the entire trip there were only two crew members on the RIB, Ian and Sarah.

Whilst all three of us remained calm, I knew that Ian realised, like me, that this was a fast-deteriorating and highly dangerous situation. He made several attempts to bring *Everest One* alongside to take a tow, but with both boats rising and falling at least three metres, if the sharp pointed bows of *Freethinker* didn't rip the rubber tubes of *Everest One* to shreds, then there was every possibility that *Everest One*'s hull could crash down onto my boat and smash it to pieces.

'Geoff, I want you to try bearing away a few degrees – if it's OK, we'll make for another harbour,' said Ian over the VHF.

I couldn't reply because I simply could not take my hand off the tiller long enough to transmit a response without losing control of the boat.

As instructed, I let the mainsheet go slightly. But now, sailing off the wind and at right angles across the waves, *Freethinker* was travelling too fast and she was highly unstable, each wave passing under my starboard beam nearly flipping me over sideways.

Trying to gather my thoughts and my strength, I let go of the mainsheet completely and heaved to. Even completely de-powered and stationary in the water, the violence of the waves was tossing *Freethinker* around like a cork. It was now 1800 hours and I knew we would be losing light soon.

Running out of options, Ian again tried to come alongside, with Sarah hanging precariously off the port side of the RIB. But each time the boats bashed into each other with enough force to break Sarah's hand were she not quick enough to move it in time. For the first time in a lifetime of sailing, I realised that I was frightened. *Everest One* was my only route to safety, and it was so frustrating being sat in my boat, looking at Ian and Sarah in the relative safety of the RIB but unable to help me. I could see the desperation in Ian's eyes, which began to worry me too. It was not like Ian to show any sign of concern.

In one last-ditch effort they came alongside again. An enormous wave passed beneath us, lifting both boats simultaneously, and for a fraction of a second my hull was parallel to theirs. Quicker than I could follow with my eyes, Sarah slipped a rope through the two-inch eye at the end of my towing bridle. A second later, as the wave passed and both boats once again separated, I could see that she had managed to secure the tow rope. Whatever happened now, at least I was attached to *Everest One*. I breathed a sigh of relief, but the situation was anything but over yet.

For the next forty-five minutes I was towed at no more than 2 knots directly into the wind and mountainous waves. With every wave that passed beneath us, the tow line snatched tight and jerked my boat forward. I was the wettest and coldest I had been the entire trip, and so tired I could not stop myself being overwhelmed by a sense of fatigue. As much as I fought to stay awake, my eyes would close, and then another wave would pass by. Another lurch, and another spine-shattering pain would shoot down my neck as my head was thrown backwards.

So when we finally arrived on a calm and sheltered beach adjacent to Dunbar at dusk, and I was met by a group of Rotarians all offering their congratulations, oblivious to the events which had been occurring out to sea a matter of minutes earlier, I was so dumbstruck by the contrast that I could barely speak.

'Bed. I need to go to bed,' was the best I could manage.

In many ways it was fortunate the weather on the following day was above our limits. Every muscle I could feel ached, and even those I couldn't feel were probably aching too. The events of the day before had scared me a great deal, certainly enough to make me tearful with hindsight. At least from now on, if a similar deterioration in the weather arose again, for the rest of the trip there would be ports of refuge – the leg from Arbroath to Dunbar was the last long exposed sea passage. Which was just as well. I couldn't go through that again.

Now that Mike had turned up with the replacement motorhome in Dunbar, at least the crew could get back to some semblance of normality, and it was not long before the horsebox was emptied and the new motorhome stuffed to the ceiling with clothing and supplies.

Day 81, Wednesday 8 August 2007, Berwick-upon-Tweed:

> This morning, in the absence of a slipway at Dunbar, the special lifting crane on the Land Rover was put into action for only the second time. Fabricated by John Beardsley's firm in Leeds with a man-riding winch, it hoisted me over the fifteen-foot harbour wall and into my boat, to much local interest, including the RNLI.
>
> This afternoon, seven hours later, again in the absence of a slipway, it was in use once more to hoist me up the twenty-foot harbour wall here in Berwick-upon-Tweed, our first stop in England since we left Ilfracombe sixty days ago. We had a great reception here in Berwick from Rotary and the RNLI.
>
> Meanwhile Eddie drove a 200-mile round trip to Aberdeen to drop Annie's horse box back, only getting home at 1900 hours.

We had got used to the Rotary contacts now. With David Cheatham having got the bit well and truly between his teeth, he and Elaine had a great system going, and the advance notice to Rotarians was working like a dream. David was in a unique position to ask for help on our behalf, and we no longer had to worry about lining up for photographs on arrival. We were getting real offers of help.

Having been hoisted up the harbour wall in Berwick and lifted by Elaine into my wheelchair, still slightly numb and disorientated from my day at sea and still wearing my wet sailing gear and lifejacket, I was introduced to a couple of local Rotarians, both smartly dressed in suits and ties. We had been talking quietly for a couple of minutes, exchanging pleasantries, when the peace was disturbed by a bright red open-top Alfa Romeo Spyder sports car which pulled into the car park, engine revving and music blaring. A man got out and started walking towards us. I carried on talking, aware out the corner of my eye of this chap in shorts and sandals, a v-neck sweater with nothing under it but a bit of chest hair on show and a frizzy, eighties perm, approaching and standing behind me. At which point one of the guys I was speaking to gestured towards this man with his hand and said –

'Geoff, may I introduce you to the President of Berwick Rotary Club, Michael.'

But with me still slightly surprised, Michael beat me to the introduction, extending his hand and in a broad Geordie accent proclaiming, 'Why aye man, pleased to meet you like.'

What a great bloke. We hit it off straight away and no doubt, had we stayed longer, we would have heard more of his amazing stories. To reinforce the new-found relationship with Rotary, he announced that he wanted to take the entire crew out to his favourite restaurant, 'Tony's steak hoos'.

The next morning we were preparing to leave Berwick. We were already wearing our sailing kit, the RIB was loaded with food and drink and I was just about to be hoisted into *Freethinker*, when a car pulled up and a young lady jumped out. Walking over to me, she explained –

'Hi. My name is Meaghan. I'm from Ohio in the US and I'm over here studying photography. I overhead someone in a bar last night talking about your sail around Great Britain. We have a photo assignment to hand in next week on a local news story and I was wondering if I could come with you today on the boat and take a few photos.'

Well, it was certainly short notice, and maybe that was no bad thing. Sarah, who had been going on the RIB, as it was her last day with us, sacrificed both her place in the boat and her drysuit to Meaghan, with special advice on 'visiting the solicitors' as a woman. I've no idea what the advice entailed, as I had never been behind the RIB on any such occasion, but clearly it was a tad more complicated than the routine followed by the boys.

We had a good sail down to Amble, arriving at 1900 hours. We could have done with a bit more wind, but we certainly couldn't complain about the scenery on a route that took us around Holy Island and inside the Farne Islands. And judging by the amount of photos that Meaghan was taking, she found it interesting too.

Day 84, Saturday 11 August 2007, Blyth:

> Once in Amble and fully de-rigged, we went to a local pub to say a fond farewell to Sarah, who was leaving us to take up a new job. We will all miss her very much, including Timothy, who has fallen madly in love with her – what it is to be a five-year-old. Meaghan stayed for dinner too, and we even found her a spare bed in the new motorhome.
>
> On Friday morning Sarah headed home, and, after taking some more photos, so too did Meaghan. We departed for Hartlepool at 1100 but within an hour the southerly wind had strengthened considerably. By 1300 the radio was forecasting force 6 and an increasing sea state. We immediately put into effect our 'port of refuge' plan and headed straight for the nearest harbour, Blyth. We arrived here at 1530, along with several other boats who had heard the same forecast. Our thanks to Roger here at the Royal Northumberland Yacht Club who has found us marina berthing for the boats and space in the boatyard for the vehicles – he really has been most helpful.
>
> After a good night's sleep, we are once again going to head out for Hartlepoool today, which is still a thirty-mile run. We leave here at 1030 and should arrive about 1700. There are southerly force 5 winds forecast, which will hold us up. It seems that the winds refuse to give us a break, in direction or speed – either that or we have a Jonah on the team.

With David Cheatham's help, Elaine had certainly come up trumps at Hartlepool, discovering that the marina manager was himself a Rotarian. As we rounded the headland, the shore crew, Everest Mobile, announced on the VHF that we were to keep both boats in Hartlepool Marina, inside the lock where they would be safe and there would be no problem with tides. And with all three vehicles now back together, they were to be parked alongside the marina office and would have full access to electricity, water, showers and toilets. It was just as well. Less than an hour after arriving, and anxious to know if the rumour I had heard about bad weather was true, I called Weather Online, to be told that there was indeed a bad storm heading our way and it was unlikely we would be sailing anywhere for at least a week. Once again, it felt like a body-blow and it took a while for the news to register. It was another serious setback, but perhaps better that it was clear-cut than ambiguous, which would raise, then dash, our hopes. It was 11 August, so we still had just over three weeks before Timothy started school. A week's delay would give us just over two weeks to get back. With each new holdup, I was finding it increasingly hard to find the silver linings, aware that my attempts at optimism and putting on a brave face could be confused with clutching at straws.

Upon hearing the news I was quick to tell the crew, and I suggested that if anyone wanted to take time out to go home, then now would be the ideal opportunity. Certainly for Andy it tied in well as he was going to have to leave anyway to move his belongings out of his old house, find a flat to rent, and move everything back into his new home, wherever that might be. Ian and Eddie joined him, leaving only Mike, Elaine, Timothy and myself behind.

Day 87, Tuesday 14 August 2007:

> The weather has indeed already started to deteriorate. We've heard that even the Fastnet Race was postponed by twenty-four hours because of the weather, the first time in its 86-year history. Yet another delay that we can ill afford, but there is little we can do about it. We have fourteen stops left, but with such unpredictable weather it's anyone's guess when we will actually get back.

Apart from a quick trip into Newcastle to buy a new pair of trousers, we did little that week except wait for the weather. We did

did have one group of visitors, which made a welcome break: members from the local Scaling Dam Sailability group came to have a look at my boat and to see how it differed from the Challengers they had at their centre. I think they were quite surprised. We even had an invitation from one of their members to tea one evening, so it wasn't as though we were completely forgotten, but I was getting increasingly uneasy as each subsequent long-range forecast showed no sign of improvement.

The crew had all arranged to return on Thursday 16 August, in the hope that we would be able to start the following day. The night before their return, Mike, Elaine and I had treated ourselves to a Chinese takeaway, my rapidly depleting budget stretching just enough to spoil the three of us. With money so tight, Timothy even had to share Elaine's chicken curry. After eating, I retired to bed and watched a DVD, as I often did when weather-bound. Perhaps it was my fragile state of mind, battered into submission by the endless delays and massive feeling of responsibility that I felt for my crew, but after watching it I felt as though I had been pole-axed. The film in question was *Deep Water*, the true story of Donald Crowhurst, a yachtsman who took part in the very first non-stop race around the world in 1968. It told of the mental pressure he was under to start the race, completely ill-prepared, and how, once under way, he falsified his logs and pretended to sail around the world, but in fact just sailed in circles in the south Atlantic before re-establishing radio contact and rejoining the race some months later, only to find himself in the lead. Whether it was the guilt of cheating or the shame he would face if found out, it became too much for him and he threw himself overboard. His empty trimaran was discovered shortly afterwards, floating in the Atlantic, but his body was never found. It was an incredibly tragic story for everyone concerned, obviously for Donald and his family, but also for the other competitors in the race, including the man who went on to win it, Robin Knox-Johnston. But something about the film resonated with me. It touched a nerve, and I questioned whether, if things got really bad, with the responsibility I felt to everyone who had supported me, I would have the courage to say 'That's it, enough is enough, I'm quitting.' I doubt it. And it is perhaps for that reason that I was so moved by the film.

Day 91, Saturday 18 August 2007, Bridlington:

Well, with a borderline forecast in our favour yesterday, we decided to make a twenty-four-mile dash from Hartlepool to Whitby. What started out as a potentially mundane passage was to become one of the fastest, longest, most tiring and most exhilarating of the trip so far. With Whitby to my southeast and the wind blowing 15 knots from the west and off the land, it was near perfect Challenger sailing conditions, calm flat seas with a stiff following breeze. *Freethinker* was flying. Even when punching over a knot of foul tide, I was maintaining an average of 7 knots, occasionally surfing to 11 knots.

We were off Whitby just after 1300, and with such perfect conditions, and a spring tide still to turn in our favour, we decided to push on to Scarborough, another fifteen miles. Ian phoned the ever-accommodating road crew, who were already waiting for us in Whitby, to break the news! About 1600, we arrived off Scarborough. The tide had now turned in our favour, the wind continued to be kind, and we were still managing to maintain 6 to 7 knots. My VHF crackled into life. '*Freethinker, Freethinker, Freethinker*, this is *Everest One*, over'! It was Ian, and I knew what was coming. 'What do you think of pushing on to Bridlington?' To be honest, I was getting a bit cold and tired, but the opportunity to press on with such perfect conditions was too good to miss. Once again Ian called the land crew to make our apologies, up sticks and move on to yet another destination.

What would have been the perfect day was marred only by our arrival at Flamborough Head. As we rounded the headland and turned west to Bridlington, the headland sheltered all of the northwest wind so there was none, and the tidal flow was now right onto my nose. With no wind, a tide pushing me backwards, and only one hour of daylight remaining, I had no option other than to take a short tow the final two miles. But sailing sixty miles in ten hours was pretty good going. We arrived at sundown and did not get into the motorhome until gone 2200. With no time to arrange facilities with the local Rotary group, we parked in the only place we could, a car park next to a pub which had a Sex Pistols punk tribute band playing till gone midnight. I fell asleep to the alternative version of *God Save the Queen* – very patriotic.

So we are stuck here in Bridlington – amusement arcades, ice-creams and a fun fair. Timothy's going to have fun.

With Andy still in Southampton and not due back until Sunday 19 August, we only had Mike, Elaine, Ian and Eddie to move the three vehicles and to crew *Everest One* for the trip down from Hartlepool. Luckily for us, one of the Scaling Dam Sailability instructors, Graham Wing, volunteered his services for three days, desperate for a chance to crew on the RIB. Because of our limited numbers there could only be two on the RIB that day, and Ian, wanting an experienced crew, chose Eddie – so Graham was detailed to driving duty, with the promise that he could crew the RIB from then on. When we arrived in Bridlington and heard that we were in for another period of bad weather likely to keep us there for up to five days, there was nothing we could do except apologise to Graham, who made his way back to Hartlepool. It was a disappointment for him and us, but he had made himself useful and fulfilled an essential role, entitling him to become an honorary member of the Personal Everest crew, albeit only for one day.

By the time Andy returned from his trip home, our vehicles had been temporarily re-sited in the car park of the Bridlington Marine and Coastguard Agency, with both boats moored in the harbour below. Andy arrived back looking annoyingly happy – fresh, clean, no sign of tiredness, in complete contrast to the rest of us. Clearly the break had done him the power of good and, reinvigorated, he was back to his old self.

Timothy too was on good form, but for him the pleasure was all about living in the shadow of the Coastguard HQ. With Sarah having left, Timothy now fell in love with Bev, one of the Bridlington Coastguards – oh, the fickleness of youth. And despite our concern that his enthusiasm to learn all things 'coast-guardy' would soon wear the patience of our hosts, Bev and her team were actively encouraging him. On the second day we were there he appeared from his bunk at 0730, announcing –

'Mummy, can you please make me some sandwiches for

lunch. I need to be at work in a minute.'

I quickly dispatched Elaine into the neighbouring coastguard building without Timothy seeing, just to check they didn't mind.

'Oh no, that's OK,' said Bev. 'We told him we'd love to have him. Don't worry, we'll keep him busy.'

We did worry, but Bev was as good as her word, and he appeared at 1700 hours for his tea, complaining of being tired.

'Well, how did it go?' I asked eagerly, and partly tongue-in-cheek. 'Anything interesting happen?'

'Oh Dad,' he sighed reluctantly like some disinterested teenager, 'if you must know, we had one mayday, but it was mostly watching the radar and speaking on the radio.'

Sometimes with Tim, as with all kids, you are not sure if they make things up, but this time Elaine and I suspected he was telling the truth.

And Bev confirmed his story when she left work that night, showing us photos they had taken of him at his workstation and telling us that the mayday had been a small boat seen in danger by nearby rocks. The caller had even said they thought it might be 'Geoff Holt'.

'I can assure you it's not Mr Holt,' Bev advised the worried caller. 'At this very moment he's sitting in our car park.'

Day 93, Monday 20 August 2007, Bridlington:

The MCA have been wonderful hosts and they have a new recruit in the form of Timothy, who is their newest and biggest fan. Bev and her team have given Tim the complete tour of the ops room, the vehicles and equipment, and he's now our resident expert on safety at sea. I know he's only five but I sincerely hope that he remembers these experiences when he's older – he really is very lucky indeed, but at least we're getting plenty of photos to jog his memory. He is completely and utterly smitten with the coastguard and has added it to his list of jobs he wants to do, along with lifeboatman, fireman, prime minister and clown, although not too sure if the last two aren't the same thing.

Exactly a week after our arrival, and having spent almost every hour checking the forecast for any hint of an improved weather situation, finally an opportunity presented itself for us to leave. My personal forecaster had been very specific, and advised us of a new series of low pressures coming our way, but if we could get south, perhaps to Norfolk, by the end of the weekend, there would be a high-pressure system building which could potentially last a week. With only twelve more scheduled stops ahead of us, and with favourable weather, we might just make it.

After an 0500 wake-up call on Friday 24 August, day 97 of our voyage, with the tide at its lowest, we launched the boats down the huge expanse of beach at Bridlington, faced with a new problem – daylight, or rather the lack of it. As every day went by and we moved ever closer to the autumnal equinox, so the days shortened and our sailing window lessened. With the tide so far out, the Land Rover had to tow *Freethinker* out across the sand, and I was then pushed at least 400 yards out to sea by Eddie in his fetching green waders before there was sufficient water for him to lower my centreboard and drop my rudder. Only then could I turn and make a course for Grimsby.

Day 98, Saturday 25 August 2007, Grimsby:

It was a long, fairly uneventful forty-four-mile trip to Grimsby, although the natural sand spit of Spurn Head, which sticks out far into the Humber estuary, was a remarkable sight. We arrived at the appropriately named Grimsby Fish Dock Number 2 at 1600 hours, where a large ominous sign above my head read, 'If you fall into the water, you must seek urgent medical treatment', a reference to the poisonous algae that populate it.

Amongst the welcoming committee were representatives from Cleethorpes Rotary, who had arrived some hours earlier and helped the road crew set up. Not only did they take some laundry for us (I slept on ironed sheets, a real treat) but they kindly fed the entire crew with a wonderful home-made meal, including wine. The Humber Cruising Association and Grimsby Marina laid on all the facilities. It was extremely kind, and people's generosity and support for this project never ceases to amaze us.

Having written my blog early that morning, I emerged from the motorhome at 0600 for yet another leg, a marathon fifty-mile sail across the Wash to Wells-next-the-Sea in Norfolk. I was becoming numb to the fact that each of these huge legs was as long as I'd ever spent in a Challenger dinghy before starting the Personal Everest voyage, and then of course I was a much younger man. On the two occasions that I had sailed around the Isle of Wight in the 1990s, both massive personal challenges for me, I had damn near wrecked myself in trying. Now I was sailing these huge distances regularly, and often consecutively, back to back. I had no idea where I was getting the stamina or energy from. Although I was arriving each night physically and emotionally drained, after a few hours' sleep I was finding inner strength from somewhere. Whilst at sea, apart from the obvious physical difficulties of steering, pulling ropes, being wet and cold, one of the toughest challenges for me is actually state of mind. You can only talk to the support team on the VHF so much, and with no radio, music or other means of occupying my mind, I consciously employed the tricks I had learned immediately after my accident and shut everything out of my mind. I'm not sure whether I had found some ability to meditate, or whether the exposure to the elements had finally frazzled my brain, but somehow I managed eight, nine, ten or even more hours, cooped up in my tiny cockpit, with nothing but my thoughts.

Day 98, Saturday 25 August 2007, Wells-next-the-Sea:

> As we headed east down the river Humber, I saw the first perfect sunrise in years, not a cloud in the sky, it was spectacular. The wind was blowing about a force 3 off the land and I had a superb sail down the coast. Although I've seen thousands of seals in my time, most of them on this trip, I have never before seen what happened today – a common seal swimming at speed popping up alongside my floats, first the port side, then starboard and so on, and every time he surfaced about four feet from me and looked straight at me. He only stayed a couple of minutes but it was a great treat.

After eleven hours at sea, we arrived at Wells-next-the-Sea at 1700 hours. I was drunk with tiredness and, as I sailed the last mile or so up the narrow winding river, in the distance I could see people, hundreds of them, lining the harbour wall. 'Oh no, not another goldfish-bowl situation, that's all I need right now,' I thought, somewhat presumptuously. As I rounded the final turn in the river, my slipway about 500 yards ahead, I noticed a large pack of dogs, dozens of them, huge black things, barking excitedly and leaping into the water from the marshy bank to my left and swimming across in front of me, their big football-sized heads bobbing their way to the harbour wall on my right where all of the people were shouting and cheering. It was somewhat surreal, and being so tired I wasn't sure whether my eyes and mind playing tricks on me.

I arrived at the slipway to be met by Elaine, who told me that I had just sailed through some annual festival in which Newfoundland dogs, for some unknown reason, swim across the river at Wells. I lifted my visor and looked at her in disbelief, but realised she wasn't joking. Only I could pick the one day in the year when the river is heaving with enormous dogs. Damn lucky I didn't run any over – not sure how I'd explain that on my insurance claim form.

20

By 1997, I was the busiest I had ever been in my life. When I wasn't at work doing my day job of running a marketing department for an international firm of accountants, I was on some committee somewhere in the world representing disabled sailing. And when I was busy then so too was Elaine, providing me with essential care and support so I could fulfil those roles. Quite oblivious to the potential consequences of such a workload for Elaine, I was firing on all cylinders and had a diary full from cover to cover to prove it. Life was hectic, bordering on manic, and, although I didn't realise it yet, it was slowly spinning out of control.

On top of everything I was doing already, I decided that I wanted to better the time I had set five years earlier when I first sailed around the Isle of Wight. I had always known that fourteen hours, although credible in the circumstances, was not acceptable to me. I set about replicating the attempt, this time equally unimaginatively called Challenge '97. Armed with a couple of hundred pounds in sponsorship from my employer, I set off in *Billy* at 6.30 a.m. one breezy August morning for a memorable sail. It was so fast that I was back in time for lunch, a total time of seven hours fifty-five minutes. Lessons learned from my previous attempt had ensured that I found a better way to eat and drink on the trip, and, with new improved clothing, better skin protection and better planning of the tides, it proved that I was able to make good progress on a sail of sixty miles without feeling too exhausted at the end of it.

Once again the attempt attracted a lot of publicity for me, for my employer and for RYA Sailability. I felt on top of my game, and despite my disability I felt a sense of invincibility. I had begun to take things for granted, not least the daily assistance I was getting from Elaine.

Deloitte & Touche were thankfully very considerate, allowing me time to attend my many sailing commitments. I was highly conscious of that, and would regularly work beyond my normal hours at the office to compensate. In addition, I took my laptop with me when I travelled so I could keep on top of my increasingly busy workload. But of course it was not just me. Having the van had provided me with a new form of independence, and had removed the need for Elaine to lift me in and out of a car and act as my personal taxi service, but she still had to support me whenever it meant an overnight stay or travelling abroad, which I was now doing more frequently. To add to the strain, there were also the very early mornings and late evenings, on top of holding down a full-time job of her own as an insurance claims adviser, not to mention housework and all of her other commitments as a full-time wife and carer. She certainly had no spare time for herself.

It was early the following year I realised that Elaine was struggling. In fact, it was not so much me, but friends who first pointed it out. I was too close to notice the slow deterioration in her, but, not having visited us for several months, our friends saw straight away how poorly she had become. Elaine exclusively provided all of my personal care, and this was a double-edged sword. On the up side, it gave us both the flexibility to do what we wanted, when we wanted. But critically, it also put us outside the social care system, which meant no support for Elaine. To this point in time, fourteen years after my injury, I didn't even have a social worker assigned to me, let alone appear on any register of 'at risk' people. We had no help whatsoever, not even any respite care so Elaine could have the occasional break from the punishing workload. To be honest, if it were offered, I'm not sure we would have taken it, but it meant that when Elaine did eventually break down with exhaustion there was no system in place to look after me. Elaine's illness was bad enough for her to be hospitalised for several weeks, during which time social services and my local health authority fought between themselves to decide who was responsible for the £1,500 per week nursing bill that it was costing just to look after me.

The health authority suggested that I should go into a care home or residential hostel whilst Elaine was recovering, but I refused. I wanted to stay at home. I wanted to continue to go to work. In the ten weeks that Elaine was in hospital, I had thirty different care staff in my home. Thirty strangers who would come to get me up, to cook me lunch or to put me to bed. But now it was at times to suit them, not me. There could be no more getting up at 6.00 a.m. to be in Southampton at my desk by 8.00 a.m. There could be no more staying up to 11.00 p.m. working. I had to fit in with their hours, and that presented the biggest hurdle of all, getting to work on time. For the first time since gaining employment as a disabled person in 1987, I was now exposing my weakest flank to my work colleagues, something I had worked hard at keeping private for years. But now it was out of my control and I could hide it no longer. My disability, or rather the inability to provide the essential care I needed as a result of my disability, was preventing me from getting to my job and doing a day's work like all of my 'normal' work colleagues. It troubled me that they would be judging me or, worse still, making allowances for me. I did not want that.

After a night sleeping alone in my house, helpless in the event of an emergency, the earliest that any of the carers managed to get me up, showered and dressed was 10.00 a.m. And even then I would be without a tie because none of them knew how to tie one. The earliest I was getting to work was 11.00 a.m., and I felt underdressed and dishevelled all day. If my leg bag became full during the day, there was no one to call to come and empty it. On more than one occasion, I made an excuse to leave work early so when the condom did inevitably blow off and my suit trousers became saturated with urine, I could at least sit in the privacy of my own home until the evening carer came in at 9.00 p.m.

I managed to visit Elaine in hospital a few times, but fitting in with visiting hours and the arrival of my evening carer, who came to put me to bed, never left me much time. Elaine was in the right place, and I did not want her to worry about me, so I always made light of my situation when I spoke to her on the phone or during visiting hours. I reassured her that everything was OK, but it wasn't. In fact, it was desperate. What made it worse was that I could not share my desperation with anyone. The eyes of friends and family were rightly on Elaine and the need for her to get better, so it was inappropriate for me to claim a share of their sympathy. It was a lonely time for me.

I explained everything to my employers, and thankfully they were very understanding and allowed me greater flexibility with my work hours. With the exception of Sailability, I then put on hold my workload for just about every sailing committee that I sat on by appointing people to represent me, which relieved me of a huge burden.

As if things couldn't get any worse, whilst Elaine was still in hospital my stepfather John Holt, whom I had been very close to, died of cancer after a short illness. The day I heard I was sitting at home on my own, making plans to see Elaine in hospital that afternoon. I was already feeling extremely fed up, dirty and hungry. I had not eaten properly for days because one of the carers who was working for me didn't even know how to cook rice or boil potatoes and there was barely any food in the house. When I heard the news about John, I was in the bedroom looking at myself in the mirror. I was horrified at the scruffy mess I had become and now, on top of everything I was going through, John had died. I was beginning to feel very ill – not sickly, but as though I were descending into some kind of dark abyss. It was completely at odds with my normal character and it began to frighten me. Reluctantly, but knowing I needed help, I telephoned my doctor's surgery and got an appointment to see the doctor that afternoon.

The moment I entered his surgery and he closed the door, I just broke down. I was powerless to stop myself. I was inconsolable, just hunched over, crying more than I have ever cried before.

It had taken fourteen years to happen, but the effects of my disability, my reliance on other people, had finally hit me. For all those years, for all the bravado and all the pretence that I was 'OK', dare I say 'normal', it was as though I was trying to hide my disability, albeit unintentionally, behind Elaine, frightened that people might think differently of me. Events had finally forced me to accept that without assistance I could never be anything other than a helpless, paralysed body. Even with a procession of so-called professional carers, even with the good ones, I couldn't get to work on time, let alone look respectable and have food to eat. Life had been too easy. I had not understood just how lucky I was to have Elaine's love and care underpinning everything I did. This was my wake-up call, and it was like being shot between the eyes with a twelve-bore shotgun. I realised that everything we had worked so hard for was built on such fragile foundations. It was a house of cards and it was crashing down around me.

Once I had finally accepted the reality, I slipped quite quickly into a depression. For the first time in my life, my mind went to some dark places. Something deep within me had changed and absolutely nothing could lift my mood. It was a horrible feeling and, the longer it went on, the more I wallowed in self-pity. I didn't know what I wanted – to be honest, I didn't care.

On the suggestion of my doctor I tried to go back to work, but I couldn't concentrate and, to make matters worse, due to the poor care I was receiving at home I now developed a very bad pressure sore on my heel, so bad you could see the bone. But in a strange way it was that pressure sore which was to start me on the road to recovery. The sore was so painful and sensitive that I asked one of my carers to cut a big chunk out of the heel section of one of my expensive black leather work shoes so it didn't rub. By disguising the problem, once again I would be living a pretence with my employer that I was 'OK'. That day, whilst wheeling around the office, the modified shoe slipped off my foot and onto the floor. Rather than ask anyone to pass it to me or risk the embarrassment of them seeing me with one shoe on, one shoe off, I put a paper bag over the shoe on the floor and wheeled back under my desk, intending to wait out the day until normal home-time. Within an hour, the heel was hurting a great deal as it rested against the footplate of my wheelchair, blood now seeping through my sock and dripping on the carpet. I started to get the first signs of an autonomic dysreflexic attack: my skin was going blotchy, I had the beginnings of a piercing headache, and I could feel my blood pressure rising. I felt extremely unwell. Still I sat there, despite the potential consequences, not wanting anyone to notice. But then, all of a sudden, like some kind of epiphany it dawned on me: exactly who was kidding whom here? What the hell was I playing at? For years I had been hiding aspects of my disability for fear of what people thought. But at that point in time, sat in my office, something happened which changed my outlook completely. I could no longer give a damn about what people thought of me. I was the person I was and I needed to be proud of that, not ashamed.

Confidently, and without feeling the need to explain, I asked a colleague to pass me my shoe, which was still under the paper bag. I put it on my lap and went home. That evening I wrote letters of resignation to all the sailing committees that I sat on and, slowly, over the following days, as the responsibilities and workloads lessened, I started to feel the pressure lift.

I mustered the courage and explained to my employer that I was not prepared to go on pretending that there wasn't a problem. It wasn't fair on them and it wasn't fair on me. I talked through all the difficulties I faced and explained that allowances had to be made. They needed a full-time marketing manager, and it was clear that I could no longer fill this role. We agreed that the only solution was for me to take time out to get better and, when I was ready, to let them know what I could and could not do, at which point we would re-evaluate the situation. They were tremendously understanding, and it relieved me of a major responsibility that I had been feeling.

With the pressure easing, slowly, ever so slowly, I could see some light at the end of the tunnel. And when Elaine did return home from hospital, social services had finally sorted out a care package so that Elaine could receive the help and support she needed.

It was a tough few months but I learned a lot, and finally, after more than fourteen years, I was forced to face up to my disability. But having gone through all of that, the darkest period of my life, it gave me a self-confidence that I had not really felt before. It also made me truly value and appreciate the support that Elaine was providing for me – and continues to provide to this day.

Once Elaine came home, our lives slowly got back to some sort of normality, but we were both still very shaken by the events earlier that year. We had done a huge amount of soul searching and had a lot of very open and frank discussions about what had gone wrong and what needed to change; neither of us could go through that again. Although it had brought the two of us much closer together, both of us felt as though we were walking on eggshells, each of us aware of how much those few dark months had taken out of us emotionally, and desperate to find ways for it not to happen again.

Both of our employers had agreed to give us more time to get better, but, despite relinquishing just about all of my committee duties, there was still one monkey perched on my shoulder that had been there for nearly twelve years. Thankfully my court case against Endless Summer Charters had not reared its head during those difficult months, but just as we were getting our life back to normality so an instruction arrived from the Caribbean to make ourselves ready for trial.

In the intervening years we had made a couple of visits to Tortola to meet with my lawyers and to go over evidence, this on top of the countless phone calls and letters, but progress was painfully slow. This time I would actually be sat in a courtroom in front of a judge: it was going to be my big opportunity to give my version of events. For more than a decade the prospect of a court case and the potential to get justice had affected many aspects of our lives – decisions about holidays, moving house and so on, all put on hold because of the possibility of being called to trial. Now my time had come. It was a long time since that day when Barry Rice stood in my front room in Southampton and infuriated me to the point of starting this legal action. Hopefully this would now conclude what had been a long, drawn-out and upsetting period for me.

We were met at the airport in Tortola by a government official, who took us to our hotel in the capital, Road Town. That evening he instructed us to attend Government House to meet the Governor himself, but no reason was given other than it was 'urgent'.

As Si O'Callaghan, who was with us as a key witness, pushed me up the steep drive to Government House, it seemed strange to be back there again. In 1984, Sean and I had attended a fairly wild party hosted by the previous governor's daughter. Having danced till the early hours, I had eventually crashed out on, and with a discarded cigarette almost set light to, what I later discovered was the bed the Queen had slept in during a visit some years earlier. Those were happier times. My meeting that night with the new governor was much more formal. We sat out on the magnificent veranda overlooking the harbour below, the ships' lights twinkling and the silhouettes of neighbouring islands slowly disappearing in the fast-encroaching darkness. It was hot, sticky and humid and we had to talk loudly to make ourselves heard above the noise of the tree frogs.

'Mr Holt, you need to know that we have become aware of threats being made against your personal safety,' he advised me. 'We know the person involved and they have received a police caution – I am not at liberty to disclose their identity. I can tell you that it was not Mr Rice. You need to understand that taking on a yacht charter company is a big thing out here, Mr Holt. A lot of people could be affected by the wrong result. It will have repercussions across the board.'

I was completely taken aback. And I wasn't entirely sure whose side he was on. 'What? Me?' I asked. This was like something out of a James Bond novel.

Before passing me his business card, he took a pen and wrote a number on the back. 'This is the number of my personal security guard. Call him immediately if you have any problems at all.'

To be honest, I was really shocked. Who on earth would threaten me, and why? What possible reason could there be to threaten me? My case was based on what I believed to be a simple breach of contract. But maybe it would bring to light some practices that the yacht charter industry would prefer to keep hidden, not least the preference to use foreign white crew rather than local black West Indians, who were supposed to be given priority when filling job vacancies. And then there was the matter of insurance for crew members: who knew exactly what insurance was, and was not, being provided to protect the crew of these charter yachts? The charter business in the Caribbean is a huge industry, employing thousands of people and earning millions of dollars for all involved, including the local community. And for the owners of the companies based in this tax-free haven there was a lot resting on the outcome.

My day in court was an anticlimax. It felt as though all of those present were just going through the motions purely to satisfy due process. Even the judge looked bored and, as the stenographer tapped away as I gave my evidence, it grew increasingly hot and you could almost sense a complete disinterest from the defence counsel and even my prosecuting counsel. After I delivered my evidence and had been cross-examined, it was all over. Mr Archibald QC told me it had gone well in his view but the judge would need a few days to consider his verdict.

Once back in the UK, despite constant pressure from me, it actually took the judge more than a month to deliver his verdict – and when it did eventually come it was not the news I had hoped for.

In the judge's opinion, because I had entered the territory as a tourist by self-declaring it on my entry visa, even though I was directed to do so by Barry Rice, and even though I had been recruited by Barry Rice a week earlier in the UK, no breach of work contract could have occurred because, as a tourist, I could not have been working. Rice had persuaded me to falsify my entry visa and, in so doing, I had, according to the judge, signed away any entitlement I may have had.

In my view it was a politically motivated judgment. It was both unfair and unjust. I remain convinced it was a cover-up. It was an easy way out for the BVI government and the charter industry to sweep aside my legitimate claim without any repercussions for either of them. The day I received the judgment, Archibald advised me that I had the option of an appeal and, in his view, I had good grounds to appeal on the basis that my contract actually began back in England when I met Barry Rice for my interview. But this time, in order to progress the appeal, he would need some $20,000 placed on security in case the petition was unsuccessful, money he knew I did not have.

Elaine and I talked it over and came to the conclusion that the time had come to let it go. We could have borrowed the $20,000 but, regardless of the outcome, it would have prolonged the stress and worry. In a strange way, the day that the deadline for the appeal passed it felt as though a huge weight had been lifted from my shoulders. OK, so I had lost forever my chance to prove that I was wronged, but I had had my day in court. I had said what I had wanted to say. I still believe firmly that I had a legitimate claim and that those concerned will have to live with it on their consciences for the rest of their lives. Even if I had won, I doubt I would have received any money and, whatever we achieved in life, at least we could now hold our heads high and say that we had earned every single penny ourselves, without compensation and without support from anybody else. It would make our achievements that much greater.

21

Our departure from Wells-next-the-Sea was not as straight-forward as our arrival. We had planned an 0500 start the following the morning, and even Mike Gallon, the good friend who had masterminded Rotary's involvement with my project, had driven all the way from Rutland with his wife Sylvia special-ly to see me off at first light. But the northerly wind which had blown us so quickly down from Grimsby had now become our gaoler. The entrance to the tiny Norfolk harbour faces due north, and we would have to head out through a long narrow passage of nearly a mile in length between low sand banks before exiting and turning eastwards.

We set off as planned, waving goodbye in the darkness to Mike, Sylvia and the road crew, and made our way down the river to the harbour entrance, but the northerly force 4 made it completely impassable. We managed to anchor *Freethinker* in less than a metre of water in a sheltered area just inside the harbour entrance whilst Ian took *Everest One* into the channel to see what the sea conditions were like. He need not have bothered. I could see from the way large fishing boats, in their attempts to leave, were being thrown high into the air by the two-metre standing waves, nearly flipping them over backwards – there was no way I could make the same journey. It was frustrating. The impass-able section was no more than a mile long, and beyond that the sea conditions would have been quite acceptable for sailing, but the tide would be turning against us soon – so we had to accept that for today at least we would be going nowhere.

The road crew had quite a surprise when they learned we were headed back, only forty-five minutes after starting. It was the only time on the entire trip that we had to return before we had even set off, and unfortunately we got back to find that Mike and Sylvia had already left for their return journey home.

Blog entry, Day 100, Bank Holiday Monday, 27 August 2007:

100 days....!!! Blimey, can you believe it? Nearly a third of a year living in a motorhome or, in Ian's case, living in the back of the Land Rover – ours is luxury in comparison. For those 100 days, Elaine, Tim and I have slept in the van every single night, only breaking for the one night we spent in the Isle of Man, when we had no choice. It's going to be weird to get home and not be dodging wheelchairs, moving all of our belongings from bed to settee each morning then back again at night to make living space; trying to live and cook with electronics, boat parts, wet weather clothing and Tim's toys strewn everywhere. It's a miracle Elaine knows where anything is in this eight-foot-square box. But stowing everything is just another job she has in addition to permanent motorhome driver, part-time cook, washerwoman, personal carer, cleaning lady, mum, boat launcher/recoverer etc – the list goes on. We've all put up with huge inconveniences and discomforts to see this through, and it's a credit to all of the crew who have put up with it so valiantly without complaint. Now the finish line is nearly in sight it seems scarcely believable that the hardship will soon be over. With only seven more scheduled stops, we could be home within a fortnight – but having been so badly affected by bad weather so many times this year, we're not going to make any promises on ETA until we actually cross the finish line.

It was 1700 by the time we arrived at the Royal Norfolk and Suffolk Yacht Club in Lowestoft on the night of Monday the 27th. After a very uncomfortable and wet departure through the passage at Wells, the same passage that had imprisoned us the day before, we made it out into clear water at 0630. A first on the trip, and a first for me, was sailing through the wind farm off Great Yarmouth. I weaved my way through at least thirty monster wind turbines, spinning at great speed. It was very spectacular, but I was careful not to venture too close. We made the trip to Lowestoft in just over ten hours, barely sailing below 5 knots and often reaching in excess of 10 knots, even punching a foul tide. It was yet another punishing voyage, the enforced lay-day the day before providing just enough respite to recuperate and replenish physical reserves to complete the fifty-eight-mile journey without any major difficulties.

Taking advantage of the favourable wind, and after a good night's sleep, at 0600 on Tuesday 28 August we headed out of Lowestoft for our next destination, the tiny Suffolk harbour of Felixstowe Ferry, a few miles north of Harwich and just inside the difficult entrance to the River Deben. With a fast-flowing southerly tide and good wind, both in our favour, we made the thirty-mile journey in just under six hours and were back ashore in time for lunch. There was great news awaiting our arrival. Spike had called to say that because we had taken so long in our circumnavigation, he once again had some leave owing to him, and he could join us in Ramsgate for the final run of legs along the south coast. It would be great to have Spike back again. For the first time since Sarah left us in Amble, we would be operating with a full compliment of crew again – though I continued to have personal doubts whether the expedition was ever going to be completed.

Personal diary note, Day 101, Tuesday 28 August 2007:

> Great news. Spike to rejoin in Ramsgate. Still not sure we are going to make it. This bloody weather is likely to screw everything up.

Once again faced with the problems of leaving a harbour due to insufficient water, Felixstowe Ferry gave Ian one of his most challenging calculations. As at some other destinations, tidal state and daylight were the main problems. We needed the full six hours of tide in our favour to make the forty-five-mile journey across the Thames Estuary and weave our way through the notorious Goodwin Sands to Ramsgate. But we needed to leave at low water, which was at 0530, and sunrise was not until 0600. As if this were not challenging enough, Felixstowe Ferry lies in the River Deben, a river with a shallow sand bar that moves with such frequency that no printed chart remains current for long enough to be relied upon, and the only way to ensure safe passage is to confirm its latest position with the harbour master.

At 0530 on the morning of Wednesday 29 August 2007, day 102 of our voyage, and in complete darkness, Ian and I tentatively allowed the last of the ebb tide to slowly drift *Everest One* and *Freethinker* down the River Deben towards the notorious sand bar. Unable to see what lay ahead in the pitch black, all I could hear was the terrific rush of water breaking over the sand bar somewhere in front of me. Having taken local advice, and using his GPS, Ian cautiously steered *Everest One* just outside the portside channel marker. My depth sounder showed a rapid shallowing of water – six feet, five feet, four feet. I needed only one foot of clearance, but the RIB needed at least three feet. It wasn't a dangerous situation but I could feel my heart thumping, knowing I was within inches of running aground in the dark. My depth sounder then showed three feet. I was right over the bar. I radioed through to Ian, who was drifting some ten yards behind me.

'I think I'm over. It dropped to three feet but it's rising again sharply,' I said.

'Yep, we are coming up on it too,' he replied. 'Five feet, four feet, four feet, four feet, three feet, I can feel the hull touching the sand, we're aground – but it's OK, we're still moving. Three feet, three feet, four feet, five feet – it's OK Geoff, we're over.'

With that, Ian notified the road crew, who had been warned that we might be back sooner than expected. 'Everest Mobile, this is *Everest One*. We are over the bar. See you in Ramsgate.'

I heaved a huge sigh of relief.

It was a fairly good run with a strong tide and wind in my favour, but with so many course alterations to avoid the Goodwin Sands it was a very complex navigational passage. Our early start and rapid progress across the Thames Estuary caused only one problem. Bill Southgate, head of Bishop Skinner Insurance, one of my suppliers, had planned a surprise rendezvous with us. He kept his yacht on the River Orwell, a few miles to the south of us, and had been keeping track of our movements on my website with the intention of meeting up for a surprise sail together.

We departed Felixstowe Ferry almost an hour earlier than I had stated on my blog so by the time Bill emerged into the North Sea and called us up on the VHF, we were nearly ten miles ahead of where he expected. Even through binoculars we couldn't see him astern of us, so we made do with an early-morning chat on the radio. It had been a good idea of Bill's, but sadly it didn't happen as he had planned.

We arrived in Ramsgate at midday. It was like being on a different planet. The sun was out, it was warm, and there were people, hundreds of them, wearing shorts, T-shirts, summer dresses. It really felt most strange, and seeing road signs to Brighton and London, ice-cream vans and people sat on the quay eating fish and chips, it was like rediscovering civilisation. Having endured such a terrible summer, and having been stuck in car parks and fields for most of it, it was reassuring to see real life again.

And waiting for us on the slipway was Spike. It was great to see him again, and Timothy, who had arrived with the road crew an hour earlier, had already latched onto his long-lost friend. But there was another surprise waiting for Tim. On 14 May, the day of my aborted start all those weeks earlier, he had given an interview which was broadcast live on national BBC television. When asked by the interviewer if he wanted to be a sailor when he grew up, like his dad, he had replied, 'No, I want to be a fireman.'

Later that same day, I received an email from Neil Parr, a fireman in Ramsgate, who had seen the broadcast and offered to give Timothy a tour of the fire station when we arrived there. It was such a long time ago that I had all but forgotten, until I received a call from Neil the day before our arrival wanting to follow up on his promise. So Timothy was picked up by Neil and taken to the fire station, where he had a private tour.

Blog entry, Day 102, Wednesday 29 August 2007:

Timothy came back laden with goodies and stories about the dangers of fire. A big thanks to Neil Parr and his colleagues at Kent Fire Brigade. You'll be pleased to hear that Timothy has now narrowed his career choice down to coastguard, lifeboatman and fireman – unfortunately the world of clowns will have to make do without him, as will our country if he's not going to be PM.

Arriving so early in Ramsgate, despite having been at sea for six hours, Ian and I hatched a plan to sail on the afternoon tide, a further fifteen miles, to Dover. Never before had I attempted to sail two separate legs in one day, nor would it be easy on the road crew, but with favourable conditions we needed to press on at every opportunity. The forecast from Weather Online had been spot on. We had got ahead of the poor weather system to the north of us, but despite high pressure building over the south coast, the forecast was for stronger winds later in the week.

Getting me ready for the second sail of the day, Elaine noticed the beginnings of a pressure sore. The news sent shudders down my spine. 'Oh no, not a pressure sore, not now,' I murmured to myself. Luckily, it was on my heel, not my backside, but that didn't make it any less serious. It was still only an angry red area of skin, not yet ulcerated, but the correct treatment would be to keep the heel dry and free from any pressure whatsoever until it was fully healed. Allowing it to rest in a salty wet rubber boot for hours on end was not ideal, but I had no option. Along with an increasing number of mechanical niggles on the RIB, my pressure sore was clear evidence of the toll that the trip was beginning to take on us all. There was a lifting in mood now we were on the south coast, but you could see the general tiredness in everyone – except Spike, of course, who had returned looking infuriatingly healthy.

We left Ramsgate at 1730, arriving in Dover three hours later and in darkness. The road crew had performed heroics of their own, having decamped in Felixstowe Ferry early that morning, driven 130 miles to Ramsgate, established a base there, only to decamp again and head for Dover late that afternoon. Once again, they were dutifully waiting for us on our arrival, the motorhomes already parked and connected to power and water.

With the boats safely moored in the outer harbour, and as

we finished yet another Chinese takeaway, Ian announced that we would once again be making an 0400 start for an 0500 departure the following morning, our sixth consecutive early start. Exhausted, we were all asleep by 2300.

Now that we were back on the south coast, the chances of actually completing the challenge were increasing by the day. Once the most optimistic of people, I found myself secretly harbouring a belief that the expedition could still fail. We were six stops away from the finish line, at least another week of sailing. I knew there was a distinct possibility that with just one more delay the weather window could be closed for the rest of the year. Good runs of fair weather are few and far between from September onwards – I knew that – so I was the last person to be envisaging the time when I would finish.

Although I couldn't muster up the enthusiasm, it was essential that plans were put in place for my homecoming. If I was to finish, then it was only right that the achievement should be recognised, not so much for me but for my crew and all of my supporters. Luckily for me the homecoming was in the hands of my sponsor, my press officer, members of the local Rotary club and the officers of the Royal Southern Yacht Club. It was as infuriating for them as it was for me trying to establish a date for my return. For several days I had been arriving in port, tired and hungry, to be met with a long list of emails and phone messages all demanding to know when we would be back, and at what time. Six months earlier, I would have guestimated a date and hoped for the best, fairly confident of my prediction. But taking a leaf out of Ian's book of realism, and having been burned so badly by the weather, I refused to commit to a date. The homecoming party organisers agreed that Wednesday 5 September would be ideal, but I would give no assurances. I knew they would be investing both time and effort in the planning, but I was still unsure that I would even finish the damn voyage, so the last thing I could commit to, emotionally, was my homecoming. I would not allow myself to be hurt again. Not until I knew that our return was definite would I give myself the luxury of acknowledging it.

'Arghhh!' came the cry from Spike.

It was 0500, it was dark, and we were down on the pontoon just outside Dover marina, rigging the boats getting ready to depart. Out of the corner of my eye I saw Spike lose his footing and slip, the crossbeams on *Freethinker* breaking his fall into the water.

'I think I've winded myself,' gasped Spike.

Ian and Eddie were quick to help pull Spike out of the water and onto the pontoon, where he lay on his back wearing his drysuit and lifejacket, holding his ribs, clearly in a lot of pain.

Hoping to work it off, he elected to continue on RIB duty with Andy and Ian, but he didn't look good.

Day 103, Thursday 30 August 2007:

The run itself from Dover to Eastbourne was a trip of two halves. The first half to Dungeness was fantastic, *Freethinker* consistently powering at about 10 knots for nearly two hours. The stiff breeze was blowing off land so the sea state was calm, which made it an invigorating, wet and fast sail, I was completely soaked through but sailing so fast I was on a real high. By Dungeness, the wind had died, it had headed us, and as if that was not bad enough the tide turned too, so it was long drag into Eastbourne – but thanks to the Bexhill Sailing Club guys who popped out in their RIB to say hello. Thanks too to Eastbourne Marina for allowing us to use their wonderful facilities, and to Eastbourne Rotary.

By the time we arrived at Eastbourne, Spike's condition had not improved, and if anything he was looking particularly grey. He had only rejoined us the day before, and now he had badly injured himself. He spent all of the trip lying on his back in the bow section of the RIB, unable to move. When we finally docked in Eastbourne, Eddie drove him to Brighton Hospital, where he was x-rayed and found to have broken two ribs. Not that a few ribs would stop him wanting to continue – and thankfully, having been bandaged up and given a few pain killers, Spike elected to spend the remaining days on road-crew duty.

Day 104, Friday 31 August 2007:

> Well, the finish is within sight, but the weather gods are not going to let us get away that easily. We set out from Eastbourne bound for Shoreham, clearing the lock at Sovereign harbour and enjoying a good sail to Beachy Head – what a spectacular sight from the sea, with its red and white stripy lighthouse on the beach with the white cliffs behind – but then the winds became more westerly and the tide turned, so our trip was foreshortened and we made for Newhaven.

I was right to be concerned about the weather. Being forced to foreshorten our journey to Newhaven was proof that even so close to home it was the weather that would dictate the date of our return, not us. And on top of Spike's injury in Dover, Ian had hurt his back in Eastbourne. With no slipway, the marina provided the only option for getting me in and out of my boat, and this entailed a difficult two-stage lift. With Ian taking my heavy upper body, and Elaine taking my legs, I had to be lifted up from the cockpit of my boat at sea level to the pontoon three feet above, and then lifted again up into my wheelchair, with Ian and Elaine balancing on a wobbly, metre-wide pontoon. Departing the following day, the precarious routine had to be reversed, so it came as no surprise that something would give – and unfortunately it was Ian's lower back. The relentless pace was only adding to the fatigue that was affecting us all, and mistakes were beginning to be made.

The following morning, Saturday 1 September, we headed out from Newhaven into the English Channel, this time bound for Chichester. We were making good time, but the winds slowly built during the day and, with the tide about to turn, the prospect of beating for another six hours into two-metre-high waves was daunting. I was prepared to give it a go, but I too was beginning to make irrational decisions.

We were an hour past Shoreham when Ian radioed through –

'Geoff, I'm not happy, this is only going to get worse. Can you turn around? We're going back to Shoreham.'

Part of me was relieved. The pressure sore on my heel was now causing me a lot of pain, and I was extremely tired and cold. But part of me was willing to endure another six hours of discomfort for the sake of making ground. I was fast reaching the stage when I just wanted to get the whole project over and done with. I was now well outside my comfort zone. I was in unknown territory as far as my physical and mental state were concerned. At times it felt like I was on auto-pilot, just going through the motions, zombie-like, out of control. At other times I felt in control enough to realise the scale of what I was achieving, and how lucky I was to have such a supportive crew. But I remembered Donald Crowhurst. Did I have the courage to say if and when I had endured enough? At least now, with only a few stops to go, there was an increasing likelihood of actually finishing this journey. Maybe there was also a part of me which didn't want the journey to end. It would mean a return to normality, whatever that was.

Our return to Shoreham may have been a welcome break from the choppy seas for me and the crew on the RIB, but it was mental torture for the road crew. They had already crossed the Sussex border and were now back in our home county of Hampshire and only ten miles from our next destination, Hayling Island, when they took the call to about-turn and return to Shoreham. According to Elaine, that was a tough call.

With a choice of three slipways in Shoreham, we plumped for the Sussex Yacht Club, where, coincidentally, their annual Sailability day had ended less than an hour earlier. It was a shame to have missed the opportunity to meet everybody, but there were several members who had stayed on who were pleasantly surprised to find the Personal Everest circus arrive on their doorstep, and they had a rare opportunity to inspect *Freethinker*.

An early-morning call to Weather Online on Sunday 2 September confirmed that a force 6 would be blowing through that day. As disappointing as it seemed at first, we were advised that thereafter there would be a prolonged period of settled weather, lasting well beyond the proposed end date of Wednesday 5 September. With only two more destinations to the finish, there were signs that we might finish on time after all.

But there was another reason to be glad about not sailing that day. It was Joyce Pennell's eighty-third birthday, and her three daughters, Wendy, Val and Jenny, had organised a surprise lunch for her at a restaurant no more than twenty miles from the yacht club we were staying at. Elaine had spoken with Jenny to arrange our surprise visit, and it was imperative that we arrived last, since my only mode of transport was a huge motorhome covered in sponsors' logos, and to have arrived before them would have ruined the surprise. It was so good to see them again. We had spoken occasionally on the phone over recent weeks but here they were, my family, whom I had missed so much – it was a great day. I knew our arrival home later that week would be hectic, with little chance to speak to anybody, so it was like having our own private homecoming party. But it was slightly odd when it came to saying goodbye and returning to Shoreham, knowing that we had many more miles to sail before finishing.

Day 106, Monday 3 September 2007:

> We left Shoreham at lunchtime, when there was just enough water on the slipway, and I had one of the best sails of the trip. With a northerly offshore wind blowing a good 15 knots, the Challenger was screaming along for several hours, often exceeding 8 knots, even against a foul tide.

Sitting so low in *Freethinker*, I could make out two headlands in front of me. To my right was Selsey Bill, and to my left was the eastern end of the Isle of Wight. As I made my way towards Selsey on a starboard tack, ever so slowly the grey featureless silhouette of the coast took shape and I could see the houses clearly lining the beach. I chose quite a tight course, cutting in close to the shore but then heading out into the Solent for a marker denoting the Looe Channel to avoid the very shallow ledge that sticks out from the Bill.

As I slowly rounded the headland, so the Hampshire coast-line opened up to my right, and there in the distance was the unmistakable Spinnaker Tower in Portsmouth. And even further in the distance I could see the tall chimneys of Fawley oil refin-ery billowing out smoke and flames, with the row of ladder-like red lights running up their length. It was at that point, for the first time on the entire trip, that I allowed myself to accept that I would actually complete Personal Everest, and that I had indeed circumnavigated Great Britain. I lifted my visor and just stared at the chimneys at Fawley in disbelief. Not exactly the most beauti-ful of landfalls, but those chimneys indicated that I was home.

Having taken my mind off my sailing for a fraction of a second, I was jarred back into reality by the huge overfalls in the Looe Channel, which struck me unawares. They were as big and as violent as any I had seen in the whole trip, and it was a rough, wet and stomach-churning twenty minutes as *Freethinker* was tossed and pounded. I let go of my mainsail and the tiller and just leaned forward, head between my knees, holding on for dear life as my boat was spat through the overfalls at more than 6 knots on the tide alone. It seemed never-ending but ever so slowly the sea state lessened, and once clear I regained my com-posure, pulled in the mainsheet and headed north for Chichester Harbour entrance, finally coming ashore at the Hayling Island Sailing Club at 1800.

The sailing club was deserted, apart from our vehicles and trailers. It is one of the RYA's centres of excellence – and no wonder. It is a simply magnificent facility, perfectly situated at the mouth of the harbour with views out across Chichester Harbour and the Solent. Alan Davies, a Rotarian but also a sailor whom I had known for many years through Sailability, had helped negotiate with the club to provide the facilities, and he was on the slipway along with the shore crew to bring me ashore that evening.

Rather than make one long sail to Hamble, we decided to put in a ten-mile sail around to Gosport on Tuesday, with a final fifteen-mile leg left for Wednesday 5 September. Ex-crew members Sarah and Joel had both taken time out from their jobs and would rejoin us in Gosport for the final leg to Hamble. That night in Hayling Island, the joyous mood was tangible. None of us could contain our grins, knowing the heartache was about to end, soon to be replaced with an outpouring of rejoicing. It was enough to give me at least a bout of nervous excitement. That night we were left alone, in peace, just the crew. It was a beautiful evening, with a clear sky, and most of the crew sat on the wall that surrounds the club along the top of the beach, drinking beer and wine, throwing pebbles into the sea, talking about what we were looking forward to most about getting home and what we would be doing next. The consensus seemed to be looking forward to sleeping in a decent bed, but for me it was seeing my friends, getting out of the limelight and going fishing. In terms of what we did next, none of us could think that far ahead. For the first time since Brixham I felt myself relax, and I allowed myself to start enjoying what remained of this epic journey.

The following morning dawned as beautiful as the previous evening had ended. But this time, facing east, we watched as the sun rose directly ahead of us over Chichester Harbour. It was such a still morning, the only noise coming from the engines of the fishing boats making their way out of the harbour. This was our penultimate day. Later we would be heading around to Gosport, but for the time being everyone was quietly going about their business. It was just like any other day on the Personal Everest voyage.

With our arrival back on the Hamble now only a day away, my phone had been red-hot with messages from journalists wanting to do stories with me. I obliged where possible, but it was quite ridiculous to think that I could juggle press interviews when the biggest day of my sailing life was only a day away. One of the interviews I agreed to was with my local BBC TV station. They had supported me and my project long before I even got to the start line, and both Sally Taylor and Roger Johnson had kept in touch with me regularly during my trip. So when the BBC asked if I would give an interview at 0830 on Tuesday 4 September from the Hayling Island Sailing Club, I willingly agreed.

The reporter that morning was Danni Sinha, just she and Jo, her cameraman. I had done many interviews over the years, and most had been about some project or ambition I hoped to achieve, but this was different. I didn't need to self-promote this time – my actions had done that for me. I was on the verge of achieving something amazing, and I was really calm and relaxed. Jo set the camera up, showing me from the waist up, facing east, the morning sun giving my face a warm, orangey glow as I looked towards it, squinting slightly.

Danni asked me her first few predictable questions, but then she asked me a question which completely took the wind out of my sails –

'When did you have your accident?'

It was not a deliberately loaded question, and under normal circumstances I would not have given it a moment's notice. As I opened my mouth to give her the date, my mind was already a split-second ahead of my mouth. I quickly recalculated the date in my mind, and then it hit me. I realised the significance of finishing the following day, 5 September. That was the date I had broken my neck twenty-three years earlier. I sat there, frozen, looking out to sea, a couple of tears rolling down my cheeks, the camera still rolling.

'I'm sorry,' I said, quickly wiping away the tears with the sleeve of my jumper so they didn't see. 'I'm sorry, it was twenty-three years ago tomorrow, I didn't realise.'

I quickly tried to regain my composure, feeling completely stupid. I had been so relaxed and happy, then her question hit me like a punch in the stomach. I had not even given it any thought until that moment, but suddenly it dawned on me. At the age of eighteen an accident had robbed me of a career in sailing and then, twenty-three years later, to the very day, I would reaffirm myself as a yachtsman, both in my own eyes and in the eyes of my peers. I guess Mike Gallon would call it synchronicity.

Aware that they had inadvertently captured on film a rare moment of private emotion on my part, and worried that the broadcast would be of me weeping, not sailing, I made a special request of Danni when it came time for her to leave –

'When editing your piece, be kind to me, please.'

She knew what I meant. She smiled and nodded.

With the film crew gone and a handful of well-wishers watching from the top of the slipway – including my dad, Robin Hoad – I set sail for the shortest, and least stressful, sail of the entire voyage. It took no more than a couple of hours to sail around to Portsmouth Harbour, the last time the RIB crew and I would be able to sail together, alone at sea. Tomorrow that would all change.

There were not many pleasure boats on the Solent that afternoon, just the usual hustle and bustle of commercial traffic, ferries and hovercraft, all of them going about their business. I had to dodge a few of them, but it was terrific to be sailing along Southsea seafront, looking at all the familiar sights including South Parade Pier and the war memorial on Southsea Common. Like all sailing vessels, I was forbidden from sailing through Portsmouth Harbour entrance, so I was taken under tow for the final stretch into the harbour and around into Gosport Marina.

Joel and Sarah were already there waiting for us, along with the road crew and a few friends. For the first time I had every single member of my crew together. It was like a family reunion. It was funny to look at the crew, myself included, in comparison to everyone else on the shore that day. We looked so weather-beaten, hair bleached by the sea spray and wind, our sailing clothes and lifejackets faded by the UV light at sea. It had taken a long time, we had come a long way, and tomorrow was going to be our big day. After having our last supper of the trip at a nearby pub, we all returned to the motorhomes for the last night. Tomorrow we would be sleeping in real beds.

22

Having now been signed off work on a semi-permanent basis, and with all my committee responsibilities and the court case behind me, for the first time in many years I felt in control of myself and my life. I was also so much more confident in the person I had become, and there was no more pretence, least of all to myself.

It was shortly after the death of my stepfather, John Holt, that another door of opportunity opened up. We had arranged for his personal possessions to be valued for probate by a local auction-eer, and I was helping the valuer as she examined the items we had in our front room.

'Oh, that's a lovely Susie Cooper vase,' she exclaimed. 'Probably dates to about 1930 and is worth between £200 and £300. And that's –'

'Hang on, hang on,' I said, cutting her short as she was about to value the next item on the shelf. 'How do you know that? You've not even picked it up. How do you know that?' I was amazed, watching her work, just standing in the middle of the room, notepad in hand, identifying and valuing all these items by sight alone.

'Experience,' she laughed. 'Oh yes, and I did a degree in fine arts valuation at Southampton Institute.'

Within thirty minutes of her leaving, I had called the Institute and spoken to the Dean of the Faculty. Qualifying as a mature student, I bypassed the normal academic requirements and enrolled on the spot. I also paid my course fees with a credit card the same day, before even setting foot on the premises. The fol-lowing week I attended the first of my classes, which, part-time, were to last a total of five years.

By choosing to do it part-time, I found that the pace of work suited me fine, just one day a week – but I wished it was more. I absolutely loved it. I would sit in lectures and just soak up the information like a sponge. Ceramics, furniture, jewellery, art, I couldn't get enough of it. Considering I had never had an interest in antiques before – I didn't even know my kings and queens of England – it was at first strange to find myself suddenly doing a degree in the subject. But it was perfect, and my only regret is that I had not chosen to study it at an earlier age. Even though I enjoyed it, however, it wasn't easy. I had never read so many books and written so many essays in my life, but we had enthusiastic lecturers and a great group of students in my class, young and old, and the whole course helped give me a different perspective on life.

Once again life was back on track. With the additional care being provided by social services, a heavy load had been taken off Elaine's shoulders too. We were at one of those junctures in life, normally born of a feeling of contentment and security, where we were considering where to go next.

For some time Elaine had talked about the idea of starting a family, but I hadn't felt ready for the prospect of parenthood and I was worried about the extra workload it would put on Elaine. I knew she would have loved to have children, and for many years I felt guilty at not wanting even to explore the possibility. But her patience paid off, and by the year 2000 I was at last ready to think about it.

One August morning in 2001 I was sitting in my office at home when Elaine brought through the pregnancy test stick. There had been half a dozen other mornings just like this, most ending in tears for Elaine, though I would allow myself a little, private, sigh of relief as I comforted her. But this morning the indicator went straight to the blue line within seconds. Neither of us could believe it at first. She opened another tester kit and repeated the test. There was no mistaking it – she was pregnant. I even surprised myself, realising that I was excited at the prospect, and happy too.

It was 10.45 in the morning of 22 April 2002. I was sat on my own in a private room in Winchester Hospital watching *Bargain Hunt*, of all things, on the TV. Elaine was in the delivery suite next door having a caesarean due to the baby being in a breach position. Suddenly the doors to my room opened and the midwife pushed through a trolley with Timothy wrapped tightly in blankets, a plastic tag around his ankle and a tiny woolly hat on his head.

'Congratulations, Mr Holt, you've got a lovely son.'

A previous scan had shown that it would be a boy, and we had already decided on the name Timothy. Partly because we liked the name, partly in memory of Tim, Roy and Joyce's son-in-law, who had been such a dominant male figure in my early years.

'Is he OK? Is he healthy?' I asked anxiously.

'He's absolutely fine. We'll bring Mum through shortly.' And with that she left the room.

Nothing had prepared me for this moment. I wasn't sure how I was going to feel but, sat there, looking at my new, perfect, son – just me and him – it was the best moment of the best day in my life.

For some bizarre reason I had been having nightmares that, because he was my son, he might be paralysed like me. A ridiculous and irrational thought, I know, but one I couldn't get out of my head for weeks leading up to the birth. I put my index finger in his tiny hand, and he squeezed it tightly, and I watched his tiny toes as they wiggled and his legs kicked. He was half-me, half-Elaine. He was just perfect. All of a sudden, life made sense. I didn't matter any more. What mattered more than anything in the world was my new son and his future health. I can't remember all that I said to him, but I promised him everything. I promised him that I would always be there for him and I would love him forever. I was overcome with joy and happiness. I even recall thinking that I would go through everything again, all the pain and all the anguish of my accident, all the hardships I had faced in my life – I would willingly go through them all again for this moment. Whatever I had been through was worth it for that little chap that lay before me. And I felt a love for Elaine so deep and so strong for providing such a perfect little boy. We had been through so much together. We deserved this happiness.

Our lives had changed forever, but definitely for the better. Having a new baby around created a few practical complications – after all, Elaine only has two pairs of hands – but we weren't complaining. Every moment with him brought us both joy and, with Elaine being the only one able to attend to all the night feeds and nappy changes, it suited me fine. Despite having a new baby in the house and all the pandemonium that ensued, I managed to complete my degree and graduated later that year as a qualified valuer and auctioneer. Quite how I found the time and the patience, particularly to research and type my 20,000-word dissertation in a house full of toys, nappies, constant visitors and a demanding baby, is beyond me, but it was a huge relief finally to have the pressure of exams off my shoulders.

We wanted to celebrate Timothy's birth with our friends and family, but with neither of us believing in god we felt it would be hypocritical to have him christened in church. We opted for a Humanist naming ceremony, which we held in our garden on a gloriously sunny day in August 2004. Over a hundred guests came and it was a memorable day, especially to be able to sit in front of everybody, my son on my lap, and to make our pledges to him. Elaine read aloud a short piece of text:

If a child lives with tolerance, he learns to be patient.

If a child lives with encouragement, he learns confidence.

If a child lives with praise, he learns to appreciate.

If a child lives with fairness, he learns judgement.

If a child lives with acceptance and friendship, he learns to give love to the world.

Timothy, we hope to teach you the value of kindness, tolerance and honesty, and hope you will come to love us not only as parents but as friends.

One of the gifts Timothy received that day in August 2004 was a blank family-tree book for us to complete. As we went to bed that night Elaine made some lighthearted quip about it being impossible to complete on my part, and this began to play on my mind. Over the next few months, the suspicions I had always had about my true, biological father were making me increasingly restless. For Timothy's sake, if not for my own, I had to find out the truth. I needed to know who my father, his grandfather, was. Robin Hoad was always going to be my 'Dad', and he was always going to be Timothy's 'Granddad' – there was never any question about that – but I needed to put this ghost to rest.

Aware that my quest might lead me into some sensitive areas, especially for Robin, in January 2005 I telephoned my brother Richard and asked him if he would agree to a DNA test to at least prove or disprove whether we shared the same father.

Always one for a confrontation, Richard decided the easiest way was actually for him to phone my mother and ask her outright. It was a brave move. Like me, he had not spoken or had contact with her for nearly twenty years. Seconds later he called me back. 'Yep, you're right. She told me your real father was someone else, but she refused to tell me who. She'll only talk to you.'

I immediately tried calling her number, but my stepfather Andy answered and he refused to let me speak to my mother. I tried several times over the following weeks, but every time the phone was either put down on me, or I left messages on the answerphone which were never returned.

On 24 February 2005, my thirty-ninth birthday, a large package arrived from Scilly, but this was no ordinary birthday gift. Amongst all the personal effects, photographs and letters she had collected which charted my life over the years, my mother included a note which named my father as one Ernest Read. The letter went on to state in a matter-of-fact way, 'He was a green-grocer, he was 60 years old at the time and will be dead now. Do not contact me ever again.' There was no address given for him, no further clues, nothing. Some birthday present that was.

I found it all very traumatic. On the one hand I had the name of my father, whilst on the other, if she was telling the truth, he would almost certainly be dead by now. But the way in which she disclosed the facts was also hard to take.

Armed with only the most basic of information – a name, an occupation and an idea of age – I spent many weeks sat in public records offices looking through directories and electoral roles. I had an early stroke of luck when I discovered an E Read, greengrocer, living in Farlington, a few roads away from where I lived, in the year I was born. It was definitely the right person, but a year later the record showed that he was gone with no forwarding address. After two more months of searching I had exhausted just about every avenue and so, in a last-ditch effort, I wrote into the 'Where are they now?' section of the *Portsmouth Evening News* with brief details of my search. Six weeks later, and quite by surprise, I took a call from a lady who knew Ernest, or Ernie as he preferred to be known. She broke the news to me that both he and his wife had died many years earlier, which didn't really come as a surprise. I thanked her and was about to put the phone down, accepting that this was a chapter in my life that was gone forever, when she told me that Ernie had a son called Ted who lived in the New Forest, less than twenty miles from me. She even gave me his phone number.

Unwilling to phone over such a delicate matter, I tracked down an address and wrote what was quite a difficult letter to Ted. I kept imagining what it would be like to receive such a letter. How would Ted feel on learning he had a new brother? Or, worse still, what if my mother had lied to me, or if it was some terrible mistake? That would have been simply awful. Those close to me questioned whether it was the right thing to do in the first place. 'Why not just let go of it?' they asked. But I needed answers – I had harboured a sense of being different since childhood, and now was my opportunity to find out if my feelings had been well-founded. Before I wrote, I made a point of telling Robin face to face what I had discovered, and I called Richard and Lucy to tell them the same. I laboured the point that, no matter what, Richard would always be my brother, Lucy my sister, and Robin my dad. Although he didn't know my true father's identity, it became clear that Robin had known all along that it wasn't him, and, for whatever reason, that he had chosen not to share it with me. I guess it's not the sort of thing that one would chose to discuss voluntarily – but once again the feeling that others around me knew and kept the information from me was hurtful. No one seemed to understand why knowing the identity of my true father was so important to me.

Luckily, in the letter he wrote back to me, Ted seemed quite relaxed about the prospect of having a brother, but he quite rightly suggested that we confirmed our relationship scientifically before jumping to any conclusions. I telephoned a paternity testing centre and was advised that a DNA test was not the most accurate test for our circumstances. For two brothers seeking to determine the same biological father, a Y chromosome test would prove or disprove the matter with a high degree of accuracy. The test itself was a simple matter of taking a swab of saliva and sending it back to the laboratory. The kit arrived the day before our meeting and I put one set in my bag to deliver personally to Ted. It would mean a wait to confirm the results, but we both agreed it would be better to meet anyway

An hour before Ted and I were due to meet for the first time, I thought I ought to raise the subject of my disability. After all, it was going to be hard enough for both of us, without expecting the poor guy to deal with the whole wheelchair thing as well. I'd deliberately not mentioned it before, there seemed no reason to.

I wrote an email that was short but to the point: 'Ted, so there's no surprises, I think you ought to know that I use a wheelchair. See you shortly.'

Almost instantly I got a reply: 'I know, I'm not stupid. I Googled you days ago. I was wondering when you were going to mention it.'

I rocked back in my chair with laughter when I read his note. Cheeky bugger, I thought, researching me – but then it was no more cheeky than the searches I had done on him. Were these the first signs of shared characteristics?

An hour later I turned up at the Haywain pub in Cadnam, on the edge of the New Forest, on my own, and wheeled into the bar. It was a strange feeling, nervous but not worried. I was too pragmatic to think there was going to be any sort of emotional reunion, and with Ted a bit older than me, and potentially from the same stock, I suspect he was feeling the same way. I spotted him immediately, sat in a corner, black trousers, black polo-neck, a pint of Guinness in his hand.

'Thanks for meeting me, Edward,' I said.

He laughed. 'Ted – everyone calls me Ted. Well it's not every day you get a letter from someone claiming to be your brother. I thought it was one of those scams until you mentioned Farlington in 1966, I was fourteen years old, and I remember something happening in the family.'

We mostly talked about our families, and a potted history of our lives. In the short time we had on that first meeting we were unlikely, and unwilling, to start getting into detail. But, as we talked, it seemed really odd sitting next to this guy who was my brother. The biggest shock came when I asked Ted about my father.

'So what can you tell me about Ernest?' I asked.

Again he laughed. 'Our dad was called Ernie. Everyone called him Ernie.'

'Our dad.' That seemed such a strange thing to hear. No longer was it a stepdad or legal-guardian dad. Our dad. My real dad. It just seemed such a good thing to hear, comforting in a way.

Ted turned the question around. 'Well, what do you know about him?'

'He was a greengrocer,' I replied, confident and rather proud that I had done my research.

For a third time Ted laughed. 'You've no idea, have you?' he said, seemingly surprised that was all I knew. 'Ernie was in the Army Air Corps and posted to the Parachute Regiment in 1940, where he was promoted to Warrant Officer. He served in Palestine and fought at Arnhem. After the war he worked as a camp boss for various oil companies around the world. Only much later did he become a greengrocer for a short while before becoming a publican and secretary of a couple of local golf clubs. He died in 1985 and his ashes are buried in the Allied Cemetery in Oosterbeck.'

Bingo – it all made sense. All those confusing feelings I had harboured since childhood when I looked at Richard and his contentment with his life compared to my wanderlust, my hyperactive need to challenge myself. We were both brought up the same way so it could only mean that I was wired differently – and that proved my belief that it was nature, my DNA, that was the driving force behind my restless outlook on life, not nurture.

Ted later told me that he saw the family resemblance straight away, claiming I 'looked like Ernie but sat in a wheelchair'. As if our physical similarities were not proof enough, a week later the lab results came back, confirming with 99 per cent certainty that Ted and I were indeed brothers. I was finally able to lay to rest the nagging doubt about my father, but I also gained an added benefit in the shape of Ted and his family, my new extended family. We quickly became good friends, and for the first time I saw photographs of my father, a good-looking man with strong features. Perhaps strangely, I did not feel any real sadness at not knowing him. No – that was then, this was now. I'd found Ted, and that was enough for me. We could at last make a start on that family-tree book of Timothy's.

In many ways, having Timothy after my accident meant that I had less worry as a parent than those who have had accidents when they are already parents. I read BBC journalist Frank Gardner's excellent biography, *Blood and Sand*, chronicling the events before and after he was shot in Saudi Arabia in 2004. Frank had children before the shooting, and I would have found that very difficult – I'm sure he did too – coping with kids who have known the 'daddy that can walk' and then the 'daddy that uses a wheelchair'. I know that children are highly adaptable, but at least Timothy, growing up with a dad who uses a wheelchair, has known nothing different. On the flip side, I have never had the opportunity to kick a ball with him, to run after him in a park, to take him swimming, to hold the saddle of his bike to steady him on his first solo run. Even flying a kite or wiping drips of ice-cream from his chin – I couldn't even do that. But I would never dream of letting him see that it hurts me to just sit in my chair whilst my friends and family did all of those things that I can never do with my son. Ever since he was old enough to understand, I have explained that Daddy had a swimming accident and it hurt my neck, which means that I will never walk again. We don't make a big deal of it, and I hope it doesn't worry him, but there are times when I wonder. Occasionally, during those special few minutes in the morning between him waking up and coming through to our bedroom for a morning cuddle and us all getting up, I get the odd difficult question that knocks me sideways. 'Daddy, when you dream, do you dream that you are walking? And if you do, does that mean you would rather dream than be awake?' The innocence of youth. At times like that I could squeeze him for being so cute and so innocent.

Elaine and I have always had an open and forthright relationship with Timothy. We don't hide anything from him, least of all about my disability, but equally we don't go out of our way to expose him to every personal detail. He'll often see Elaine empty my leg bag of urine or lift me into my wheelchair, but he hasn't seen Elaine change the suprapubic catheter which goes through my abdominal wall into my bladder, for example. But, at six years old, he's mature enough not to talk about personal things that happen at home whilst outside of the house or when he's at school. I'm half-expecting that at some stage my disability might be used against him in playground spats – kids are capable of the most horrid things – but thankfully he's already the tallest in his class and, if he grows to my height, he'll have no problems looking after himself.

Of all the new experiences that he has tried, the one I really wanted to be involved in was sailing. He has always known that Daddy was a yachtsman, he has seen the photos and heard the stories and, from the age of two, he would often ask if he could go sailing too. This had to be more than just sending him off for a sailing experience – it was as much for me as for him. I hadn't given it any thought as the three of us made our way up to Rutland Sailing Club, where I had been asked to a meeting at the club which coincided with their Sailability sailing session. We hadn't even intended to go out on the water, but the meeting finished early and one of the volunteers asked if I wanted to go for a sail. I suddenly remembered that the club had a new type of boat, the Access 2.3 two-seater – I recalled signing a cheque for a grant towards it when I was a trustee with Sailability. I'd never sailed one before, but I asked if I could take Timothy with me. In many ways it was better that events unfolded in that way – there was no time for nerves on anyone's part, Elaine's, Timothy's or mine. Actually, what I felt was not so much nerves as fear that I would be responsible for a highly active two-year-old, out on the reservoir, on my own. And neither of us could swim.

A tiny lifejacket was found for my son in the back of the club's sail locker, and I was hoisted out of my chair and down into the boat. Once I was settled, Timothy was next in. I ordered him not to move – visions of him trying to dangle over the side to look at the fishes were worrying me senseless. With the sails set, the bow was pushed off and I bought her round onto a course headed out to the centre of the enormous reservoir. Dodging ducks and mooring buoys, in a light breeze of about 10 knots, we sailed out.

We must have looked like a pair of grinning idiots – Timothy because he found it highly amusing trying to steer into the ducks, and me because I was so happy. I simply could not stop smiling. A hundred and one emotions were running through my mind. Sailing had been my life, and it was still incredibly special to me. Because of the path my life had taken, and because of Sailability, these special boats existed. So when Timothy came along, even though I had to watch him grow up doing all the normal kids' things without really being a part of it all, I was the one who took him for his first sail, on my own, despite everything. It was a very special moment for me indeed. Twenty years ago, if anyone had said that a high-level quadriplegic would be able to take his two-year-old son out sailing on his own, they would have been laughed at, it would have seemed easier to put a man on the moon. But here I was doing just that, it was happening.

We spent about an hour on the water, sailing to no particular destination, just back and forth with Timothy steering and both of us laughing. Getting back alongside the pontoon, I could see that Elaine had been moved by it all. She knew how much it meant to me. I was bursting with pride and couldn't wait to get home and show everyone the photographs.

But any chance of enjoying the moment vanished the following day when I took a call from the brother of my lifelong school friend Simon Lawton –

'Geoff, it's Jeremy. Jeremy Lawton.' The moment I heard his voice I knew what was coming next.

'I'm sorry Geoff, but Simon died yesterday.'

So the drink had finally killed him. I thanked him for letting me know and put the phone down. 'You stupid bastard, Simon,' I said to myself repeatedly. I'd known it was only a matter of time. Every time we met or spoke over the years, he got worse. At first it was sclerosis of the liver, then diabetes through drinking so much alcohol, then partial paralysis and partial blindness through the diabetes, and if the spirits and beer weren't going to get him, then the forty fags a day were, and he developed cancers in the throat and the base of his brain. What a terrible waste. He was barely forty years old, and now he was dead.

I got in my van and drove to my special place in Lower Swanwick, along the foreshore where we played as kids. As I sat in my van in the car park, from where I could see right down the river. I could hear our voices and picture us as though it were yesterday, wading through the mud, fishing, laughing, having fun, right in front of me. It was such a beautiful spot, and the memories were flooding back quicker than I could do them justice. Growing up he had been my best mate, and friendships like that don't just die because you get older and move on. Part of me felt guilty for not seeing more of him over the years but we both knew that he had an illness that made it impossible to have the same relationship we had enjoyed as kids. And on those rare occasions when we had met, I would sit there thinking how ill he looked – yet, perversely, it would be Simon who would get emotional about what had happened to me. I found it very hard to come to terms with the fact that he had died. It was so final, but I would always treasure memories of him.

It was whilst sitting in my van, leaning forward with my arms folded on the steering wheel and my chin resting on my arms, just staring at the boats on the river, reminiscing about Simon, that I wondered if he died with any regrets. I had always promised myself that when the time finally came I didn't want to have any regrets. Simon was less than a year older than me, and it just proved that anything could happen at any time. It was not so much a regret, but I did harbour one ambition, and that was to sail around Great Britain. Realising the enormous undertaking that such a scheme would represent, I'd purposefully not given it much thought until now – but perhaps now was the time to look at exactly what such a dream would entail.

23

I slept surprisingly well that last night in Gosport. I had fallen asleep at about 2300 hours, listening the some of the crew outside, chatting and laughing. As a child, I remember the excitement and anticipation that I would feel the night before Christmas, and as I snuggled into my quilt that night I had that very same feeling.

Although we were not scheduled to leave until 0700, everyone was up by 0500, even Timothy. Elaine and I barely spoke as she got me washed and dressed and, for the final time, pulled the neoprene neck seal of my Henri Lloyd dry-top over my head. As good as it was, possibly the most important piece of clothing I owned, on more than fifty occasions, usually within minutes of emerging from my warm and snug bed, I had had to endure that damp, cold and salty neck seal being pulled over my head, ripping out my hair and digging itself into my warm skin.

'Do you know the first thing I'm going to do when I get back?' I asked Elaine.

'No, what?'

'Burn this damn thing. I couldn't have survived without it, but I never want to see it again,' I laughed.

With my heel carefully bandaged to avoid aggravating the pressure sore, and with my lifejacket secured, I realised that this was possibly the last time I would ever be in the motorhome. I took a good look around, and the memories of the past 109 days came flooding back. We had endured many inconveniences, but still we, a family of three including a five-year-old child and me with my wheelchair, had made this our home for nearly a third of a year. It was here that we had laughed, cried, cooked, eaten, slept and made all of the decisions about our trip.

'I'm going to miss the motorhome,' I said, without considering Elaine's feelings on the matter.

'What? Are you out of your mind? It's been a complete nightmare.'

She was right, of course. It hadn't been easy, and the only reason we had coped without killing each other was because Elaine had made it work as a home, albeit a very small one. And secretly, I think she was going to miss it too.

And with that I unfolded the hydraulic ramp and, for the last time, left the motorhome.

Outside, the crew were already dressed in their sailing clothes and *Freethinker* was rigged and ready to go. There was a slight change of crew responsibilities today. Having been unable to go on the RIB since breaking his ribs a few days earlier, Spike would act as one of the road crew, as would Elaine, who had driven the motorhome for the entire trip and wanted to finish it the same way as she had started. All the rest – Mike, Joel, Sarah, Andy, Eddie, Ian and Timothy – would travel by sea. Ian, Eddie and Andy were on *Everest One*, whilst the others would travel on another RIB.

It was a beautiful morning although the weather forecast, not for the first time, looked set to plague us. But not this time with too much wind – on the contrary, we would be lucky if we saw 5 knots of breeze all day.

In recognition of my achievement, and to try and avoid a repetition of the press scrum which saw me nearly drowned a few months earlier, the Royal Yachting Association had kindly agreed to lay on a fleet of four jet-skis. Led by Andrew Norton, the RYA's motor cruising manager, the jet-skis, all rigged with flashing blue lights, were to provide a safety cordon around me as I sailed to Hamble.

At 0630 on Wednesday 5 September 2007, 109 days after setting off from Hamble, I was lifted into *Freethinker* for the last time and launched down the slipway adjacent to the marina. I felt fine and relaxed doing my radio check with Ian, but when I saw the jet-skis arriving, their blue lights flashing, my heart skipped a beat and I could feel the butterflies in my stomach.

'*Freethinker, Everest One.* Ready to go, Geoff?' asked Ian.

'As ready as I'll ever be,' I replied.

'OK, let's do it,' said Ian, and with that we made our way out slowly past the marina into Portsmouth Harbour.

No sooner were we in the main channel, than the harbour police launch, a large 35-foot motorboat, hurried towards us, clearly alerted by this strange mix of vessels at such an early hour. Unable to change frequency on my VHF, I could see Ian talking on the VHF from *Everest One*, presumably to the police.

'Geoff, I've just explained what we are doing to the harbour police. They already knew about you and have asked if they could have the honour of escorting us out through the harbour entrance,' said Ian.

With that, the police launch took up position at the head of our small flotilla and led us out, through the narrow entrance and into the Solent. Portsmouth Harbour, steeped in maritime heritage, had seen many arrivals and departures in its history, and now mine could be added to that list. I allowed myself a moment of private amusement, for six months earlier the same police launch had reprimanded me for crossing the harbour entrance in my motor fishing boat, and now I was being given the celebrity treatment. The significance of their support was not lost on me, and it added to a memorable day.

As soon as we had cleared the entrance the police launch headed back to Portsmouth Harbour and we set a course for Spithead. Almost at once I noticed the early-morning Wightlink ferry leaving the harbour behind me, headed for Ryde on the Isle of Wight. She was some way off, but in the still morning air I could hear the ship's passenger-announcement speakers transmitting a message. I couldn't hear it all, but I distinctly heard the words 'Geoff Holt'.

As I turned to my left to look, I saw a number of passengers on the top deck of the ferry, looking in my direction and waving. And then the ship itself gave a series of long blasts on its ship's horn to wish me well. It really was a fantastic feeling to know that whilst we had been away, people back home had been following my story and knew who I was.

It was a long and sometimes tedious drift around the coastline past Lee on Solent and Hill Head. We had estimated that we would reach the South Cardinal Buoy, the exact spot where I had been tipped out of my boat, at 1100. But with hardly a puff of wind, it was unlikely that we would make it until nearer midday.

For those last few hours, I relived every leg, every mile and every destination on our journey. I still couldn't quite comprehend the significance of what I was about to achieve, and I was wondering how I would feel when I crossed the finish line. I chose not to pre-empt my feelings, but just to see what happened when it happened. Unlike other triumphant explorers or sailors, who could jump about, hold flares or do back-flips when they achieved their ambition, I could do little more than lift my arms and smile, but I knew that I would be doing all those things inside my head.

With still an hour to run, spectator boats started to arrive. At first just a yacht or two, then a motor cruiser, a couple of RIBs – and it wasn't long before there were nearly two dozen boats on the water, all waving and shouting 'well done Geoff!'

Andrew Norton's jet-ski cordon was doing its job perfectly, but every now and then someone would slip through to try and capture a quick photograph. In the end, it was my sailing tactics that kept the boats at bay. Realising the tide was at its weakest inshore, I purposefully sailed *Freethinker* in as close I could, tacking in and out. Aware that all the boats were listening to my transmissions on channel 77, I gave a running commentary on my depth. Sailing in such shallow water, at times down to eighteen inches, meant that I was out of range of help from *Everest One*, but Ian realised my motives. By transmitting my depth I was also keeping all other boats with deep keels away from me.

At last I could see the South Cardinal Buoy about a mile away. Using both of their boats, the River Hamble Harbour Masters had created a finish line, with one boat stationary by the buoy, the other about twenty yards away. With the wind disappearing completely, it was anyone's guess when I would cross it.

My friend Jonathon Savill had organised a surprise for me. When I first saw the familiar red and white of Lee on Solent coastguard rescue helicopter, I hadn't realised it had been launched especially for me. In fact, I heard its powerful motors long before I saw it, then with only a few hundred yards to the finish, it came and hovered directly above me. To my surprise, they were patched through to my VHF frequency.

'*Freethinker*, *Freethinker*, this is the coastguard helicopter Whisky Bravo. Over.'

I grinned from ear to ear.

'Whisky Bravo, *Freethinker*, go ahead.'

'*Freethinker*, Whisky Bravo, on behalf of the Coastguard Agency and all of us at Lee on Solent, we'd like to offer you our congratulations on your magnificent trip. Well done. We are now about to leave station. Over.'

Leave station? The downdraft from the helicopter was providing me with enough wind to sail.

'Whisky Bravo, *Freethinker*. Thank you for your message, very much appreciated. Could I ask that you remain on station for another minute so that I can use your downdraft to cross the finish line. Thank you. Out.'

And using their wind, at 1145 hours, I sailed *Freethinker* across the line. The River Hamble Harbour Masters sounded a foghorn to mark the event, and with that there commenced a deafening cacophony of sirens, foghorns and hooters, all being blasted by the spectator boats.

For the first few seconds, I was dazed. I let go of the mainsheet, took my helmet off, rested it in my lap and looked around me.

'I've done it, I've bloody done it,' I said quietly to myself, almost in disbelief, as though I needed to hear that confirmation from my own lips.

I looked around me, and everywhere people were standing in their boats, waving their arms. I could see my crew all hugging each other. I couldn't believe it. Together, we had done it.

First alongside was a RIB carrying the BBC. Pointing a microphone in my direction, Sally Taylor shouted, 'Well done Geoff, you've done it. How does it feel?'

Quite where my response came from, I'll never know – but I suddenly recalled Steve Redgrave at the end of one of his Olympic campaigns. I replied, 'What did Steve Redgrave say? If you ever see me near a boat again, you have my permission to shoot me.'

I then wanted to pay tribute to my crew. I tried but was overcome with emotion and could barely get my words out without getting choked up.

Everest One was quickly alongside, and Ian leapt on board *Freethinker* and shook my hand. So typically Ian. I wanted to give him a hug, and deep down I think he would have done too, but that wasn't how Ian showed emotion.

'Thanks mate, I couldn't have done it without you,' I said to him sincerely.

'That's OK,' he laughed. 'Just remind me not to go to any more boat shows' – a reference to our first meeting.

I had barely crossed the finish line when Ian pulled my mainsail down ready to tow me back to the yacht club. But we had a private joke to play. On great nautical occasions, boats often run a series of code flags up their masts; it's called 'dressing overall', and we wanted to do the same on *Freethinker*. But rather than link a series of flags together in no particular order, we wanted to convey a message. In a reference to my capsizing on 14 May, we had carefully pre-selected a number of flags which, when hoisted, read 'This way up Geoff'. It was an in-joke, and it was only the crew who saw the funny side.

With the flags hoisted and *Freethinker* made fast alongside *Everest One*, we made our way back up the River Hamble, a river that had become so entwined in my life and that occupied such a special place in my heart. As a child I had played along its banks with my friend Simon Lawton, and it was on the Hamble that I first set foot on a sailing boat. My stepfather John Holt had kept his yacht *Gulliver* on the Hamble, and we would travel up and down the river each school holiday. I even learned to sail in my Mirror dinghy on the river. It was from the River Hamble that I set off in *Morag Mhor*, my first ever job at sea, and it was from the Hamble I left on *Challenger* for my first trip across the Atlantic. A few months later I again left the Hamble, this time on *Rampant*, for my second transatlantic crossing. And then, years later, it was on the River Hamble that I had my first sail as a disabled yachtsman, thanks to the wonderful Tid Campbell, and I scattered her ashes on the same river when she died. A few months ago the River Hamble had nearly claimed my life when I was thrown into it – and now here I was heading back up the Hamble, my river, after successfully sailing around Great Britain.

And as we made our way up the river towards the Royal Southern Yacht Club, men working on the surrounding marinas were downing tools and waving, people working up masts, hanging there in their bosun's chairs, were waving, and there were scores of people lining jetties and the river bank, all shouting and cheering. Even *Te Quiero*, a beautiful boat I had fallen in love with in the Mediterranean some twenty-five years earlier, was there, her crew waving.

It was an overwhelming sensation of accomplishment and pride, not just for me, but for my crew too. They had stood by me and never let me down, even though the promised 60 days had extended to 109.

As we rounded the final jetty and lined ourselves up for the slipway, there were Elaine and Spike, waiting for my fifty-first and final arrival. As always, they were dressed in crew kit, the motorhome and the Land Rover parked, ready and waiting. But proceedings were interrupted, forgivably, for the press photographers to get their shots.

Elaine and Timothy both clambered their way onto my boat and we had the most public private family hug ever. Even Timothy found it in himself to give me an unprompted kiss and say 'well done, Dad.' It was all overwhelming and very emotional.

As my boat was pulled up the slipway, at my request, I was sprayed with champagne. I had seen it done a thousand times on TV, usually at the end of a Formula 1 car race, and I had always criticised them for wasting good champagne. But this was going to be my only chance in life to test my theory – and never have I been so wrong about something. It was a fantastic feeling to be completely doused in the stuff. It made my hair a bit sticky but it really added to the occasion. And I could hear the beautiful tones of the Southern Union Chorus. On my failed start back in May, crew member Mike had organised for his barbershop group to sing Louis Armstrong's 'What a wonderful world', but in all the chaos I never got to hear it that day. Now, resplendent in their bright red shirts in the glorious sunshine, they had come again, and this time I enjoyed every note of the song. It was indeed a wonderful day.

There were hundreds of people gathered in the car park, most of whom I recognised as members of my family and my friends. It was so good to see them again, I didn't realise how much I had missed each and every one of them. And there, in the crowd, were two people in wheelchairs, my friends Juliet from Devon and Alan from Wales. The two people who had inspired and motivated me, when I felt like giving up, had come to welcome me home.

I had called my adventure Personal Everest. But having completed my challenge, I realised that, more than just climbing the highest mountain in the world, I was standing on top of the world itself.

Epilogue

On 5 September 2007, after a journey of 109 days and 1,445 miles, quadriplegic yachtsman Geoff Holt reached the summit of his Personal Everest. He and his volunteer crew of nine had taken their three vehicles, two vessels and two trailers to 51 different destinations around the country during one of the worst summers on record. Geoff's average speed at sea, in his trimaran dinghy *Freethinker*, was 3.4 knots.

Within a few days of getting home, all of the crew had returned to their jobs and their loved ones, and to some semblance of normality. Timothy was a week late in starting school, but his head teacher forgave him. Most of the equipment and vehicles were returned or sold, except *Freethinker*, which was donated to the Dan's Dream Trust – and she is now used around Europe to promote the Challenger dinghy as a prospective Paralympic class boat.

In recognition of his achievement, Geoff has received many high-profile awards. He was voted the BBC TV South Sports Personality of the Year 2007, and was presented with the award by Sir Robin Knox-Johnston, the sailor whose single-handed voyage around the world had inspired Geoff as a boy. He was also named Tetraplegic of the Year by the REGAIN charitable trust, and was shortlisted for the prestigious Yachtsman of the Year trophy – which was won, ironically, by Sir Robin Knox-Johnston. He continues to support his local Rotary group, and in March 2008 he was awarded the Paul Harris Fellowship, Rotary International's highest award for service.

Geoff still works hard in support of the charity RYA Sailability, but he has also developed a new career as an inspirational speaker. Drawing on aspects of his life story, and identifying parallels between his Personal Everest and issues facing businesses, he has been much in demand delivering lectures and keynote speeches around the UK.

The legacy of Personal Everest extends much further than a shelf full of trophies or the special memories shared by Geoff and his team. Thousands of people read, saw or heard about the challenge, and many realised that they had witnessed something special. Personal Everest has inspired a number of disabled people to take up sailing, and it has even prompted many to completely re-evaluate their perceptions of disability.

Afterword
by Dame Ellen MacArthur DBE

Geoff –

I was deeply moved by your book, and truly inspired as I found myself glued to its pages.

It is beautifully written and honest. You give the reader a total insight into your life in a way which makes them feel like they are living it with you. Not only did I learn how amazing you are aside from your public profile, but I learnt what makes you who you are. Your relationships with others speak volumes. Your humour, shown in desperate times, and your persistence, which will not let you give up, are clearly cornerstones to your character.

I am lucky to understand many of your recent voyage experiences, having also sailed solo round Great Britain. It is a route which many people underestimate. At the end of the day it's generally the coastline and rocks that sink boats, not the open ocean, and the Round Britain route is no exception. It's an extremely difficult challenge, with difficult weather, lee shores, tides and treacherous harbour entrances. When I sailed it in 1995 we had all manner of hairy moments and close shaves. It's an unforgiving route, that's for sure, but an incredibly rewarding one.

I can also say that the craft you chose was not the most forgiving. Multihulls are fast and powerful, but they are hard work to sail. The motion, in any sea way to speak of, is violent and tiring. On my little *Iduna* I had a cabin and a place to shelter. You had no such luxuries.

You are one of the most incredible people I have met. You will never be the person who pushes himself to the front, but the one who silently goes about his business – and lifts himself so high in doing so that you tower way above the rest.

Your latest voyage was nothing short of exceptional, but to me that journey is simply a reflection of you.

Ellen MacArthur

Personal Everest 2007
Supporters and sponsors

My crew
Ian Clover
Andy Cockayne
Eddie Edrich
Mike Golden
Elaine Holt
Timothy Holt
Sarah Outen
Mike 'Spike' Spencer
Joel Whalley

My sponsor
Blake Lapthorn
    Tarlo Lyons

Special thanks to
Peter Harrison

My technical suppliers
Henri Lloyd
Raymarine
Marinetrack

Official suppliers
Admiralty Leisure
Aladdin's Cave
Bishop Skinner
Boat Launch

Crewsaver
Department of
    Medical Engineering,
    Salisbury Hospital
Gecko Headgear
Hyde Sails
Ohmex
Screen 169
Weather Online

Yacht clubs, sailing clubs and marinas
Amble Marina
Brixham Yacht Club
Campbeltown Sailing Club
Dover Port Authority
Gosport Marina
Grimsby Marina
Hartlepool Marina
Hayling Island Sailing Club
Holyhead Marina
Humber Cruising Association
MDL Sovereign Harbour,
    Eastbourne
Peterhead Sailing Club
Plymouth Yacht Haven
Ramsgate Marina
Royal Lymington Yacht Club

Royal Norfolk & Suffolk
   Yacht Club
Royal Northumberland
   Yacht Club
Royal Southern Yacht Club
South Caernarvonshire
   Yacht Club
Sussex Yacht Club
Stonehaven Sailing Club
Tenby Sailing Club
Wells-next-the-Sea
   Sailing Club
Weymouth & Portland
   Sailing Academy
Whitehills Marina

RNLI stations
St Ives
Fishguard
Arbroath
Dunbar
Berwick-upon-Tweed
Stonehaven Maritime
   Rescue Institute

Photography
OnEdition
Mark Lloyd Photography
Andy Cockayne
Hamble Valley Rotary
Meaghan Spann
Personal Everest

HM Coastguard
MCA Bridlington
Search & Rescue Helicopter
   Whisky Bravo,
   Lee-on-Solent

**Rotary Clubs and
their members**
Amble
Arbroath
Banff
Bangor
Berwick-upon-Tweed
Blyth
Bridlington
Bridport
Brixham
Buckie
Bude
Campbeltown
Cleethorpes
Dunbar
Eastbourne (Sovereign)
Fakenham
Falmouth
Felixstowe
Fishguard & Goodwick
Hamble Valley
Hartlepool
Havant
Holyhead
Lowestoft
Lyme Regis
Lymington
Melcombe Regis
Oundle
Padstow
Penryn
Peterborough
Plymouth
Poole Bay
Portland
Pwllheli
Ramsgate

RIBI: ComVoc and Website
Rochford
Rushen (IOM)
Shoreham & Southwick
Stranraer
Tenby
Weymouth

Other businesses and individuals

Abersoch Boatyard Services
Alan Thomas
Andark Diving
Andy Cassell Foundation
Boatability
British Waterways
    (Crinan Canal)
Challenger Class Association
Dan's Dream
Deucoch Caravan Park, Abersoch:
    Norman and
    Audrey Winteringham;
    Ruth, Andy and
    Rebecca Pullen
Gosport Boatyard Ltd
Graham Wing
Grapefruit Graphics
Hamble Ropes & Rigging
Hampshire Motorhomes
Helen Fretter
INSPIRE
ITS Magic
John Mclaughlin
Jonathon Savill
Juliet Prentice
Mark Tyrrell
Mendez Marine

Mike Gallon
Mylor Yacht Services
National Boat Shows
On Edition
Pennyfarthing Tools
Peter & Sue Sonksen
Peter Harrison Foundation
Peter Sanders Sails
Puffin Dive School, Oban
Ramsgate Fire Service
Richard Trebilcock
Rick Stein
Royal Yachting Association
RYA Sailability
Selby Engineering & Lifting
    Services Ltd
Shockmedia Productions
Southampton Round Table #4
Southern Union Chorus
Susan Preston-Davies
Sweeney
UKSA
West Wales Windsurfing and
    Sailing
White Formula

Harbour masters and port authorities

Lymington
Portland
Bridport
Brixham
Salcombe
Plymouth
Falmouth
Newlyn
St Ives

Padstow	Peterhead
Bude	Stonehaven
Ilfracombe	Arbroath
Tenby	Dunbar
Dale	Berwick-upon-Tweed
Fishguard	Amble
Aberystwyth	Blyth
Abersoch	Hartlepool
Morfa Nefyn	Bridlington
Holyhead	Grimsby
Peel	Wells-next-the-Sea
Portpatrick	Lowestoft
Campbeltown	Felixstowe Ferry
Ardishraig	Ramsgate
Crinan	Dover
Oban	Eastbourne
Fort William – Lochaber	Newhaven
Laggan Loch	Shoreham
Dochgarroch	Hayling Island
Nairn	Gosport
Whitehills	Hamble

There is always a risk when listing people, groups, organisations and businesses that some will be inadvertently missed. I have tried my best to identify as many of you as I could, but with so many people playing a part in the success of Personal Everest, it is inevitable that I have overlooked others. I offer my heartfelt thanks to everyone, whether on the list or not, who played a part in the success of this memorable expedition. Thank you all.

Also from

SEAFARER BOOKS and SHERIDAN HOUSE

www.seafarerbooks.com   www.sheridanhouse.com

ICE BEARS AND KOTICK

PETER WEBB

This is the story of an impossible boat journey that two men
made for the fun of it. They rowed and sailed through pack ice,
and survived polar bears, whales, starvation and capsize – and in
so doing they completed the first circumnavigation of the Arctic
island of Spitsbergen in an open row boat. Along the way they
learned about themselves, about life, and experienced a wilderness
that will most likely disappear before the century is out. A story for
small-boat sailors, lovers of ice and snow, and anybody who knows
anybody who wanted to run away to sea.

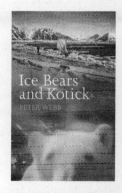

Illustrated · UK ISBN 978-1-906266-03-5 pbk
USA ISBN 978-1-57409-264-6 pbk

DIVER

TONY GROOM

An honest, moving and sometimes hilarious account of a hair-
raisingly exciting career, both in the Royal Navy and in commercial
deep-sea diving – training the most unlikely of raw recruits ...
handling unexploded bombs while under air attack ... living for
months in a pressurised bottle with a voice like Donald Duck ...
commuting to work through a hole in the floor in the freezing,
black depths of the North Sea. Tony Groom joined the Royal Navy
at the age of seventeen, determined to become a diver. As a member
of the Fleet Clearance Diving Team, he found himself diving for
mines, dealing with unexploded bombs and being shot at in the
Falklands War. He left the Navy in 1985, and has since travelled the
world as a commercial diver.

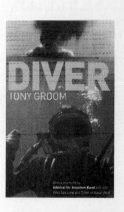

**'The Royal Navy Clearance Divers, not the SAS, are the
British mystery unit of the Falklands War'**
Major General Julian Thompson

**'Wide-ranging, illuminating and sympathetic ... This tale fills
a massive gap and is long overdue'**
Commodore Michael C Clapp

**'Epitomises the *esprit de corps* of the Royal Navy's Clearance
Diving branch, as well as the close-knit camaraderie of the
commercial offshore diver'**
Mick Fellows

Illustrated · UK ISBN 978-1-906266-02-8 pbk
USA ISBN 978-1-57409-269-1 pbk

THE MARINER'S BOOK OF DAYS 2009

EDITED BY PETER H SPECTRE

Now in its 18th year, *The Mariner's Book of Days* has been hailed as the best and most entertaining nautical desk diary and calendar to see print. An invaluable reference, each annual edition is completely different from its predecessors, and all have become collector's items. Opposite every diary page, with notes on the nautical significance of each date, is a collection of nautical miscellany. Richly illustrated with sketches and engravings, *The Mariner's Book of Days* takes readers on a 365-day voyage through history.

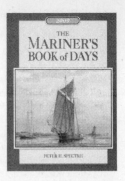

'This nautical desk diary and calendar is an ever-growing encyclopedia of marine fact, fiction and folklore. Entertaining and informative ... a keeper well after the year is over and done'

     Sailing Magazine

Illustrated · ISBN 978-1-57409-252-3 pbk

SKELETONS FOR SADNESS

A novel

EWEN SOUTHBY-TAILYOUR

It is September 1980. Edward Casement, sailing with his crew towards Cape Horn and the Pacific in his ketch *Nomad*, calls in at the Falklands. Things do not go according to plan, and, having lost his crew, he ends up spending longer in the islands than he had intended, sailing on charter for the Governor in the company of an English nurse. In an atmosphere of growing intrigue, not all is as it seems, and then comes the Argentine invasion. A story of love, espionage, a yacht, and a war in the South Atlantic.

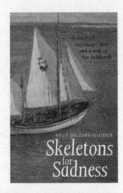

'A breathtakong thriller ... highly original and beautifully written'

     Lt Cdr Tristan Lovering MBE RN

Illustrated · UK ISBN 978-1-906266-02-8 pbk
USA ISBN 978-1-57409-260-8 pbk

AFTER YOU, MR LEAR
In the wake of Edward Lear in Italy

MALDWIN DRUMMOND

This is the story of a journey in search of the character and
work of the Victorian polymath Edward Lear (1812–1888).
Best known today as a nonsense poet and humorist, Lear
was also a talented and celebrated topographical landscape
painter. On the 150th anniversary of Lear's appointment
as Queen Victoria's drawing master, Maldwin and Gilly
Drummond set sail in their yacht *Gang Warily*, from near
Osborne house, Queen Victoria's home in the Isle of Wight.
They cross the Channel, navigate the rivers and canals of
France to the Mediterranean, and follow the coast of Italy
from Lear's adopted home at San Remo south as far as
Calabria. A fascinating account of a voyage of discovery,
richly illustrated, and including some of Lear's own most
accomplished drawings and paintings, as well as the author's
photographs and sketches. Packed with new insights into the
life and work of a remarkable man.

Illustrated · UK ISBN 978-0-9550243-7-5 pbk
USA ISBN 978-1-57409-255-4 pbk

JOSEPH CONRAD: MASTER MARINER

PETER VILLIERS

Before he published his first novel in 1895, Joseph Conrad
spent 20 years in the merchant navy, eventually obtaining

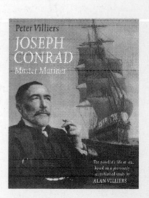

his master's ticket and
commanding the barque
Otago. This book, superbly
illustrated with paintings
by Mark Myers, traces his
sea-career and shows how
Konrad Korzeniowski,
master mariner, became
Joseph Conrad, master novelist. Alan Villiers, world-
renowned author and master mariner under sail, was
uniquely qualified to comment on Conrad's life at sea,
and the study he began has been completed by his son,
Peter Villiers.

'A book that finally does justice to Conrad's time at sea'
Traditional Boats and Tall Ships

Illustrated with 12 paintings in full colour by Mark Myers RSMA F/ASMA
UK ISBN 0-9547062-9-3 pbk
USA ISBN 1-57409-244-8 pbk